Peer Play and the Autism Spectrum

The Art of Guiding Children's Socialization and Imagination

INTEGRATED PLAY GROUPS FIELD MANUAL

Peer Play
and
the Autism Spectrum

The Art of Guiding Children's Socialization and Imagination

INTEGRATED PLAY GROUPS FIELD MANUAL

Pamela J. Wolfberg

Foreword by Adriana L. Schuler

Autism Asperger Publishing Company
P.O. Box 23173
Shawnee Mission, Kansas 66283-0173
www.asperger.net

© 2003 by Autism Asperger Publishing Co.
P.O. Box 23173
Shawnee Mission, Kansas 66283-0173
www.asperger.net

Publisher's Cataloging-in-Publication
(provided by Quality Books, Inc.)

Wolfberg, Pamela J.
    Peer play and the autism spectrum : the art of
guiding children's socialization and imagination :
integrated play groups field manual / Pamela J. Wolfberg;
foreword by Adriana L. Schuler.
    p. cm.
    Includes bibliographical references and index.
    Library of Congress Control Number: 2002115281
    ISBN: 1-931282-17-X

    1. Autistic children–Rehabilitation. 2. Autism in
children–Patients–Rehabilitation. 3. Play. 4. Social
skills in children. 5. Imagination in children.
I. Title.

RJ506.A9W65 2002   618.92'898203
        QBI02-200836

This book is designed in Marker Felt Wide, Minion and Lucida Casual

Managing Editor: Kirsten McBride
Editorial Support: Ginny Biddulph
Illustrations: Eddy Mora
Cover and Interior Design & Production: Tappan Design

To the many children
whose social and imaginary worlds
reside deep within my heart and mind

and

To all my siblings
who made my first play circle complete

Acknowledgments

I wish to thank the many people who made this book possible. I am deeply indebted to all of the children who allowed me to explore their play cultures and portray their stories. My heartfelt thanks also go to their families who gave generously with their patience, understanding and support.

I am eternally grateful to my dearest mentors and collaborators, Adriana Schuler and Therese O'Connor, whose voices are enmeshed within these pages. Without their wisdom, fortitude and unfailing encouragement this work could not have been accomplished.

I wish to extend wholehearted thanks to the many talented practitioners who helped us refine our practice. I owe special thanks to Tara Tuchel for openly sharing her experiences as an apprentice play guide – she is clearly a role model for all. I am also grateful to Glenda Fuge and Rebecca Berry of Developmental Pathways for Kids for creating a most remarkable program based on their clinical expertise.

Much appreciation goes to numerous others from the following schools and programs: Autism Support Kensington – London, U.K.; Clackmannanshire Council Psychological Services – Scotland; Erinoak Preschool Autism Services – Ontario, Canada; Essex County Council Learning Services – Essex, U.K.; Hope Technology School – Burlingame, CA; Marin County Schools – CA; Phoenix Education Center – Belmont, CA; Region IV Education Service Center – Houston, TX; Region VIII Education Service Center – Austin, TX; San Bruno Park School District - CA; San Francisco Unified School District – CA; San Mateo County Schools – CA; Santa Clarita School District – CA; Taipei Teachers College – Taiwan; Twin Cities Autism Society of America – MN; Wings Learning Center – Half Moon Bay, CA; Yayasan Pemberdayaan Penyandang Autism – Jakarta, Indonesia.

My deep appreciation also goes to my colleagues and former professors who provided thoughtful commentary and support at various phases throughout this venture: Joseph Campione, Julie Donnelly, Cheryl Fletcher, Jean Gonsier-Gerdin, Mimi Lou, Lorraine McCune, Kathryn Orfirer, Charles Peck, Cathy Pratt, Barry Prizant, Suzanne Pemberton, Kathleen Quill, Kathy Small, James Stone, Tsung-ren Yang and Craig Zercher. I am also grateful to Cerissa McNichols, Emily Burnell Petrou and Jane Schisgal for their assistance with media production and research, and Olga Norman for her graphic design creations that originated with the Integrated Play Groups project.

I dedicate a special note of heartfelt thanks to the memory of Robert Gaylord-Ross, James Russell Podratz and Carlos Barerro, whose gifts to the field will forever be cherished and live on in the spirit of play groups.

For their generous contributions, I wish to express my gratitude to the Glenna B. Collins Scholarship Foundation of the Autism Society of America, the Sandra L. Bailey Memorial Fund of the Illinois Autism Society and the San Francisco Education Fund.

I also wish to express sincere thanks to Kirsten McBride, Brenda Smith Myles and Keith Myles for thoughtful reading of this manuscript, sensitive and careful editing, and seeing this work through to completion. Thanks also to Kim Tappan and Eddy Mora for illustrations and cover art.

Finally, I am forever grateful to my family, friends and faithful canine companion for their unconditional support, friendship and love throughout this endeavor.

– Pamela J. Wolfberg

Foreword

About fifteen years ago Pamela Wolfberg was one of our most promising students at San Francisco State University, and I was fortunate, if not destined, to be her major professor and mentor. The communicative behaviors and socialization of children on the autistic spectrum had long been the focus of my own training and research activities. Childhood autism had remained one of my major sources of intrigue and specialization, and the rumor was that Pamela's classroom had attracted a fine collection of students with outright diagnoses of autism as well as students with confirmed autistic features. Pamela's school site was located within close proximity to our college campus and had been recognized as a primary focus of the local school district's integration efforts, noted for its extensive disability awareness programs. Pamela had shared her intentions with me; she was wanting to take advantage of the opportunities for interactions with typically developing peers. Encouraged by her preliminary play encounters, she had invited typically developing peers to spend big chunks of their recess time in Pamela's most inviting play area, and was planning to turn these first integrated play activities into a more cohesive and systematic program development effort. Pamela wanted to create a mini-play community by inviting two groups of three peers to interact with two of her students in highly structured, yet child-initiated play groups that would meet twice a week.

A prime consumer of the professional literature, I wasn't optimistic about the chances of teaching pretend play to individuals whose primary disability was captured by impairments in reciprocity and imagination. Nevertheless, I encouraged Pamela, as I believed that mere participation in enjoyable activities with typically developing peers would reduce these children's social isolation and establish some recreational skills, even if pretend play would not have occurred and all the trained play activities had been scripted and memorized.

The best thing that happened is that Pamela proved me wrong; her students turned out to be much more capable than I had ever imagined once the multiple supports were established in intense initial coaching sessions. Even more rewarding – it was very difficult for outsiders to tell Pamela's students apart when engaged in playful interactions with their peers; their faces looked so joyful and their voices appeared to have lost their "mechanical" qualities.

Nevertheless, despite the most encouraging advances it was unclear if these play activities could be sustained, and most important, it was a difficult for Pamela as well as her observers to explain the forces at work and to train others to follow in her footsteps. There were no guidelines or principles to be spelled out, let alone a training manual. It took fifteen years for the theory to follow the practice. It took extensive research and demonstration efforts for the principles to be crystallized. Now a dissertation and many videos, lectures, chapters, and articles later, Pamela is able to inaugurate others into her domain.

Pamela has completed an awesome task, operationalizing seemingly intuitive classroom-based pre-intentional hunches into a formalized, researchable training format that allows her not only to share her practice with others but also to refine her own knowledge and understanding. Here is a training manual that was inconceivable fifteen years ago, a manual that speaks to the power of classroom-based, qualitative research with quantitative trimmings and reflective practice. Explore and enjoy!!!

– Adriana L. Schuler, Ph.D.

Table of Contents

Phase I - Embracing the Spirit of Play
IPG Conceptual Foundation

Phase II - Setting the Stage for Play
IPG Program and Environmental Design

Phase III – Observing Children at Play
IPG Assessment

Phase IV – Guided Participation in Play
IPG Intervention

Prologue

A Good Play

We built a ship upon the stairs
All made of the back-bedroom chairs,
And filled it full of sofa pillows
To go a-sailing on the billows.

We took a saw and several nails
And water in the nursery pails;
And Tom said, "Let us also take
An apple and a slice of cake;"
Which was enough for Tom and me
To go a-sailing on, till tea.

We sailed along for days and days
And had the very best of plays;
But Tom fell out and hurt his knee
So there was no one left but me.

– Robert Louis Stevenson, *A Child's Garden of Verses*

Watching children play generates feelings of delight and endearment in most of us. As we consider the origins of such feelings, we may touch upon memories of our own play in childhood. Many of us will picture a special playmate, a favorite plaything, a secret place and precious time when nothing else mattered but the world of make-believe we created in our minds as well as with friends. Some of us may even long to go back in time to recapture those seemingly endless moments of pure pleasure and well-being.

Now picture a childhood void of the joyful images and sensations we associate with play – a childhood lacking in curiosity, diversity and symbolic meaning – a childhood without playmates or friends. Many of us may be aware of children who do not naturally play and socialize in typical ways – children who appear confused, distracted or uninterested in the company of peers. We may even feel uncomfortable observing their seemingly aimless repetitive motions or preoccupations with particular objects or themes. Because of the unusual ways in which these children express themselves in play, they may be perceived by peers as outsiders – lost souls on the fringes of playgrounds and other social gathering places.

Over the years, my colleagues and I have had the opportunity to observe countless children in a variety of social and cultural settings. While watching children who are given free reign to play and socialize with one another, we can easily detect who is thriving and who is at risk in their development. Children on the autism spectrum are among those who are at greatest risk as they face serious challenges learning how to play in both social and imaginative ways.

Autism is a complex condition that impedes children's spontaneous development of reciprocal social interaction, communication, play and imagination. Defining features of autism include a "lack of varied, spontaneous make-believe play" as well as a "failure to develop peer relationships" appropriate to developmental level (American Psychiatric Association, 2000). Many children on the autism spectrum (including children with Asperger Syndrome and pervasive developmental disorder) spend inordinate amounts of time alone pursuing repetitive and unimaginative activities. Without appropriate intervention, they are especially vulnerable to being excluded from their peer group and leading impoverished play lives.

Play's significance is far-reaching as a social and cultural context through which children acquire symbolic capacities, interpersonal skills and social knowledge (Vygotsky, 1966, 1978). Moreover, peers perform a distinct role in play by fostering opportunities for learning and development that cannot be duplicated by adults (Hartup, 1979, 1983; Wolfberg et al., 1999). Through shared experiences in play children acquire many interrelated skills that are necessary for attaining social competence and forming meaningful friendships. Particularly within a social pretend framework, children practice and assimilate these skills while exercising their imaginative potential. Children on the autism spectrum are highly unlikely to reap the benefits of play under the same conditions as typical children.

About This Field Manual

Peer Play and the Autism Spectrum: The Art of Guiding Children's Socialization and Imagination is a field manual for practitioners and caregivers seeking to address the unique and complex challenges children on the autism spectrum experience in peer relations and play. This practical guide offers an introduction to the basic principles, tools and techniques that comprise the Integrated Play Groups model.

The Integrated Play Groups (IPG) model was conceived out of deep concern for the many children who are missing out on peer play experiences as a vital part of childhood. Integrated Play Groups are designed to support children of diverse ages and abilities on the autism spectrum (novice players) in mutually enjoyed play experiences with typical peers and siblings (expert players). Small groups of children regularly play together under the guidance of a qualified adult facilitator (play guide). Children's socialization and imagination are guided through a carefully tailored system of support, with an emphasis placed on maximizing children's developmental potential as well as intrinsic desire to play, socialize and form meaningful relationships with peers. An equally important focus is on teaching the peer group to be more accepting, responsive and inclusive of children who relate and play in different ways.

Since its inception, the Integrated Play Groups model has undergone a number of transformations in an effort to keep pace with burgeoning knowledge about autism spectrum disorders and more than a decade of research and practice.[1] (See Appendix B for a review of efficacy research on Integrated Play Groups.) The model's objectives and methods are consistent with recent findings of the Committee on Educational Interventions for Children with Autism by the National Research Council (2001). The authors of this ground-breaking report include the teaching of play skills with peers among the six types of interventions that should receive priority in the education of children with autism spectrum disorders.

The strength of the Integrated Play Groups model hinges on the fusion of philosophy, theory, research and practice (see Figure-Prologue). The model is grounded in a philosophy that places tremendous value on the purpose and place of play in childhood. At the same time, it is guided by current theory, research and best practices that reflect an understanding of the nature of play and the autism spectrum in the context of childhood development, culture and social policy (for an in-depth review of guiding theory, research and practice, see Wolfberg, 1994, 1999). In the conception of Integrated Play Groups, it is impossible to disentangle these as they continually inform, guide and build on one another.

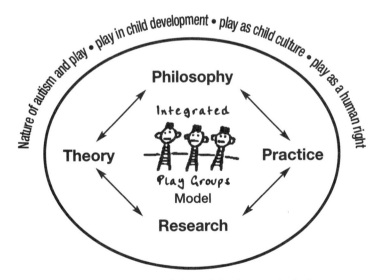

Figure – Prologue. Unifying principles of the integrated play groups model.

---

[1] The Integrated Play Groups model originated in 1987 as a pilot project with partial funding from the San Francisco Education Fund. The model was subsequently expanded and supported in part through a grant from the United States Department of Education, contract #HO86D90016. Points of view or opinions stated herein do not necessarily represent official policy of the U.S. Department of Education.

Peer Play and the Autism Spectrum: The Art of Guiding Children's Socialization and Imagination represents the latest evolution of the Integrated Play Groups model, following in the footsteps of my first book, *Play and Imagination in Children with Autism*, which is based on award-winning research (Wolfberg, 1999). This field manual essentially picks up where the last book left off by translating theory into effective and meaningful practice.

A major aim of this manual is to expand and refine existing best practices for children on the autism spectrum. It is my sincere hope that it will inspire individuals to initiate peer play groups for children in school, home and community settings. While this manual offers a starting place for applying the practices of Integrated Play Groups, additional formal preparation will aid in implementing the model with quality assurance. For this I extend a warm welcome to anyone interested in participating in seminars or courses offered through the Autism Institute on Peer Relations and Play – Center for Integrated Play Groups (see Appendix A for more details).

In the spirit of play, I encourage you to explore the concepts and methods presented in this manual – to be creative, experiment and have fun while learning how to guide children's participation in social and imaginary worlds together.

How the Book Is Organized

This field manual is divided into four phases as follows.

Phase I: Embracing the Spirit of Play – IPG Conceptual Foundation provides a theoretical framework. Chapter 1 explores the nature of the autism spectrum and the complex problems children experience in play (with and without peers). Chapter 2 looks at play from multiple perspectives in order to understand the principles and concepts that underlie the Integrated Play Groups model. It is within this conceptual framework that we introduce the art of guiding children's socialization and imagination through peer play.

Phase II: Setting the Stage for Play – IPG Program and Environmental Design offers detailed instruction on how to get started. Chapter 3 focuses on the initial stages of the planning process. Chapter 4 concentrates on gathering and preparing the players to participate in groups. Chapter 5 centers on preparing the play setting. Chapter 6 focuses on structuring play sessions. At the end of Phase II are hands-on activities that correspond to tools and field exercises to aid in the design of Integrated Play Groups.

Phase III: Observing Children at Play – IPG Assessment presents tools and techniques for conducting quality assessments in Integrated Play Groups. Chapter 7 details the assessment approach by introducing the observation framework and corresponding instruments. At the end of Phase III are hands-on activities that correspond to tools and field exercises to guide the assessment process.

Phase IV: Guided Participation in Play – IPG Intervention introduces key intervention practices for facilitating Integrated Play Groups. Chapter 8 focuses on the practice of monitoring play initiations. Chapter 9 describes the practice of scaffolding play. Chapter 10 centers on strategies for guiding social communication. Chapter 11 describes a set of play guidance techniques. Finally, Chapter 12 presents case illustrations to show how these practices come together to support children of diverse ages and abilities in Integrated Play Groups. At the end of Phase IV are hands-on activities that correspond to tools and field exercises to guide the intervention process.

The book concludes with an epilogue and appendices that include additional information and resources to offer further guidance and support.[2]

---

[2] Please note that names of people and places have been changed throughout this manual to protect the privacy of those involved.

PHASE I
Embracing the Spirit of Play
IPG Conceptual Foundation

We don't stop playing because we grow old;
we grow old because we stop playing.

- George Bernard Shaw

CHAPTER 1

Nature of Play and the Autism Spectrum

Chapter Highlights

This chapter introduces theory on the nature of the autism spectrum and the complex problems children experience in play (with and without peers). The following topics will be highlighted:

► Autism Spectrum Disorders in a Nutshell

► Developmental Play Patterns and Variations

► Peer Cultural Influences on Children's Play

CASE VIGNETTE:
Jamie – a.k.a. Little Salvador Dali

I first met Jamie when he entered my program for children with autism in a public elementary school. He was 6 years old – a period I fondly recall in my own childhood when life revolved around friends and the imaginative play worlds we created together. But friendships and make-believe play were not a part of Jamie's early childhood experience. His parents and former teachers described him as a passive child who lived in a world of his own. He accepted and enjoyed certain forms of physical contact, including being picked up and held by his adult caregivers, but rarely initiated social contact of his own accord. Jamie also never spontaneously approached or interacted with his peers, although he sometimes gazed at them from afar.

At the center of Jamie's universe was his unusual fascination with time. When left to his own devices, he pursued his passion through ritualistic activity. He drew calendars, schedules and clocks of every kind. On the playground he surrounded himself with colorful sidewalk chalk drawings that resembled the famous paintings of dripping clocks by the artist Salvador Dali. In his classroom he delighted in the prank of throwing drinks at the large clock mounted on the wall. Each conquest resulted in an eruption of giggles that only intensified when he was admonished. Jamie's intrigue with time made everybody wearing watches fair game, as he would tug on their wrists to inspect the coveted object up close.

Children who were not familiar with Jamie found his behavior perplexing. While most of his peers tended to ignore or avoid him, a few actively teased and taunted him. Thus, Jamie's limited play and social skills not only exacerbated his social isolation, but also emphasized his difference from other children.

Sorting out the diverse problems children on the autism spectrum experience in play (both with and without peers) poses significant challenges for theorists, practitioners and family members. A common misconception is that by virtue of their biological make-up, children with autism are incapable of play and consciously choose to be isolated rather than in the company of peers. Yet research and experience tell us that these children indeed share many of the same impulses and capacities for play, companionship and peer group acceptance as typically developing children (for reviews, see Boucher, 1999; Wolfberg, 1999; see also Bauminger & Kasari, 2000). Nevertheless, numerous obstacles prevent children with autism from accessing the skills that would allow them to actualize their potential for play. An examination of the nature of play development in children on the autism spectrum may help to elucidate how best to overcome these obstacles.

Autism Spectrum Disorders in a Nutshell

Autism is a lifelong developmental disability that typically appears in the first three years of life. The result of a complex condition that affects normal brain functioning, autism undermines many aspects of behavior, learning and development.

Meaning of "Spectrum Disorder"

Autism is commonly described as a "spectrum disorder" that accounts for wide variability among individuals in their ability to adapt and function in daily life. Within the autism spectrum, children may exhibit different combinations of specific behaviors ranging from mild to severe. Moreover, the presence of symptoms and degree of severity may change over the lifespan. In light of this variability, obtaining an accurate diagnosis of autism is exceedingly complex (Szatmari, 1992; Wing & Attwood, 1987).

Early Detection

Children with autism spectrum disorders (ASD) appear relatively normal in the early stages of infant development. Perceptible signs of the disorder typically emerge around 18 months when toddlers fail to point, share attention, imitate or follow the expression of others. It is around 24 to 30 months that most delays or differences are noted in a child's development, specifically in the areas of social interaction, communication and play (Siegel, 1996).

Core Features

Autism is characterized by a "triad of impairments" in reciprocal social interaction, communication and imagination that are generally associated with other noted problems (American Psychiatric Association, 2000; Wing & Attwood, 1987). Specifically, children with autism exhibit restricted, repetitive and stereotyped patterns of behavior, interests and activities. They also show signs of sensory sensitivities in which one or more of the five senses of touch, sight, hearing, taste and smell may be affected (American Psychiatric Association, 2000). Also compromised is the capacity to recognize and understand mental states (such as feelings, desires, intentions and beliefs) in oneself and others. The latter affects the capacity to interpret and predict social behavior known as a "theory of mind" (Baron-Cohen, 1995; Baron-Cohen, Leslie, & Frith, 1985). See Table 1.1.

In light of these impairments, people with autism experience many difficulties communicating with others and relating to the outside world. They may show unusual responses to other people, preoccupations with objects and unusual body movements. Many are resistant to and upset by changes in routines. Some exhibit aggressive or self-injurious behavior. While symptoms may change or even disappear with age, social problems generally persist into adulthood, sometimes in subtle ways (Frith, 1989; Siegel, 1996).

Hallmarks of Autism Associated with Play

Among the defining features of autism are a "lack of varied, spontaneous make-believe play" and a "failure to develop peer relationships" appropriate to developmental level (American Psychiatric Association, 2000, pp. 66-67). While within the autism spectrum children naturally differ from one another in distinct ways, as a group they share similar struggles in their capacity to develop social and symbolic play. In sharp contrast to the rich social and imaginary play of typically developing children, the play of children with autism is strikingly detached and stark. Spontaneous, diverse, flexible, imaginative and interactive qualities are all noticeably lacking. (See Chapter 2 for a working definition of play.) Clearly, the difficulties children with autism experience in play are intricately linked to the central features of the disorder (see Figure 1.1).

Table 1.1

Core Features of Autism Spectrum Disorders

Core Challenges	Characteristics
Social Interaction	• Failure to use nonverbal social cues such as eye-to-eye gaze, facial expression, body postures and gestures to regulate social interaction • Failure to develop peer relationships appropriate to developmental level • Lack of spontaneous seeking to share enjoyment or interests with others • Lack of social or emotional reciprocity
Communication	• Delayed or no spoken language development. No attempt to compensate through alternative modes of communication such as gesture or mime • Inability to sustain conversation with others • Stereotyped, repetitive and idiosyncratic language patterns – uses words without attaching the usual meaning to them
Imagination	• Lack of varied, spontaneous, make-believe play or socially imitative play appropriate to developmental level • Literal orientation
Restricted, Repetitive and Stereotyped Patterns of Behavior, Activities, Interests	• Preoccupation with restricted interest that is unusual in intensity or focus • Inflexible adherence to specific, nonfunctional routines or rituals • Stereotyped and repetitive motor mannerisms (e.g., hand or finger flapping, whole body movements) • Persistent preoccupation with parts of objects
Sensory	• Sensitivities in sight, hearing, touch, smell, and taste to a greater or lesser
Theory of Mind	• Inability to take into account social perspectives of others • Failure to recognize and understand that others possess feelings, desires, beliefs that are different from one's own • Vulnerability to trickery and deception

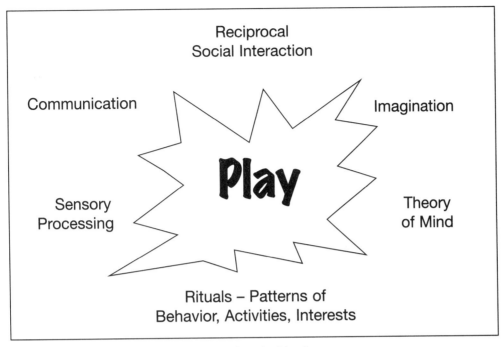

Figure 1.1. Hallmarks of autism associated with play.

Developmental Play Patterns and Variations

CASE VIGNETTE
Typical Developmental Play Patterns

Alexandra is a typically developing child. Tracing the path of her development, we see snapshots of a rich play life.

- At 10 months, she plays peek-a-boo and patty-cake with her Nana.

- At age 2, she plays beside her cousins pouring sand in and out of plastic containers of various sizes.

- At age 4, Alexandra pretends to play house and prepares a meal on the play stove with her preschool classmates.

- At age 7, she transforms her bedroom into a hospital with her friends, tending to all her stuffed animals and imaginary turtle.

- At age 10, Alexandra and her sister create an elaborate miniature world with a secret language and map to hidden treasures.

Tracing the course of symbolic and social play in typical childhood development provides a context for understanding play patterns and variations in children with autism. Typical play development reflects the child's growing understanding of objects, social awareness of self and others, emotional attachments and relationships with adults and peers. As children develop, play radically transforms in form, function and degree of complexity.

It is commonly accepted that play follows a generally consistent developmental sequence (Garvey, 1977; Piaget, 1962; Rubin, Fein, & Vandenberg, 1983; Vygotsky, 1978; Westby, 2000). Various play forms emerge and peak at different points across the age span, many of them continuing in some fashion throughout life. However, it is important to keep in mind that play does not develop as a discrete set of skills independent of other developmental attainments, nor does play develop in a step-by-step manner along a linear path. Rather play, like other aspects of behavior and development, "depends on and emerges out of a nexus of closely connected developments in [language], cognition, emotion, and social interaction ..." (Bloom & Tinker, 2002, pp. 5-6). Like a fine tapestry woven from an intricate network of fibers, play emerges in overlapping layers, each layer inextricably entwined with the next, enmeshed in color and texture, steadily unfolding into a complex design. Table 1.2 gives an overview of typical play patterns as well as variations in children with autism.

Symbolic Dimension – Typical Play Patterns

The symbolic dimension of play reflects cognitive features of play governed by developmental trends. Early signs of play are at first vague and difficult to distinguish, but progressively become more differentiated and clear. Particularly during the preschool years, children's play becomes increasingly active, varied, elaborate, representational and integrated. As children reach middle childhood, play capacities are fully formed and continue to unfold in more sophisticated ways.

Manipulation play. Manipulation play, also referred to as exploratory or sensorimotor play, is evident in early life when babies discover pleasure in sensory experiences with objects, self and others. Playful behavior is at first reflex-oriented as babies engage in whole-body movements and manipulate their mouths and hands in response to physical sensations. Infants as young as 8 weeks have been shown to smile and coo at objects that respond to their own body movements (e.g., kicking to activate a mobile tied by a ribbon to the infant's leg) (Watson, 1976). Babies soon discover pleasure in patterns of activity involving physical movement and sensory exploration of body parts.

Babies' actions gradually become more differentiated, conventionalized and organized around manipulations extended to objects. Simple manipulations are initially applied to single objects in a seemingly random and haphazard manner – such as gazing, mouthing, patting, swiping, grasping, shaking, banging, turning and dropping. Through repeated actions, babies learn to anticipate the effects of their behavior on the objects. They also gradually learn to apply more complicated schemes by combining and exploring the relational properties of objects, such as banging two blocks together, pulling, twisting and turning knobs, carrying, filling and dumping. Guided by sensory information, this type of play helps the baby assimilate information about the physical properties of objects.

Functional play. The capacity to spontaneously engage in functional play emerges by the end of the first year. In this type of play, children display the appropriate use of an object or conventional association of two or more objects – such as rolling a car on a surface or placing a cup on a saucer (Sigman & Ungerer, 1981). The child relies on objects and props with logically related properties, including constructive materials and realistic replicas. Functional play ranges from simple to more complex and elaborated forms (Williams, Reddy, & Costall, 2001).

Functional play is also sometimes referred to as simple pretense. That is, it includes a quality of delayed or deferred imitation as the child mimics familiar actions as applied to objects, self and others in everyday life. The child possesses a mental image of the object in terms of what it can do, but has not yet separated the object from the physical action itself.

Examples of functional play include simple or complex actions with constructive materials – such as placing a peg in a hole, stacking blocks, combining a train track or building with Legos. Children may also enact isolated schemes using realistic props – such as pushing a broom along the floor or putting a doll in a bed. Functional play may also involve self-directed action schemes – such as brushing one's own hair with a toy brush, trying on hats, holding a telephone to one's ear and saying "hello." Finally, a more complex form of functional play involves reenacting isolated schemes and simple scripts directed at people and dolls – such as feeding mommy with a toy spoon, brushing a doll's hair, placing a blanket on the teddy bear.

Symbolic-pretend play. Spontaneous symbolic-pretend play (also known as advanced pretense, make-believe and imaginary play) first emerges between 2 and 3 years of age. Leslie (1987) describes three fundamental forms of symbolic play:

- Object substitution – using one object to represent another (e.g., pretending a banana is a telephone)
- Attribution of absent or false properties (e.g., pretending that a dry table is wet)
- Imaginary objects as present (e.g., pretending that an empty cup contains tea)

Pretend-play scripts are initially organized around first-hand experiences with the aid of realistic props, such as putting a doll to bed with its pajamas, a blanket and pillow and commenting, "Baby sleeping." Play scripts later incorporate familiar events performed by others, such as grocery shopping with a baby doll.

Between 3 and 4 years of age, children rely less on realistic replicas or life-like props to pretend and increasingly use language to plan and narrate integrated play scripts. They are able to transform themselves into single and multiple roles by animating dolls and dramatizing characters. Sociodramatic play is particularly common at this stage as themes and scripts are inspired by the familiar or invented as pure fantasy. Imaginary companions are also commonly a part of children's pretend-play experiences (Taylor, 1999).

It is a mistaken belief that once children reach an age at which they are capable of engaging in "games with rules" – such as card games, board games and organized sports – they no longer pretend. The fact is that many children continue to pretend through middle childhood, and some a great deal longer. The pretend play of school-age children frequently goes "underground" as a result of societal constraints and pressures placed on them (Singer & Singer, 1990). Indeed, it is not uncommon for older children to live out their imaginary worlds in secret. They may create elaborate and detailed microcosms with dolls, miniatures, inventions and peer confidants (Cohen & MacKeith, 1991), or they may live out fantasies through more socially accepted mediums, such as art, writing, story-telling and drama (Dyson, 1991; Gardner, 1982).

Symbolic Dimension – Play Variations in Autism

Compared to typical children, children on the autism spectrum present unique profiles of play along the symbolic dimension. When given opportunities to play freely, for example, they tend to spend excessive amounts of time pursuing repetitive activities in isolation (Frith, 1989; Wing, Gould, Yeates, & Brierly, 1977). Many children get stuck on one or a few activities, which they may carry out for hours and continue over months and even years. Some children are attracted to conventional toys, activities and themes that reflect the play preferences of younger children as well as age-mates. Others develop fascinations or preoccupations that revolve around unusual objects or pedantic subjects.

Manipulation play. This type of play is present in children with autism at higher rates than functional or symbolic play, and in less diverse forms compared to children of a similar maturational age (Libby, Powell, Messer, & Jordan, 1998; Tilton & Ottinger, 1964). Children with autism are commonly attracted to play activities and materials that involve sensory experiences. Many young children spontaneously seek out physical or rough-and-tumble forms of play, such as running, jumping, spinning and bouncing.

Objects are often the focal point of sensory exploration. Manipulating toys and other objects in a stereotyped fashion is a frequently cited characteristic of autism (Tiegerman & Primavera, 1981). Stereotyped play routines range from simple acts – such as mouthing, banging, twisting, spinning the wheels of a toy car – to more elaborate routines and rituals, such as lining up objects according to size. Some children perform extraordinary feats of balance and coordination when they manipulate objects in play, for example, using a string as a lasso.

CASE VIGNETTE
Manipulation Play Ritual

Freddy sits cross-legged in a sand box surrounded by various toys ... a shovel, bucket, flour sifter, and miniature vehicles. Ignoring these toys, he scoops up a pile of coarse sand with both hands clasped together. He gazes into his hands; his eyes and mouth gradually open wider and wider as the bits of sand slowly flow through his fingers. He brings his hands closer to his face, staring at the granules with a glazed look in his eyes. He then separates his hands and releases the last bits of sand from his grasp. He closes his mouth while slowly flicking his fingers above the newly formed sand heap. (Wolfberg, 1999, p. 70)

Functional play. This type of play is less likely to spontaneously emerge in children on the autism spectrum compared to developmentally matched age-mates. Nevertheless, some children do display this capacity as demonstrated through conventional use and association of objects and toys (Jarrold, Boucher, & Smith, 1996). Functional play schemes may range from simple to complex, including acts that are directed to objects, self and others. Overall, children with autism spend less time in functional play and produce fewer functional play acts. In addition, they display qualitative differences in their functional play in terms of diversity, elaboration and integration of play schemes. Further, they exhibit fewer doll-directed functional play acts (Mundy, Sigman, Ungerer, & Sherman, 1986; Sigman & Ungerer, 1984; Williams et al., 2001).

CASE VIGNETTE
Functional Play Ritual

Teresa carries her unclothed doll to the classroom sink, repeating the phrase 'take a bath.' With the doll under her arm, she fills a bucket with water and dish soap, calling it 'bubble bath.' She submerges the doll in water, lifts it out, takes a bottle of shampoo, and squeezes shampoo onto its hair. She scrubs the doll's hair, repeating the phrase 'wash a hair.' Teresa dunks the doll in the bucket, lifts it out, and rinses the doll's hair with fresh water. She next takes a towel and wraps it around the doll with the head exposed. From a cupboard, she takes out a hair dryer, plugs it into a socket, and dries the doll's hair, repeating the phrase 'dry a hair.' She next takes her doll to the play corner and sits on the floor, placing the doll on her lap. She takes out the comb while holding a portion of the doll's hair in one hand and repeats the phrase 'brush a hair.' She combs and braids the doll's hair in sections. (Wolfberg, 1999, pp. 69-70)

Symbolic-pretend play. This type of play is least likely to surface spontaneously in children with autism (Baron-Cohen, 1987; Lewis & Boucher, 1988; Sigman & Ungerer, 1984). When these children do show capacities for pretend play, qualities of diversity, flexibility and creativity are noticeably lacking. They tend to incorporate fewer novel acts in their pretend play compared to children of a similar developmental level (Charman & Baron-Cohen, 1997; Jarrold, Boucher, & Smith, 1996). In addition, they have difficulty planning, organizing and integrating play scripts. Play scenarios are often carried out as rituals with little variation; they appear to be well-rehearsed scenes prompted by a predictable situation or context rather than spontaneously generated (Harris, 1993).

CASE VIGNETTE
Symbolic-Pretend Play Ritual

One of the things I like watching is when [my sister Aimee] plays dolls ... She lines them up and plays by herself ... She acts out movies with them. Like one day she was playing "The King and I" and lining up all her little people dolls. They said things exactly from the movie. She got mad because there weren't enough dolls. The king had 106 children. (Remes, 1997, pp. 4-5)

Social Dimension - Typical Play Patterns

Peer play is characterized by a continuum of social complexity and cohesiveness that traverses the age span (Parten, 1932). With increasing exposure to peers in the preschool years, children naturally engage in a variety of social play behaviors, and it is within this period that children begin to establish mutual relationships and form friendships. Social play continues through middle childhood as children acquire more sophisticated skills to participate in peer groups.

Early social play. Joint attention, imitation and emotional responsiveness are dominant features of early social play. Playful behavior is evident in the first few months of life when infants react to caregivers imitating their vocalizations and facial expressions (Garvey, 1977). Playful exchanges emerge as babies smile, laugh, imitate actions and take turns in social games, such as peek-a-boo and mirroring games (Ross & Kay, 1980). Objects are used to initiate play exchanges as babies develop the capacity to attract the adult's attention using nonverbal cues (Vandell & Wilson, 1982). Babies also develop the ability to respond to the emotional cues of their caregivers, which directly impacts on social as well as exploratory play (Sorce & Emde, 1981).

Emerging in tandem with adult social play, early play with peers also reflects capacities for joint attention, imitation and emotional sharing. By 6 months, for example, babies begin to take notice of other children (Hartup, 1983). They actively direct natural signs, such as looking, smiling, vocalizing, gesturing, reaching out and touching peers, and they show that they recognize familiar peers by reacting to them in idiosyncratic ways (Hay, 1985). Early social exchanges are brief and fleeting, as toddlers watch and mirror one another, offer and accept toys and initiate and respond to one another's emotional cues (Eckerman & Stein, 1982; Ross & Kay, 1980; Vandell & Wilson, 1982).

Continuum of social play with peers. With growing exposure to peers, children progressively learn how to coordinate their play activity and social behavior (Howes, Unger, & Matheson, 1992; Parten, 1932). Rather than following a strict sequence of developmental stages, children tend to cycle back and forth among a range of social play behaviors as they gain experience and skill. It should be noted that it is quite natural for children to occasionally spend time in solitary or independent play while in the company of peers. Thus, solitary or independent play (which is not to be confused with "isolate" play) is often a natural extension of social play with peers, as it enables children to imitate, practice, consolidate and use newly acquired skills. As children develop, play with peers progresses along a continuum that reflects increasing social complexity and cohesiveness.

When they first enter preschool, many children spend a significant amount of time as *onlookers*, observing peers at play before actually entering into the play. This often helps in orienting them to choose an activity and playmates to join. Older children, on the other hand, spend time watching peers in group situations in order to become familiar with the rules, roles and social patterns of the play culture.

Playing in *parallel* or proximity to peers is also a consistent feature of typical childhood development. In this type of play, the child plays independently alongside or nearby other children. While playing with similar play materials and in the same play space, the children do not join one another in play. They may occasionally look over, imitate, show an object and alternate actions with peers, but they do not interact in any apparent way. This type of play persists throughout childhood, offering ongoing opportunities for learning through modeled behavior.

The capacity to establish a *common focus* in play emerges as children engage in interactions that are loosely organized around mutually enjoyed play activities. In the preschool years, play interchanges gradually increase in length, frequency and complexity as children establish a common focus by actively sharing materials, taking turns, giving and receiving assistance, asking questions, giving directions and generally conversing about the play. Common focus is also reflected in sociodramatic play as children jointly construct imaginative play sequences.

Cooperative play involves complex social organization with shared *common goals*. The play is directed toward the purpose of making a product, dramatizing an event or playing a formal game. The children determine the agenda by generating rules or roles through explicit planning, negotiation and division of labor. The efforts of one child supplement those of another, thereby establishing a sense of cooperation and belonging to a group.

Peer group entry is a social capacity that children refine and master when they reach school age (Dodge, Schlundt, Schocken, & Delugach, 1983). This skill enables children to tactfully join peers in established play activities. For example, following a carefully timed sequence, the child observes and approaches the players, hovers on the periphery of the group, mimics and comments on the activity, progressively moves closer and finally waits for an invitation or a natural break to enter the group. Socially competent children are considered especially adept at entering peer groups, which reflects a high level of social awareness and finesse.

Social Dimension – Play Variations in Autism

Children on the autism spectrum present distinct variations with respect to developing social play with peers; however, as a group they share common traits. Specifically, the vast majority of them show delays or differences in the development of joint attention, spontaneous imitation and emotional responsiveness (Dawson & Adams, 1984; Lewy & Dawson, 1992; Sigman & Ruskin, 1999; Wetherby & Prutting, 1984), which clearly impacts on the capacity to engage in reciprocal interactions with peers. In the absence of explicit structure and support, these children are likely to remain isolated or on the fringes of peer groups.

Overall, children with autism make fewer overt initiations to peers. When they do attempt to socialize, their initiations tend to be subtle, obscure or poorly timed. By the same token, they are less likely to consistently respond to the social advances of peers (Lord & Magill, 1989). Coordinating play within a social-pretend framework is particularly complex since children with autism have problems comprehending and producing imaginative play (Charman & Baron-Cohen, 1997).

Social play styles. Wing and Gould (1979) describe three qualities of social behavior that are consistent with our clinical observations of children with autism at play with peers. Some children present patterns of social play that reflect a distinct social style that is consistent over time. Others present social styles that change over time. Still others present overlapping characteristics that may shift according to the social play context.

Children who seem to be withdrawn or avoidant of peers are considered *aloof.* Some of these children actively seek to steer clear of or maintain distance from peers. Others wander among peers but give the impression of being unaware of their presence as if they were gazing right through them. Aloof children are generally unresponsive to their peers' social gestures and speech. Occasionally they approach peers (as they would adults) to fulfill simple wants and needs, but treat them as if they were inanimate objects (e.g., motioning to a peer to open a bag of chips). Otherwise, these children typically do not show joint attention such as using eye gaze or gesture to attract a peer's attention for the purpose of sharing a social event.

CASE VIGNETTE
Aloof Social Play Style

Felix is a 7-year-old boy diagnosed with autism. He is enrolled in a special day class in a public elementary school. Described as having an aloof social style, Felix actively avoids peers and retreats when they approach him. During free play, he spends much of his time exploring play materials apart from his peers. Occasionally he peeks over at peers when they play beside him with materials that are of interest to him. He has a particular fascination with letter and number shapes, and spends much of his time filling and dumping them in and out of containers. From time to time he will grab coveted objects from peers, but seems oblivious to their reactions.

Passive children appear indifferent to peers, but may be easily led into social situations. These children are generally compliant and willingly go along with their peers when they take the initiative to play. Although they may spend time watching peers or play in parallel beside them, they rarely initiate social interaction on their own in obvious ways. They may have good speech and respond to clear and simply put questions. In many of the same ways as "aloof" children, passive children are unresponsive in their lack of joint attention with others. They seem unable to communicate their intentions through facial expressions and gestures, as well as to interpret others' intentions by reading their facial cues.

CASE VIGNETTE
Passive Social Play Style

Maya is a 4-year-old girl diagnosed with pervasive developmental disorder. She attends a typical preschool three mornings a week in addition to receiving home-based services. Described as having a passive social style, during free play Maya spends much of her time wandering among peers, peripherally watching them as they engage in activities. She willingly plays alongside peers, but rarely overtly initiates any sort of interaction. Maya is most attracted to play with figures featured in popular books and videos. For example, she enjoys gathering several figures and lining them up according to size. While sorting, she repeats the names of the characters and story lines from the respective book or video.

Children considered *active-odd* show an interest in being with peers, but do so in socially awkward or peculiar ways. They may go up to peers, including total strangers, and touch them or their toys without warning. They may attempt to carry on a one-sided conversation pertaining to a unique fascination or obsession of little interest to the peer. Some children have an idea of what to say and do to initiate or join peers in play, but have a poor sense of timing. Similar to children described as "aloof" and "passive," children described as "active-odd" lack social perceptiveness and skill in the use of social pragmatics, which are necessary for effective communication and establishing social relations.

CASE VIGNETTE
Active-Odd Social Play Style

Kato is a 10-year-old boy diagnosed with Asperger Syndrome. He is fully included in the fifth grade in a public elementary school. Described as having an active-odd social style, Kato is aware of being different from his classmates. He expresses a deep desire to make friends and questions why other children do not readily accept him. He makes frequent attempts to engage his peers, but his social initiations are generally poorly timed and fail to take into account his peers' perspectives. His social initiations include reciting facts and enacting play themes that center on his fascination with the airline industry. Kato enjoys amassing information on airplanes, travel schedules, maps, weather patterns and airline disasters. Rarely does he attempt to join his peers in activities that diverge from his own interests.

Table 1.2

Typical Play Patterns and Play Variations in Children with Autism

Play Domain	Typical Play Patterns	Play Variations in Autism
Symbolic Dimension	Spontaneous progression along developmental continuum	Delayed or atypical progression within developmental continuum
	Sensory exploration/manipulation play progressing from undifferentiated, repeated acts to varied acts and combinations	High rates of stereotyped sensory exploration/manipulation play involving fewer novel acts and combinations
	Functional play progressing from simple to complex and diverse play schemes reflecting deferred imitation	Spontaneous functional play less common – play schemes less integrated, incorporate fewer different novel acts and doll-directed acts
	Symbolic/pretend play progressing from simple to complex and cohesive play scripts by transforming objects, self and others and creating imaginary roles and situations	Spontaneous symbolic/pretend play least common – play scripts inflexible, literal, disjointed, reflecting difficulties in generating novelty, planning and organizing
Social Dimension	Joint attention, spontaneous imitation, emotional responsiveness evident in early social exchanges with adults and peers	Problems in joint attention, spontaneous imitation, emotional responsiveness emerging in early development and persisting in social play
	Play with peers spontaneously developing along a continuum of social complexity and cohesiveness across the age span	Spontaneous development along social continuum of play with peers impaired and variable with respect to aloof, passive, active-odd social play styles
	Socially competent children more readily accepted and included within peer play culture	Lack of social competence increases likelihood of peer neglect or rejection from play culture

Peer Cultural Influences on Children's Play

In view of the complex challenges facing children on the autism spectrum, the world of play must seem an especially foreign and confusing place. The fact is that children do not grow up in a vacuum – patterns of social and symbolic play development are naturally influenced by experiences with others and the social, cultural and societal contexts in which they participate (Bronfenbrenner, 1977; Hanson, Wolfberg, Zercher, Morgan, Gutierrez, Barnwell, & Beckman, 1998; Meyer, Park, Grenot-Scheyer, Schwartz, & Harry, 1998; Wolfberg et al., 1999).

The peer group or "peer culture" plays a decisive role in including or excluding children based on what is defined as acceptable or unacceptable behavior (Wolfberg et al., 1999). The reality for many children with autism is that their behavior does not fit into peer perceptions of what is "normal." For example, unconventional attempts to socialize and play are frequently mistaken as signs of deviance or limited social interest. Consequently, children with autism may be teased and taunted by intolerant peers or simply disregarded by good-hearted peers.

In a recent study that explored the peer culture of children with diverse abilities in inclusive preschool programs, we uncovered a number of themes that give insight into how children with autism experience play with peers (Odom et al., 2001; Wolfberg et al., 1999).

Desire to Belong

First we discovered that all the children with disabilities in our sample (which included several children with autism spectrum disorders) expressed the desire and/or need for peer cultural affiliation. Overall, the children displayed various forms of social-communicative and symbolic behavior signifying intentions to be with, like and accepted by peers. While some children communicated their intentions clearly through conventional verbal and nonverbal means, the children with autism generally used less refined or unconventional social-communicative strategies. Their initiations ranged from relatively subtle, passive and indirect approaches (e.g., watching, following, imitating, touching peers and their materials) to more overt and complex modes of social-communicative and symbolic behavior (e.g., sharing, gesturing, talking with peers, talking and writing about peers, and taking roles in play).

Inclusion in Peer Culture

Another significant finding was that all the children with disabilities experienced some form of inclusion in their respective peer culture. We observed a variety of circumstances in which they successfully coordinated social activity and established reciprocal relationships with peers as playmates, partners and/or friends. However, social encounters between the children with autism and peers tended to be brief and fleeting. In some cases, the ability to establish common ground around shared interests formed a basis for these children to relate to one another and engage in collective activity. More often than not, typically developing peers played a major role in facilitating the inclusion of the children with autism through their own social behavior (e.g., interpreting and responding to social cues, normalizing unconventional behavior, helping, guiding, and caring for children).

Exclusion from Peer Culture

Exclusion from peer culture was also a reality that the majority of children with disabilities encountered in their preschool classrooms. Peer cultural exclusion took many forms, ranging from passive neglect to overt rejection. In some cases, this was reflected in segregation of children with disabilities from those without disabilities. As a result, some children with disabilities remained isolated from the larger peer culture within their preschool classes. Just as the social behavior of typically developing peers influenced the inclusion of children with disabilities, this resulted in incidents of exclusion (e.g., apathy and indifference, misinterpreting and overlooking social cues, conflict over space and property, and tattletales, gossip, and cliques).

Transactional Nature of Peer Cultural Participation

The process leading to children's inclusion in or exclusion from the peer culture is transactional. Differences among children with autism in social and linguistic competence, play development, language acquisition, and exposure to and experience with peers will likely influence how they initiate entry into, and ultimately experience inclusion in or exclusion from the peer play culture. Interpreting the codes and conventions of the peer play culture may be especially complex for children with autism to comprehend and master without explicit guidance. Without this tacit understanding, however, the potential to "fit in" or conform to the expectations of the peer culture is greatly diminished.

By the same token, differences among typically developing peers in social perceptions, skill, experience, language, motivation and/or intuitiveness will likely influence their capacity to accommodate children's differing abilities and needs. The ways in which peers respond to and/or support children with autism, in turn, will naturally impact the degree and quality of their participation in peer cultural activities.

Chapter Summary

In this chapter we explored the nature of autism and the complex problems children with ASD experience in play (with and without peers). Autism is a spectrum disorder characterized by a distinct constellation of features that are intricately tied to atypical patterns of social and symbolic play development. For example, the impulse and potential for play, while not entirely absent, is difficult to discern compared to typically developing children. The unusual ways in which children with autism relate to objects and people often set them apart from their peer culture. As a result, they may become caught in a cycle of exclusion, which deprives them of opportunities to learn how to socialize and play in more conventional and socially accepted ways.

With these key points in mind, in the next chapter, we explore the major principles and concepts that underlie the Integrated Play Groups model as a way to counteract the unique and complex challenges facing children with autism spectrum disorders.

CHAPTER 2

Making Play
a Priority

Chapter Highlights

This chapter explores play from multiple perspectives to introduce the major principles and concepts that underlie the Integrated Play Groups (IPG) model. The following topics will be highlighted:

► What Is Play?

► Play's Prominent Role in Childhood

► The Art of Guiding Peer Play

► Essential Features of the IPG Model

We were taught to say that play is the work of children.
But, watching and listening to them,
I saw that play was nothing less than Truth and Life.

– Vivian Paley (1999)

One of the major hurdles my colleagues and I encounter as educators, consultants and practitioners is convincing those who make decisions on behalf of children with autism to include play, and especially peer play, on their list of priorities. On the surface it seems ironic that until recently few have embraced play as a relevant concern for children with autism, particularly in view of play's pervasive role in the lives of children. Yet history has shown that perceptions of play's purpose and place in the education, treatment and family life of children are forever shifting with the Zeitgeist – the winds of time.

There is no doubt that we live in an age of the "hurried" (Elkind, 1981) and "scheduled" (Bartlett, 1999) child. What this means for many children on the autism spectrum is that days are jam-packed with school, therapy sessions and all the shuttling back and forth this entails, leaving little room for play. But even when time for play is included in their busy agenda, it is questionable whether children with autism are gaining access to "genuine play." This reality is most disturbing if we consider what children miss out on when they do not have either the opportunity or the means to play.

What Is Play?

One of life's many mysteries is the question, What is the true meaning of play? Although we think that we can easily recognize when a child is playing, defining play is notoriously difficult. Play comes in many forms. Philosophers, psychologists, anthropologists and educators are among those who have studied play without reaching consensus on a single definition. Play definitions typically reflect one's theoretical orientation. For our purposes, it is essential to make a distinction between *what play is* and *what play is not* in order to support children with autism in the best ways possible. Our working definition of play draws on several well-known researchers who characterize play's prevailing characteristics in children's development (Garvey, 1977; Rubin et al., 1983; Smith & Vollstedt, 1985).

Play Is Pleasurable

When children play, it is clear to us that they are enjoying themselves. Signs of positive affect, such as smiling and laughter, naturally reflect children's delight in play. Children may exhibit other signs as well, such as blissful humming or singing. But a blatantly cheerful demeanor does not always accompany children's play. Children can look quite serious and subdued while deeply engaged in the joy of play.

Play Requires Active Engagement

Children become deeply absorbed in activities as they explore, experiment, create and share roles in play. This is in contrast to inactive or passive states, such as wandering aimlessly or lounging for extended periods. In some cases, daydreaming may reflect active engagement when children indicate that they are playing with ideas or inventing a fantasy.

Play Is Spontaneous, Voluntary and Intrinsically Motivated

In play, children freely choose the activity – it is impossible to force a child to play. The motivation to play comes from within the child and occurs without external demands or rewards.

Play Involves Attention to Means Over Ends

In play, the focus is on the process rather than the attainment of a particular goal or outcome. Children set their own agenda, which is self-imposed and open-ended rather than externally imposed and directed by others.

Play Is Flexible and Changing

Children are free to do the unexpected, change the rules, and experiment with novel combinations of behavior and ideas in play. Play is forever transforming as children vary, elaborate and diversify existing themes. This quality of play is in contrast to highly rigid, repetitive and inflexible behavior that we associate with stereotyped activity.

Play Has a Nonliteral Orientation

This characteristic distinguishes play from nonplay behavior as children treat objects, actions or events "as if" they were something else. Children give clear signals to one another to indicate this nonliteral orientation. In pretend play, for example, children can tell what is real and what is make-believe. They learn to make this distinction even before they start pretending – such as figuring out the difference between real and feigned aggression in rough-and-tumble play. It is this aspect of play that enables even young animals to read and interpret social codes and cues that help them adapt to group life.

Play's Prominent Role in Childhood

Play as a Universal Phenomenon

While for centuries questions have endured regarding the functions and value of play, the fact remains that play exists and is ever present in childhood. Children play regardless of culture, ethnicity, socioeconomic status and whether they are raised with or without siblings, in urban or rural settings or in healthy or unhealthy conditions.

In the best of circumstances, children benefit from a key person who plays and encourages play – a person who inspires and sanctions play and shows trust, acceptance and delight in children's capacity for playfulness (Singer & Singer, 1990). Children also need space and open-ended, unstructured time to explore and carry out their fantasies in play. In addition, props are fundamental to play, ranging from simple objects to elaborate toys and even pets. Nevertheless, Singer and Singer (1990) propose that even when left alone with no encouragement to play, no place to play, and nothing to play with, children will still find ways to play because they are naturally inquisitive.

There are many examples of children who have grown up under less than optimal conditions with documented histories of highly imaginative games and toys. In the United States, for examples, children of African origin who grew up as slaves on plantations had an immensely rich play culture, which continues to inspire children's play today (Smith, 1963). Similarly, Appalachia, a largely economically deprived region, has an elaborately documented collection of creative games and toys (Page & Smith, 1985).

Even children who are victims of the most devastating circumstances such as natural disasters, war and genocide have been known to play. George Eisen (1988) provides the most compelling testimony of children playing during the Holocaust as he documents the almost surreal imaginary play worlds created by children living in the Jewish ghettos and the heart-breaking scenes of children engrossed in play just moments before entering the gas chambers.

Another universal aspect of play is that children are drawn to play with one another whenever the opportunity arises. Around the world it is common to see children of all ages playing together in groups. In many cases, the older children integrate the younger ones into their play while caring for them. The props and themes incorporated in the play represent the tools, patterns and rituals of daily life activity within their society and culture. For instance, when I traveled through Nepal I came across a group of children on the street playing with flower petals. Flowers have great significance in Nepali life as they are used in many religious ceremonies. By comparison, it is interesting to note that the most popular themes in our Integrated Play Groups here in the United States revolve around shopping.

Play as a Universal Phenomenon

- Children from virtually all walks of life play
- Optimal conditions for play include a key person, places, time and props
- Children strive to play even in the face of misfortune
- Children are drawn to play with one another, often in mixed-age groups
- Props and themes in play reflect tools, life activities and rituals of society and culture

Play as Children's Culture

When children join together as a group, they construct a peer culture that is uniquely their own (Corsaro, 1985, 1988, 1992; Wolfberg et al., 2000). An essential feature of this peer culture is that children develop a sense of collective identity in which they recognize themselves as members of a group created exclusively by and for children. Although the adult world is often represented within the context of children's peer culture, children pursue social activity that is most meaningful to them on their own terms regardless of adult expectations. For instance, a group of young girls may sneak off during school hours to put on make-up like grown-ups while knowing full well that they are contradicting the wishes and values of grown-ups. Since play is the leading social activity in the lives of children, it is the very essence of their peer culture.

"Play culture" more accurately describes that realm in which children create and live out their social and imaginary lives (Mouritsen, 1996; Schuler & Wolfberg, 2000; Selmer-Olson, 1993; Wolfberg, 1994, 1999; Wolfberg et al., 2000). It is based on active participation in those social activities that are most valued by the peer group. In a sense, play culture is living folklore that manifests itself in the rituals, narratives and creations children produce and pass on to one another. The skills, values and knowledge acquired through peer play experiences are a part of the cultural tradition transmitted to each new generation of children. For instance, the games that children play on the streets and playgrounds of America – such as hand-clapping songs, jump rope, jacks – can be traced back through the generations to many lands (Smith, 1963).

Play as Children's Culture

- Play is the most valued social activity in children's peer culture
- Play is the realm in which children create social and imaginary worlds apart from adults
- Play is living folklore as expressed in rituals, narratives and creations, passed on from one generation to the next

Play in Children's Development

It is within the culture of play that children learn and develop in a multitude of ways. For example, a plethora of research connects play to advances in children's cognitive, language, literacy, social, emotional, creative and sensory motor development. (See Table 2.1 for an overview of play's contributions to child development; for a more in-depth review, see Wolfberg, 1999.) Vygotsky (1966, 1978) regarded play as instrumental to the child's growing capacity for social understanding and symbolic representation. He further recognized active participation in play with others as critical to the process. (A more detailed discussion on Vygotsky's influence in this area follows.)

Peers perform an especially critical role when it comes to play as they foster opportunities for learning and development in ways that cannot be duplicated by adults (Hartup, 1979, 1983; Wolfberg et al., 1999). After all, when it comes to play, children are the true experts. By watching, following, imitating, sharing space and materials, coordinating activities and pretending with peers, children gain a host of interrelated skills that are necessary for attaining social competence and forming meaningful friendships.

Social pretend play is an especially important vehicle for children to acquire symbolic capacities, interpersonal skills and social knowledge. Within a social pretend framework, children integrate progressively complex actions and roles to achieve interpersonal coordination in play. For example, while collaborating on play scripts, they mutually explore social roles and issues of intimacy, trust, negotiation and compromise – such as sorting out what roles and themes to act out while playing dolls with friends. By constructing a shared understanding of literal and nonliteral meaning, children also deepen their communication skills and understanding in social pretend play. This represents the child's growing awareness and appreciation of the existence of mental states (such as feelings, desires, intentions and beliefs) in oneself and others, known as a "theory of mind."

Play as a Human Right

Play also has meaning for all children, as it is a fundamental human right. This notion has existed for over half a century as a tenet of the United Nations Declaration of Human Rights.

The child shall have full opportunity for play and recreation,
which should be directed to the same purpose as education; society and
public authorities shall endeavor to promote the employment of this right.

United Nations Declaration of Human Rights, 1948, Principle 7 (adopted 1959)

A number of respected organizations, such as the International Association for the Child's Right to Play, the Association for Childhood Education International, and the National Association for the Education of Young Children affirm that play is essential for all children's healthy growth and development (see

Resources in Appendix C). Despite their dedicated efforts through education and public policy to uphold the right of all children to play, the impact on children with autism remains elusive. There is no question that when children are kept apart from their peer group and respective play cultures, they are being deprived of this basic human right.

Yet even when opportunities for peer play are provided to children with autism, it is often not enough to ensure equal access to full participation in play. Conditions suitable for most typical children to spontaneously play – providing access to space, time, props and peers – may not be sufficient for children on the autism spectrum who lack an apparent predisposition to play in typical ways. The Integrated Play Groups model offers these children explicit guidance and support in an effort to fulfill this basic human right.

Table 2.1

Play's Contributions to Children's Development

Developmental Domain	Developmental Acquisitions
Cognition	Knowledge of functional, spatial, causal, categorical relationships; problem solving, mental planning, flexible and divergent thinking; association, logical memory, and abstract thought
Social Competence	Verbal and nonverbal communication, perspective-taking, social awareness; exploration of social roles and issues of intimacy, trust, negotiation and compromise to form friendships
Language	New vocabulary; forms and functions of language; complex language structures; rules of conversation; metalinguistic awareness
Literacy (Reading and Writing)	Interest in stories, knowledge of story structure and story comprehension; narrative competence; understanding of fantasy in books; use of symbols to represent the world
Emotional Expression	Regulation of affect and emotion; expression of thoughts and feelings; working through emotional conflicts
Creative-Artistic Expression	Inventiveness, imagination, symbolic representation; enlarged collection of novel ideas and associations
Sensory-Motor	Fine- and gross-motor skills; body awareness; sensory regulation

Play as a Path to Inclusion

Bearing in mind play's social, cultural and developmental significance raises deep concern for children on the autism spectrum, who as a group experience the most significant challenges in play. It is especially worrisome that when given access to space, time, props and peers, these children are not drawn to play and participate in their peer group in ways that we would expect of typically developing children. Consequently, children with autism are unlikely to reap the benefits of play that come naturally to most other children, even when the odds are against them. The result is a "Catch-22" situation – children with limited peer socialization and play skills are likely to be excluded from participating in play culture, yet without actively participating in play culture, they are unlikely to develop the peer socialization and play skills needed to escape their isolation.

In order to break this vicious cycle, the surrounding play culture must adapt to include children with diverse abilities and unique ways of relating, communicating and playing. While typically developing children are the true experts when it comes to play, adults must pave the way for the peer group to alter their skill, experience and perceptions so that a new play culture may emerge. Specifically, the peer group must learn to be more aware, responsive and inclusive of children with social challenges. Through Integrated Play Groups we are making a conscious effort to make this happen in a methodical and all-inclusive manner.

The Art of Guiding Peer Play

The concept for Integrated Play Groups emerged in response to the need to provide children with autism and related special needs the opportunity and means to fully participate in their peer play culture. While interventions that involve play are among the wide range of educational and treatment options available for children with autism, it remains in question whether they are actually directed to the same purpose (for reviews, see Boucher, 1999; National Research Council, 2001; Wolfberg, 1999). As objectives and methods greatly vary, it is not clear to what extent they reflect an understanding of the true nature of play and the obstacles children with autism encounter.

On the one extreme, interventions that involve play tend to be highly structured and adult-directed rather than child-initiated. Play goals are actually work in sheep's clothing, directed toward achieving a discrete set of skills. The very notion of a "play drill" is an oxymoron when one considers the real essence of play. On the other extreme are interventions that tend to lack structure altogether, led by the assumption that play is something that children simply do when they are left on their own. This clearly defies logic in light of what we know to be core symptoms of autism spectrum disorders. Even with the best of intentions, such interventions fall far short of providing sufficient support to tap into children's full potential for play and peer cultural inclusion.

The Integrated Play Groups model strives to maximize the potential of every child with autism to socialize and play with peers within the context of a jointly constructed play culture. Drawing on multiple theoretical perspectives as well as current research and best practices, the model reflects a blending of approaches to foster social interaction, communication, play and imagination in the most effective and meaningful ways possible.

Vygotsky's Influence

The ideas and approaches of many remarkable researchers and practitioners helped to shape and continue to inspire the Integrated Play Groups model (for a review, see Wolfberg, 1999; refer also to References and Selected Readings in Appendix C). A major source of inspiration for developing the Integrated Play Groups model derives from the work of Russian psychologist Lev Vygotsky (1966, 1978), who ascribed a most vital role to play's meaning in the lives of children. According to Vygotsky, play's significance extends beyond that of merely representing stages of development to actually leading development:

> In play a child always behaves beyond his average age, above his daily behavior; in play it is as though he were a head taller than himself. As in the focus of a magnifying glass, play contains all developmental tendencies in a condensed form and is itself a major source of development. (Vygotsky, 1978, p. 102)

Vygotsky further emphasized that social factors mediate all learning and development. According to his theories, children develop through active participation in culturally valued social activity with others. He recognized play, and particularly pretend play, as a primary social activity through which children acquire symbolic capacities, interpersonal skills and social knowledge. Through participation in play, children construct shared meanings and transform their understanding of the skills, values and knowledge inherent to their culture. Vygotsky even considered independent play as social activity since the enactment of themes, roles and scripts reflects the child's sociocultural experiences in everyday life – such as acting out a tea party with dolls. This emphasis on the social nature of play conforms to Vygotsky's main premise that the transmission of culture through social interaction is critical to the formation of mind.

Vygotsky suggested that play creates the "zone of proximal development," whereby more experienced partners are able to maximize the child's developmental potential by scaffolding or systematically adjusting their assistance to match or slightly exceed the level at which the child is able to perform independently. He defines the "zone of proximal development" as:

> ... the distance between the child's actual developmental level as determined by independent problem solving and the level of potential development as determined through problem solving under adult guidance or in collaboration with more capable peers. (Vygotsky, 1978, p. 86)

The Integrated Play Groups model applies Vygotskian theory by infusing the notion of "guided participation" in the intervention. This concept was also inspired by Rogoff (1990), who incorporated Vygotsky's ideas in her cross-cultural research in cognitive development. *Guided participation* refers to the process through which children develop while actively participating in a culturally valued activity with the guidance, support and challenge of social partners who vary in skill and status. Thus, Integrated Play Groups create conditions for children with autism to develop while actively participating within the culture of play with more competent peers and the guidance of a skilled adult. It is within this sociocultural context that we provide individualized support that is sufficiently intensive and responsive to the child's underlying difference and unique developmental potential.

Qualities of Effective and Meaningful Practice

The process of guiding children with autism in play with peers cannot easily be translated into a step-by-step approach. Peer play guidance is an art that requires a blend of knowledge, skill, experience and intuition to refine and master. It requires adopting a flexible and holistic style involving many layers and levels of awareness and support. Play guides must therefore draw on a number of different sources of knowledge and insight to accommodate children with diverse developmental levels, learning styles, interests and experiences. The art of guiding children's socialization and imagination through peer play may be understood as involving distinct qualities of effective and meaningful practice. These qualities are summarized in Table 2.2. (For a more in-depth discussion, see Schuler & Wolfberg, 2000, pp. 262-263.)

Essential Features of the IPG Model

Table 2.2

Summary of Qualities of Effective and Meaningful Practice in Integrated Play Groups

Quality Indicators of Play Guides	
Knowledge of Autism Spectrum Disorders	Demonstrates basic theoretical understanding of nature of autism
Understanding and Appreciating Play	Demonstrates basic theoretical understanding and values play's central role in childhood development and culture
Astute Observation Skills	Well versed in informal and formal play observation techniques
"Theory of Mind"	Demonstrates heightened empathy for children with autism
Providing a Secure Base for Play	Nurtures relationships with all the children
Setting the Stage for Play	Provides external structure in the environment and play session to elicit spontaneous and flexible forms of play
Scaffolding Play	Systematically adjusts assistance to support child's emerging skills within the "zone of proximal development"

Table 2.2 *continued*

Quality Indicators of Play Guides	
Mediating Shared Perspectives	Acts as interpreter and social guide to establish common ground among novice and expert players
Dramatizing and Ritualizing Play	Uses exaggerated affect, imitation and repeated activity patterns to stimulate joint attention in play
Narrating Scripts	Expands on children's actions and verbalizations to construct a sense of story in play
Reflective Practice	Reflects on self to refine skills needed to guide children in play with peers

(Adapted from Schuler & Wolfberg, 2000)

The Case of Jamie – a.k.a. Little Salvador Dali (continued)

As introduced in the previous chapter, Jamie is a child with autism whose limited play and social abilities set him apart from his peer group. He eventually had the opportunity to participate in Integrated Play Groups along with another child with autism and three typically developing peers from his school. These groups met twice weekly for 30 minutes in his classroom with me as the play guide.

Jamie initially resisted the change in his routine. It took a lot of trial and error to find activities that would engage him. By the fourth session he had broken all the rules, including "treat the toys nicely," as he randomly removed items from the shelf and threw them about. I interpreted this as a play initiation and suggested that the children make a game out of throwing. As a result, I directed and modeled a game of tossing beanbags into boxes of various colors. I introduced cue cards showing steps for taking turns. The expert players next came up with the idea of throwing all the soft animals and dolls onto a bed sheet that they held taut to create a trampoline effect. This captured Jamie's attention for a short time until he got the idea to break another rule, "stay in the play area."

Jamie ran out into the classroom with the apparent intent of filling up a cup with water to throw it at his beloved clock. I interpreted this as yet another attempt to initiate play and shaped it into a game of chase with an expert player. Jamie and his pal found this hilarious, as they scuttled back and forth between the play area and the big clock. At a certain point the two boys began to wear down, but Jamie continued to look back at his playmate with a devilish grin, anticipating being chased again. On a hunch I suggested to the expert player (who was a rather large and stocky boy in comparison to Jamie) that he simply pick up Jamie from behind and carry him back to the play area. Like magic, Jamie relaxed in his arms and went along for the ride.

Jamie remained calm and eagerly awaited the next event. As his peers became immersed in pretending to play school, it took no coaxing at all for Jamie to join them in the role of writing up the schedule for the day on the chalkboard. He impressed the other children as he skillfully composed the text and drew clocks denoting the times for each activity. From that day forward, Jamie never left the play area as he found joy in playing with his peers while participating in a wide range of creative activities. Jamie had been fully accepted as a member of the play culture.

The art of guiding children in Integrated Play Groups (IPG) is enacted through a carefully tailored system of support. The following is an overview of the essential features of the Integrated Play Groups model (see Table 2.3 for a summary). Each of these components will be further elaborated and illustrated in subsequent chapters throughout this book.

IPG Program Design

An Integrated Play Group consists of a small group of children with diverse abilities (novice and expert players), who regularly play together under the guidance of a trained adult facilitator (play guide). Integrated Play Groups are customized as a part of a child's individual education/therapy program coinciding with other accepted approaches (e.g., relationship-based, developmental, speech-language-communication, behavioral, educational, social skills, sensory integration). Groups are designed to support preschool- through elementary-aged children (approximately 3 to 11 years).

Play groups are made up of three to five children with a higher ratio of expert to novice players. Novice players include children of all abilities on the autism spectrum and with related special needs. Expert players include typical peers/siblings with strong social, communication and play skills. Expert players are recruited from places where children ordinarily have contact with peers (e.g., school, family friends, neighbors, community). Playmates ideally have some familiarity and attraction to one another and the potential for developing long-lasting friendships. Groups may vary with respect to children's gender, ages, developmental status and play interaction styles.

Play guides receive training and supervision to facilitate Integrated Play Groups. They include skilled practitioners, family caregivers or other care providers experienced in working with children on the autism spectrum. Many have advanced degrees in such fields as general and special education, speech and language therapy, psychology, mental health and occupational therapy. (Refer to Phase II for more details on IPG program design.)

IPG Environmental Design

Integrated Play Groups take place in natural play environments within school, home, therapy or community settings (e.g., inclusive classrooms, after-school programs, recreation centers or neighborhood parks). Play groups generally meet twice a week for 30- to 60-minute sessions over a 6- to 12-month period. Times may vary depending upon the age and developmental stage of the participating children.

Thoughtful preparation goes into creating safe, familiar, predictable and highly motivating play environments in which children are comfortable to explore and socialize. Play spaces are specially designed based on a consideration of multiple factors including size, density, organization and thematic arrangements. Play materials include a wide range of sensory-motor, exploratory, constructive and sociodramatic props with high potential for interactive and imaginative play. Play materials vary in degree of structure and complexity to accommodate children's diverse interests, learning styles and developmental levels.

Table 2.3

Summary of Essential Features of the Integrated Play Groups Model

Features of the Integrated Play Groups Model	
Mission	To provide a haven for children with diverse abilities to create genuine play worlds together, where they may reach their social and imaginative potential, as well as have fun and make friends
IPG Program Design	
Objectives	• Foster spontaneous, mutually enjoyed, reciprocal play with peers • Expand/diversify social and symbolic play repertoire • Enhance peer-mediated play activities with minimal adult guidance
Service Delivery	• Preschool-/elementary-aged children (3 to 11 years) • Customized as part of education/therapy program • Led by trained adult facilitator (play guide)
Play Group Composition	3 to 5 children per group – higher ratio of expert to novice players • *Novice players* – children of all abilities on the autism spectrum and with related special needs • *Expert players* – typically developing peers/siblings
IPG Environmental Design	
Schedule	Play group sessions meet 2 times per week for 30-60 minutes over 6- to 12-month period
Play Setting	• Natural integrated settings – school, home, therapy or community • Specially designed play spaces – wide range of motivating materials, activities and themes – encourage interactive and imaginative play
Play Session Structure	Consistent routines, rituals and visual supports foster familiarity, predictability and a cohesive group identity
IPG Assessment	
Observation Framework	Naturalistic observation of children at play: • Social play styles • Symbolic dimension of play • Social dimension of play • Communicative functions and means • Play preferences – diversity of play
Assessment Tools	• Play Questionnaire • Play Preference Inventory • Integrated Play Groups Observation • Profile of Individual Play Development • Record of Monthly Progress in IPG (with sample goals) • IPG Summative Report
IPG Intervention	
Guided Participation	System of support to facilitate social interaction, communication, play and imagination by skillfully applying the following practices: • Monitoring play initiations • Scaffolding play • Social-communication guidance • Play guidance

Play sessions are structured by establishing routines and rituals that foster familiarity, predictability and a cohesive group identity. Personalized visual calendars and schedules help children anticipate the days and times of meetings. Basic rules for fair and courteous behavior and appropriate care of materials are presented at the outset of play groups. Play sessions include an opening and closing ritual (e.g., greeting, song and brief discussion of plans and strategies). Group membership is established by creating play group names and associated rituals. (Refer to Phase II for more details on IPG environmental design.)

IPG Assessment

The art of guiding children in Integrated Play Groups hinges on conducting quality assessments based on astute observations of children at play. Play guides must be well versed in the range of assessment tools and techniques specifically developed for use with this model. Systematic observations provide a basis for setting realistic and meaningful goals, guiding decisions on how best to intervene on behalf of the novice players, and systematically documenting and analyzing the children's progress. Thus, Integrated Play Groups assessments include a focus on social play styles, social and symbolic dimensions of play, communication functions and means, play preferences and diversity of play. (Refer to Phase III for more details on IPG assessment.)

IPG Intervention – "Guided Participation"

The intervention, *guided participation*, is enacted through a carefully designed system of support. Play sessions are tailored to the unique interests, abilities and needs of the children. The play guide methodically guides novice and expert players to engage in mutually enjoyed play activities that encourage social interaction, communication, play and imagination – such as pretending, constructing, art, music, movement and interactive games. Gradually the children learn how to play together with less and less adult support. The idea is to enhance opportunities that allow novice and expert players to initiate and incorporate desired activity into socially coordinated play while challenging novice players to practice new and increasingly complex forms of play. Play guides facilitate Integrated Play Groups by applying a key set of practices.

- *Monitoring play initiations* focuses on uncovering novice players' meaningful attempts to socialize and play by recognizing, interpreting and responding to the unique ways in which they express intentions to play in the company of peers.
- *Scaffolding play* involves building on the child's play initiations by systematically adjusting assistance to match or slightly exceed the level at which the child is independently able to engage in play with peers within the child's "zone of proximal development."
- *Social-communication guidance* focuses on supporting novice and expert players in using verbal and nonverbal strategies to elicit each other's attention and sustain joint engagement in mutually enjoyed play activities.

• *Play guidance* encompasses strategies that support novice players in peer play experiences that are slightly beyond the child's capacity while fully immersed in the whole play experience at his present level, even if participation is minimal.

(Refer to Phase IV for more details on IPG intervention.)

Chapter Summary

In this chapter we explored the many meanings of play. Play's defining features include spontaneous, pleasurable and active engagement with objects, self and others. We examined play's prominent role in the lives of children, establishing its intrinsic value and significance from a sociocultural, developmental and human rights perspective. This has powerful implications for children with autism who have neither the opportunity nor the means to play without explicit support. Within this conceptual framework we introduced the art of guiding children's socialization and imagination through peer play and the essential features of the Integrated Play Groups model.

The remainder of this book is devoted to translating theory into effective and meaningful practice. We now turn to Phase II, which focuses on designing Integrated Play Groups for children.

PHASE II
Setting the Stage for Play
Integrated Play Groups Program and Environmental Design

The stage is not merely the meeting place of all the arts,
but is also the return of art to life.

- Oscar Wilde

CHAPTER 3

Planning Integrated Play Groups

Chapter Highlights

This chapter focuses on the initial stages of the planning process for designing Integrated Play Groups programs. The following topics will be highlighted:

► Deciding if Integrated Play Groups Are Appropriate for a Child

► Initiating the Process

► Formulating an Integrated Play Groups Action Plan

► Team Planning

► Designating Roles and Responsibilities

► Other Planning Issues

How I Began Integrated Play Groups

My Background

I became involved with Integrated Play Groups when I attended an initial seminar with Pamela Wolfberg in the spring of 2000. I was inspired by her stories and her work. I run the districtwide elementary autism program at one of the local elementary schools in [my community]. I have five boys in my communication-based program. I am a speech and language pathologist with an early childhood minor. Because of my early childhood experience, I understand the importance of play in child development. Because of my speech and language background, I understand the importance of social communication skills. This is why Integrated Play Groups sounded so appealing to me that I decided to take action.

Writing Grants

I wrote a grant that would allow me to obtain advanced training, supervision and consultation time ... I was awarded that grant, and I began to learn more about Integrated Play Groups. I then wrote a second grant in order to obtain funding for toys and materials for my "play room." Thankfully, that grant was also awarded due to a very supportive community funding program ...

Setting up the Play Environment

I work in a building that was built in 1919, so there are many little "useless" rooms. I turned one of these "useless" rooms into my playroom. Over the summer of 2000, I was able to purchase recommended toys and materials and get started on the play environment.

Recruiting and Preparing the Players

By the time the 2000-2001 school year began, I was almost ready to get started. When the school year began, I sent home permission slips with my students and the peers that I chose as expert players – although one of my third-grade students actually picked his own group members. Once the permission slips were returned, and the members were in place, I had a meeting with the players in order to explain our objectives.

In October of 2000, my Integrated Play Groups were underway. I learned many, many things over the next seven months, as did everyone else involved.

Tara Tuchel – Apprentice Play Guide
(Note: Tara will share more of her experiences guiding children in Integrated Play Groups in Chapter 8)

Tara is one of the more gifted practitioners to become a qualified play guide. As her experiences as an apprentice vividly portray, a great deal of thought and preparation goes into creating successful Integrated Play Groups. Without a doubt, the best laid plans pay off in the long run. Putting forth the extra effort upfront to get organized and systematically execute a well-formulated plan will lift a tremendous weight off your shoulders when your play groups begin in earnest. Unencumbered by bureaucratic details, you may concentrate on developing your craft to guide the children in play.

Deciding if Integrated Play Groups Are Appropriate for a Child

Within the past decade there has been a rapid increase in the number and variety of interventions, therapies and approaches devoted to children on the autism spectrum. While the good news is that there are now many more choices, the task of sorting out what to include in a child's individualized education and therapy program can be daunting. This is complicated by the fact that there are a lot of mixed messages as to what constitutes viable and effective methods to meet the needs of a given child.

The one lesson that we can all agree upon is that "one size does not fit all." We fully appreciate that every child is unique, not only from a developmental perspective but also in terms of culture and social experience. Thus, the practices that comprise the Integrated Play Groups model may be appropriate for some children (at specific points in their development and life experience) and not for others.

Further, when Integrated Play Groups are deemed appropriate, outcomes are likely to differ from one child to another depending upon a variety of factors. Since Integrated Play Groups are intended to be a part of a child's education and therapy program, we make no claims to have all the answers and certainly do not hold out any promise of a recovery or cure.

So, the question remains, How do you make an informed decision on behalf of a child? As I would advise professionals and families alike, consider all the options that may potentially address a child's peer socialization and play needs. Think about the goals you have in mind for the child and compare and weigh the alternatives. The purpose here is to offer a starting place to gain information about Integrated Play Groups as one possible approach among others.

Initiating the Process

The decision to initiate Integrated Play Groups as a part of a child's educational and/or therapy program centers, first and foremost, on the child. The family naturally also plays a pivotal role in the decision-making process. Integrated Play Groups are generally recommended by a professional or parent once (a) it has been established that the child in question has specific difficulties or delays in development that impact on his capacity to spontaneously play and socialize with peers; and (b) there is agreement that the child would potentially benefit from an intensive intervention to specifically address those needs. There are a number of different ways in which to initiate the process (see Table 3.1).

Referrals

One way in which Integrated Play Groups may be initiated is through outside referrals. Referrals often derive from evaluations generated by diagnosticians, developmental specialists, school personnel, therapists and/or other pro-

fessionals with knowledge of a particular child's needs. Recommendations may be made to a school district, community agency or other service or care provider to supply the necessary resources and support to effectively implement an Integrated Play Groups program for the child.

Grassroots Efforts

One of the more common ways in which Integrated Play Groups may be initiated for children is through grassroots efforts. We have worked closely with a number of school districts, agencies and community-based programs that specifically infuse the practices of Integrated Play Groups within the range of services they provide to children with autism and related special needs. Both small- and large-scale programs have been adopted whereby one, a few or many children are served within a particular site, district or agency. We have also guided parents to launch peer play programs within their homes or community by coordinating services through family support groups and organizations.

Whatever the case, the most successful Integrated Play Groups enacted at the grassroots level are those that involve the collaborative efforts of parents, professionals and administrators based on a shared commitment to ensuring adequate preparation and support for staff. This includes providing the necessary training and field supervision as well as space, time and supplies to effectively carry out the model.

IEP Process

Integrated Play Groups are increasingly being initiated and carried out through the IEP (Individualized Education Program) process. In many circumstances, the IEP team comes to an agreement that the practices that comprise the Integrated Play Groups model are appropriate for a particular child. The IEP team decides that these practices should be adopted as an integral component of a child's educational/therapy program in order to: (a) enable the child to achieve his goals and objectives, and (b) ensure an appropriate education that includes access to typically developing peers. Once the IEP is signed off, it is the responsibility of the serving school district or agency to ensure that appropriate personnel receive the necessary training and field supervision as well as space, time and supplies to effectively carry out the practices to meet the needs of the child.

Table 3.1
Initiating Integrated Play Groups for a Child

Referrals	Grassroots Efforts	IEP Process
Diagnostic evaluations Recommendations made by professionals with knowledge of child Recommendations made by school or agency	Integrated Play Groups infused within range of services provided to children in school, home and community-based programs Collaboration among parents, professionals and administrators to initiate, implement and maintain Integrated Play Groups for a child	IEP team agrees on appropriateness of Integrated Play Groups to address goals and objectives; school or agency is responsible for enacting Integrated Play Groups with adequately prepared personnel

Formulating an Integrated Play Groups Action Plan

Once a decision has been made to develop Integrated Play Groups for one or more children, the first step is to organize a team (see below) to formulate an action plan for each child you wish to serve. The Integrated Play Groups action plan offers guidelines for the nuts and bolts of the program. This tool is available for you to photocopy for use (see Phase II Tools). The IPG Action Plan is divided into several areas that represent essential steps to the planning process including:

- Integrated Play Groups team
- Gathering and preparing the players
- Preparing the play setting
- Structuring the play session
- Other planning issues

Each of these areas includes specific questions and corresponding field exercises (see Phase II Field Exercises). The field exercises include a range of brainstorming and hands-on activities that may be carried out in collaboration with team members or other colleagues involved in developing Integrated Play Groups. Figure 3.1 offers an example of a completed Integrated Play Groups action plan.

INTEGRATED PLAY GROUPS PROGRAM AND ENVIRONMENTAL DESIGN TOOL
Integrated Play Groups Action Plan

	Integrated Play Groups Team

√	Form a team - Designate roles and primary responsibilities
	  Play Guide - Patricia, Special Ed. Teacher
	  Assistant Guide - Jorge, Instructional Assistant
	  Key Consultants - Parents, SLP, OT, Psychologist
	  Play Group Coordinator - N/A

√	Set up regular meetings/task force Meet first Monday of the month for lunch; organize task force with other schools running IPGs
√	**Gathering and Preparing the Players**

√	Determine how you will recruit the players and secure permission
	  Ask 3rd-grade teacher to suggest good expert players
	  Hold play group tryouts
	  Send out permission slips

√	Choose novice players Choose expert players
	  1. Frederico - passive child 1. Malcom - funny, teaser
	  2. Anya - active-odd 2. Hyun - outgoing, leader
	                                       3. Lily - gentle, nurturing
	                                    Alternates - Taneesha

√	Design and implement awareness and orientation activities to prepare the players
	(field Exercises 1-2).
	  Set up time for players to visit play area
	  Simulation game - "Not So Simple Simon Says"
	  Hold discussion - read book about kids with autism
	  Draw pictures - illustrate ways to play with new friends
	  Orientation - discuss what to expect when play groups start/let kids explore play area and materials

	Preparing the Play Setting
√	Choose a venue - school
√	Decide where you will set up the play area - speech and language room
√	Select and gather basic and theme-based play materials (field Exercises 3-4)
√	Design and set up the play area (field Exercise 5)
	Structuring the Play Session
√	Establish meeting times for play groups - Tuesday & Thursday (2:00-2:30)
√	Design a personalized play group schedule (field Exercise 6)
√	Establish play group rules (field Exercise 7)
√	Design opening and closing rituals (field Exercise 8)
√	Design activities to foster a group identity (field Exercise 9)
	Other Planning Issues
√	Securing administrative support - write up proposal/meet with principal
√	Soliciting and raising funds - toy drive at school, bake sale
√	Conducting awareness programs - present to PTA/hand out fact sheets
√	Recruiting staff/interns/volunteers - student interns from university to videotape; volunteers from high school to help make play materials

Figure 3.1. Example of a completed Integrated Play Groups action plan.

Team Planning

Integrated Play Groups Team

The Integrated Play Groups team is composed of professionals and parents (whenever possible), who work together to develop and implement the action plan. It is especially useful to bring together team members who may offer different perspectives based on their respective areas of expertise and direct experience with the children. For instance, when planning Integrated Play Groups for one or more children in a school setting, it is helpful to get input from the various professionals who work directly with the children, such as teachers, speech and language therapists, occupational therapists, as well as from parents and other service and care providers, including tutors, therapists and childcare workers who see the children at home or in the community.

The following is an example of a typical Integrated Play Groups planning team in a school setting:

- special education teacher (to serve as play guide)
- instructional assistant (to serve as assistant to play guide)
- speech and language therapist (to serve as key consultant)
- occupational therapist (to serve as key consultant)
- parent (to serve as key consultant)

Integrated Play Groups Task Force

When planning Integrated Play Groups for a number of children, it is often productive to put together a task force or support group composed of several teams. For instance, within a school district or agency, teams from several school sites or programs may periodically come together to support one another as they build their Integrated Play Groups programs. As Integrated Play Groups get underway, the task force may continue to meet on a regular basis so that members may exchange information, resources and ideas. The task force may initiate collaborative projects, such as organizing toy drives or developing awareness programs.

Designating Roles and Responsibilities

The first major task of the planning team is to designate the primary roles and responsibilities of its members. It is essential for all team members to be familiar with the principles and practices comprising the Integrated Play Groups model. It is especially critical for those assigned to lead roles to receive adequate preparation.

Play Guide

The most central role in carrying out Integrated Play Groups is that of the play guide, who directly works with the children. One play guide is ordinarily assigned to facilitate one group at a time. The play guide generally takes a lead role in carrying out the various tasks necessary to set up and run Integrated Play Groups, including:

- gathering and preparing the players (see Chapter 4)
- preparing the play setting (see Chapter 5)
- structuring the play session (see Chapter 6)
- conducting assessments (see Chapter 7)
- implementing the intervention practices (see Chapters 8-12)

Qualifications. The majority of individuals we prepare to become play guides have some experience working with or caring for children on the autism spectrum. Many have certification or advanced degrees. Others function in the capacity of instructional assistants, childcare providers, tutors or interns while working toward certification or a degree in the following fields:

- education (special and general)
- speech and language therapy
- psychology/mental health
- child development
- counseling/social work
- play therapy
- occupational-physical therapy
- recreational therapy
- adaptive physical education
- behavioral intervention

Is the role right for you? Our research and clinical experience have given us a deeper appreciation of how play guides view their roles at various stages of carrying out Integrated Play Groups (O'Connor, 1999; Wolfberg & Schuler, 1992). For example, we have learned that the role comes more easily to some individuals than to others. Some have a strong knowledge base as well as an intuitive sense of how to facilitate social interaction and play among children and feel quite comfortable doing so. Others require more time to develop the knowledge, skill and experience before reaching a point where they feel competent in this role. For still others the role is not well suited, as it may conflict with their own nature, beliefs or established ways of working with children. It is therefore important to recognize in oneself whether or not taking on this type of role feels right and seems feasible.

Other Roles

Assistant guide. There are times when it is not only helpful but also necessary to have more than one adult present when guiding Integrated Play Groups. This may be the case for groups that include very young children as well as for those that include children with challenging behaviors. In such cases, it is recommended that an assistant guide be present to support the play guide. It is important to highlight that assistant guides follow the lead of the play guide and only step in when indicated to do so. They may be asked to help set up play materials, take a child to the bathroom or round up an escaping child. They may also be asked to videotape the play session when all seems under control. Assistant guides often work with the children in other capacities such as instructional assistants, tutors or child-care providers. Some practitioners and caregivers begin as assistant guides to gain experience prior to stepping into a more active role as a play guide.

Key consultants. Key consultants offer guidance to the play guide based on their direct experience with and knowledge of the child or children involved. Practitioners and family members may contribute based on their respective areas of expertise as a way to establish continuity across the child's educational/therapy program. A typical scenario is the case of a special education teacher in the role of play guide. One key consultant might be the speech and language therapist, who gives advice on appropriate goals, methods and adaptive tools for fostering communication and language. An occupational or physical therapist might offer suggestions on sensory integration activities that would best meet the needs of a particular child at the start of the session. Finally, a parent might give input as to the child's unique fascinations and play behavior at home that could be incorporated into the play session.

IPG coordinator. In some circumstances, it may be practical and feasible to have someone other than the play guide act as coordinator of one or more Integrated Play Groups. This especially applies to school districts, education service centers, parent organizations and other agencies that wish to serve many children in large-scale programs. Coordinators often serve in such positions as program specialists, administrators or other supervisory roles. The coordinator oversees the administrative aspects of the program and acts as a liaison among the various professionals and families involved. They may set up schedules for training and supervision, provide awareness presentations to the public, organize a task force or support group with regular meetings, videotape play sessions and compile assessment and evaluation data for each of the children in the various play groups.

Other Planning Issues

A number of miscellaneous planning issues may be pertinent to consider in the formative stages of designing an Integrated Play Groups program.

Raising Awareness

To solicit support for starting up Integrated Play Groups it may be necessary to raise awareness within the community, school or agency within which the Integrated Play Groups will take place. This may entail making informal as well as formal contacts with administrators, service providers and parents to share information about Integrated Play Groups and how they or their children/students might potentially be involved. Awareness presentations may be conducted within schools or agencies during staff and parent meetings. Community awareness might involve presentations to family organizations and support groups, neighborhood associations, recreation centers, childcare programs or Scouting groups. When meeting with these various individuals and groups, it is helpful to provide clear and accurate information about Integrated Play Groups and your vision for implementing the model. A Fact Sheet on Integrated Play Groups is available for you to photocopy and distribute for this purpose in Appendix A.

Securing Administrative Support

An important consideration when introducing the idea of Integrated Play Groups for the first time is to follow the protocol of a given school district or agency by meeting with appropriate administrators and personnel at every level. This is a proactive way to keep the channels of communication open throughout the planning process. For instance, some school districts require getting clearance from principals or site administrators, general and special education directors and possibly the superintendent and Board of Education. Some agencies may ask that you present your plan to their board of directors. School principals may insist on maintaining regular contact with key personnel. In addition, there may also be paperwork that needs to be filled out for insurance purposes.

Funding Considerations

Funding of Integrated Play Groups is a concern for families, schools and agencies that have limited resources. The costs involved will vary, depending upon the number of groups to be developed and what resources are readily available. For schools and agencies that have devoted staff, space and materials, the major cost will be for training and supervision. Others may find that they may need to hire an outside person to run Integrated Play Groups as well as rent a space and purchase materials. The following is a list of what is typically needed to set up and run a high-quality Integrated Play Groups program.

- Initial training and follow-up/field supervision for play guide (see Appendix A)
- Hired personnel to function in role of play guide and assistant (as needed)

- Designated space for play area (see Chapter 5)

- Purchase of play materials and supplies (see Chapter 5)

- Videocamera and videotapes recommended for assessment (see Chapter 7)

- Other general administrative costs for day-to-day management

The following are a few suggestions for raising and soliciting funds.

Donations. Seek out donations from commercial businesses, corporations and philanthropists (e.g., a toy manufacturer may supply play materials).

Community events. Sponsor a school, neighborhood or community event such as a toy drive, fair, bake sale, auction, collective garage sale, quilting bee, street festival, talent show, pot-luck dinner, walk-a-thon, raffle or puppet show.

Grants. Apply for a grant sponsored by private corporations, social service and non-profit agencies, schools and universities, professional organizations and government agencies.

Formal fundraiser. Host a formal fundraiser in which patrons pay a fee to attend a black-tie dinner, celebrity auction or theater performance.

Recruiting Staff and Volunteers

In some cases it may be necessary, and even desirable, to recruit staff and volunteers to carry out Integrated Play Groups. Word-of-mouth is always a good place to start. Beyond that, announcements may be sent through the Internet or posted in newsletters put out by local organizations. You might also post signs or ask professors to make announcements in their classes at universities or colleges. Departments of psychology, special education, speech, language and communication, child development and occupational therapy are good places to recruit staff to take on more of a lead role. Volunteers might be recruited from high schools, local colleges or religious organizations where community service is encouraged.

Chapter Summary

In this chapter we focused on the initial stages of the planning process for designing Integrated Play Groups. Ways in which Integrated Play Groups may be initiated include referrals, grassroots efforts and the IEP process. The next step of the process involves formulating an Integrated Play Groups action plan for each identified child. The IPG Action Plan is best enacted through a collaboration of parents and professionals, who form an Integrated Play Groups team. Roles and responsibilities of the various members need to be delineated to fill the key positions. At this stage it is important to ensure that the play guide receives adequate preparation to become fully qualified. The IPG action plan also addresses other planning issues, such as funding. In the next chapter, we focus on the second major component of the IPG action plan – gathering and preparing the players.

CHAPTER 4

Gathering and Preparing the Players

Chapter Highlights

This chapter focuses on gathering and preparing the players for Integrated Play Groups. The following topics will be highlighted:

► Group Composition

► Choosing Compatible Players

► Recruiting the Players

► Autism – Diversity Awareness

► Play Group Orientation

To the Looking-Glass world it was Alice that said,
"I've a sceptre in hand I've a crown on my head.
Let the Looking-Glass creatures, whatever they be
Come and dine with the Red Queen, the White Queen,
And me!"

–Lewis Carroll, *Through the Looking-Glass*

Bringing together a compatible and productive group of players to participate in Integrated Play Groups is not unlike assembling a cast of characters to perform in a stage production. There are many factors to consider with regard to the interplay of each individual in forming a cohesive group. We have learned through research and practice that it is possible for practitioners to make informed decisions with regard to the selection of children when forming a group. We have also learned that there are ways in which we can orient the children so that they are better equipped to enter into their new roles as partners, playmates and friends.

Group Composition

Novice Players

Novice players include children of all abilities on the autism spectrum as well as children with other pervasive developmental disorders (PDD). They may be nonverbal or verbal, have intensive, moderate or mild forms of autism, as well as Asperger Syndrome. We believe in giving every child the optimal support to successfully participate in Integrated Play Groups; we do not exclude children on the basis of behavior unless they pose a serious threat to themselves or others even when provided with one-to-one assistance by a skilled practitioner. Such determinations are made on a case-by-case basis.

We generally do not begin an Integrated Play Group with a novice player who does not already have an educational or therapeutic program in place. In the case of a very young, newly diagnosed child, we suggest that Integrated Play Groups begin after the child has settled into a program that focuses on basic social, emotional, communicative and behavioral needs that are best addressed through adult-child interactions.

Expert Players

Expert players include typically developing peers and/or siblings who are considered to be socially competent and enjoy playing with other children. They are generally recruited from places where children ordinarily have social contacts with peers – such as school, home, neighborhood and community settings. Expert players are expected to be role models in the areas considered most challenging for the novice players, including social interaction, communication, language, play, imagination and behavior. It is therefore not appropriate to consider children with similar challenges in any of these areas as expert players.

Age Range

Integrated Play Groups are specifically designed for children from preschool through elementary-school age (approximately 3 to 11 years). That is not to say that adaptations are not possible for both younger and older children. In our practice, we tend to work with children at an age in which their peer network is beginning to expand within the context of more formalized early childhood programs (beginning around age 3). This is also a period in which the peer culture takes hold, as typically developing children are increasingly gravitating to more socially coordinated play activity. Although children hardly stop playing by the time they reach the middle school years, for pragmatic reasons we have focused our efforts on supporting children through the elementary school years (ending around age 11).

Group Size and Ratio

Each Integrated Play Group includes a minimum of three and not more than five children (see Table 4.1 for an overview of play group composition involving novice and expert players). The ratio of expert to novice players is always higher.

Table 4.1
Summary of Integrated Play Groups Composition

Group Composition	Characteristics
Novice Players	Children of all abilities on the autism spectrum and with related conditions
	Includes children who are nonverbal, verbal, have intensive, moderate and mild forms of autism/PDD as well as Asperger Syndrome
Expert Players	Typically developing peers and siblings
	Role models who exhibit competence in social interaction, communication, play and imagination
Age Range	Preschool through elementary age (approximately 3 to 11 years)
	Adaptations for younger and older children
Group Size and Ratio	Higher ratio of expert to novice players: • 1 novice – 2 experts • 1 novice – 3 experts • 1 novice – 4 experts • 2 novices – 3 experts

That means a group of three includes one novice and two experts; a group of four includes one novice and three experts and a group of five includes one or two novices and three or four experts. The group size may vary depending upon any number of factors, including a child's age, ability and experience. For some younger children, as well as children with intensive needs, three may be a more practical and manageable number with which to start off. In our experience, five seems to be a magic number for most Integrated Play Groups, as it offers the children so many more possibilities. With five, the children can form dyads, triads and even play alone from time to time, which are all natural variations in play.

Choosing Compatible Players

When forming an Integrated Play Group it is important to choose novice and expert players who are compatible with one another, as the dynamics of a group are determined by the characteristics of and interactions among its members. Mixing and matching children with respect to gender, age, development and ability, temperament, play interaction and social style, play interests and primary language offers different types of benefits and experiences. Special considerations must also be taken when it comes to choosing siblings as expert players. These variables are described in more detail below.

Gender

While there are no real advantages or disadvantages to having all boys, all girls or a mix of boys and girls, some children have a particular preference for one configuration over another. Certain children may be attracted to play activities that tend to be more desirable or popular within a specific gender group. For instance, Thomas the Tank Engine is a commercial toy that is beloved by many young boys and is especially attractive to a great many boys with autism. Some children may be too narrowly focused on only girls or only boys for play and may need to broaden their social experience by establishing relations with children of the opposite gender.

Age

Integrated Play Groups often include children who are the same or similar in age, but may also include children with diverse ages. Mixed-age groups are logical when forming groups with siblings (who are not twins), cousins or neighborhood children who do not happen to be within the same age range as the novice player. Mixed-age groups may offer more diversity. The advantage of bringing children together who are close in age is that it is traditional for children in our society to form friendships with same-age peers. Although children do form friendships with older or younger peers, it is less common once children reach school age.

Development and Ability

Mixing and matching novice and expert players with respect to development and ability offers differing benefits in the context of Integrated Play Groups. For example, novice players are more likely to spontaneously imitate peers who are more closely matched to them in development and ability. However, forming a group with all very young or immature players may not be advantageous, as the experts may not yet be expert enough to support the novices. Developmentally advanced peers are more likely to be responsive and adept in supporting and scaffolding children with fewer skills.

Temperament, Play Interaction and Social Style

It is relevant to consider how novice players with avoidant, passive and active-odd social styles will respond to peer temperament and play interaction styles when forming groups. For example, certain children may be especially responsive to different temperaments. Novice players may be mixed or matched with expert players who are quiet and reserved as opposed to loud and active. Children may also respond well to specific play interaction styles, which offer different advantages.

Expert players who take charge and lead the group may add structure and predictability to the play. This is especially important to bear in mind in the case of many children with Asperger Syndrome, who have a tendency and need to dominate. Such children will benefit by learning how to be more flexible and less domineering while taking turns being in charge with a peer who possesses strong leadership abilities. Expert players who are nurturing and even doting may be especially patient and persistent in including novices who are avoidant and passive. However, keep in mind that too much doting (a.k.a. the "mother hen" effect) can result in the novice player becoming dependent on the expert player in a state of learned helplessness. Every Integrated Play Group should include at least one player who is the life-of-the-party. Players who like to clown around and tease in a good-natured way help add humor and flexibility to the play, which may be beneficial to everyone.

Play Interests

It is especially advantageous to bring novice and expert players together with common play interests, or at least the potential to develop shared interests. Since many children with autism do acquire fascinations with or interests in activities, toys, books and films that are conventional and even popular within the peer culture, it may not be difficult to find peers who will be good matches. However, many children with autism have fascinations that are so unique that it will be difficult to find peers who can relate to them. Nevertheless, there are ways to encourage children to make play connections around arcane interests. For instance, the child who is fascinated with letters and numbers might find a play connection with a peer who likes to pretend to play school. (We will address this in more detail in Phases III and IV as we focus on assessment and intervention.)

Primary Language

As many of us live in culturally diverse communities, it is important to take into consideration the primary languages spoken among the children in Integrated Play Groups. In the case of novices who do not speak the dominant language, possibly because they are new immigrants, it is helpful to include at least one peer who shares a common language with them. This peer may not only be helpful as a translator for the group, but may also offer the novice a sense of security by speaking in ways familiar in the home environment. For some children, sign language is a primary mode of communication, in which case it would make sense to include children who are fluent in or learning how to sign.

Sibling Relationships

It is not uncommon for siblings to participate in Integrated Play Groups. In some cases siblings may include two novice players, others may include a combination of novice and expert players. In all cases it is important to carefully consider whether or not participating in an Integrated Play Group will be appropriate for the siblings involved. For some siblings, participating together in an Integrated Play Group will be a natural extension of their family play life, and thus makes logical sense. If the children enjoy each other's company, it is a strong indication that they are well suited to participate in a group together. In other circumstances, it may be an unwise choice to bring siblings together for a play group at a particular point in time. Some siblings may find it aversive to participate in a group together, possibly because they are at a stage in which they are experiencing "sibling rivalry" or coming to terms with their brother's or sister's disability. If one sibling is given the opportunity to participate in an Integrated Play Group over another, it is important to take care that the other does not feel left out, for example, by setting up a special activity or play group for that sibling. In some situations it may be appropriate for a typically developing sibling to participate as an expert player in a completely different Integrated Play Group from his sibling with autism.

Considerations for Choosing Compatible Players
for Integrated Play Groups

There are a number of variables to consider when mixing and matching novice and expert players to form a play group:

- Gender

- Age

- Development and ability

- Temperament, play interaction and social style

- Play interests

- Primary language

- Sibling relationships

Recruiting the Players

… I started up my first play group of the year today. The kids brought their permission slips back RIGHT AWAY because they were so excited to start. Most of the expert players from last year have been finding me in the hallway to ask me when play groups [are] going to start. (Tara Tuchel, personal communication)

Seek out Peers Within Natural Social Networks

The potential for developing meaningful and long-lasting friendships is a major consideration in the formation of Integrated Play Groups. It is therefore best to seek out natural peer supports from within a common social network. Whenever possible, experts and novices should belong to the same peer group – such as by attending the same class or different classes within a school, living in the same neighborhood or participating in family gatherings or other community activities. Ideally, novices and experts are familiar with one another and even share an attraction.

In cases where novice players have limited access to peers, it may be necessary to build a social network drawing upon resources in the community, such as home-schooling networks, Scouting groups, recreation centers or private schools seeking community service for their students. It is our intention to promote carry-over of the relationships formed among the players in Integrated Play Groups to other naturally occurring social activities, such as birthday parties, sleepovers and outings.

Solicit Recommendations

One way by which you might begin recruiting players to participate in Integrated Play Groups is to ask for recommendations from adults who are familiar with the children. For example, you might begin by asking teachers, therapists or parents to nominate children whom they feel would be good candidates. Familiar adults may have insight as to which children are naturally attracted to one another or beginning to form relationships. They may also know particular activities, toys, books or films that are of common appeal.

Get to Know the Players

It is always a good idea to get to know the children whom you wish to invite to join Integrated Play Groups. The best way to do this is to spend time with them when they are socializing and playing. Whenever possible, observe potential experts in the same social arena as novices, such as during free play in the classroom, on the playground, in the home or in a neighborhood park. This will give you the opportunity to observe the children in various social and play situations. Spend time getting to know the children by chatting with them about their play interests or their perceptions of which children they regard as a playmate or friend. You might also probe the children by asking if they would be interested in visiting your classroom, program or home to play with the other children you have in mind.

Hold Play Group Try-Outs

Before settling on a particular group of players, you may wish to hold play group try-outs. This might involve bringing different combinations of experts and novices together in your classroom, home or program for one or more visits. At this point it is important to refrain from making any promises to the children you invite to play. It is best already to have set up your play area with a preliminary selection of motivating play materials so that you may observe the children as they play with them (see Chapter 5). Although holding try-outs may not give you a completely accurate picture of how the children will get along once they are in an established group, it may aid in the selection process.

Extend Invitations to Players

Once you settle on a particular group of players, you will need to extend an invitation to them to join Integrated Play Groups under the condition that their parents or legal guardian give their consent (see below). Although participation is voluntary, expert players will be expected to make a commitment to meet regularly for a specified period of time (see Chapter 6 for information on scheduling). Before signing on, they must be fully informed (along with their parent or legal guardian) about what the commitment entails and be given the freedom to choose whether or not to participate. With older children it may be appropriate to write a simple contract to establish their commitment. More able children with autism or Asperger Syndrome may also benefit by taking part in expressing their commitment in the same way as the expert players.

Secure Permission Through Informed Consent

Without exception, parents or legal guardians of all of the players, including expert, must give their informed consent for their children to participate. Informed consent generally includes full disclosure of what the program entails and any potential benefits or risks to the child. Parents of novice players must be made fully aware of referrals made by doctors, teachers, therapists or administrators to authorize implementation of Integrated Play Groups as an intervention with their child. We highly recommend that parents be informed in person or by phone, as well as in writing in their native language.

It must be explicitly understood that when children are officially signed on to be a novice or expert player, their participation in Integrated Play Groups should never be held out as a reward or withheld as a punishment. Rather, they are expected to participate as they would in any other scheduled activity.

Figure 4.1 provides a sample consent letter that may be adapted according to your situation and needs. You will note that we have included a request for permission to photograph and videotape the child as a part of the program, as well as for purposes of evaluation and future training. Although such permission is not mandatory, it is highly recommended (see also Table 4.2 for a summary of steps to recruiting players to participate in Integrated Play Groups).

[Official Letterhead]

Date:

Dear Parent/Guardian:

I am a [teacher/therapist] working in [name of school/program]. Your child has been selected by [name of teacher] to participate as a[n] ["expert"/ "novice"] player in a program called Integrated Play Groups. This program supports children who have special needs/require extra assistance ("novice players") in play with children who have advanced skills ("expert players"). The primary purpose is for the children to learn and make friends while having fun together.

Novice players may benefit from this program by developing their social interaction, communication and play skills. Expert players may benefit by enhancing their self-esteem as role models while learning how to accept, include and help children with differing abilities.

I would like to invite your child to participate in Integrated Play Groups with [2/3/4] other children. These groups will meet [e.g., in my classroom on Tuesdays and Thursdays from 10:30 to 11:00 a.m. each week].

To help us evaluate the program and train future practitioners, I would also like to ask your permission to photograph and videotape your child while participating in this program.

If you give permission for your child to participate in Integrated Play Groups, and also to be photographed and videotaped, please sign below. If you have any questions or would like to learn more about Integrated Play Groups, feel free to contact me at [phone, e-mail].

Thank you for your time and consideration.

Sincerely,

[Your name]

_____

I give permission for my child, _____, to participate in Integrated Play Groups and to be photographed and videotaped for evaluation and training purposes.

Parent/Guardian Signature _____ Date _____

Figure 4.1. Sample letter of consent to participate in Integrated Play Groups.

Table 4.2

Recruiting Players to Participate in Integrated Play Groups

Recruitment Steps	Suggested Strategies
Seek out Peers Within Natural Social Network	• Draw from school, neighborhood, family relations, community • Emphasize potential for developing long-lasting friend-ships
Get to Know the Players	• Observe, hang out with and talk to peers while they are playing and socializing with one another
Solicit Recommendations	• Ask familiar adults, such as teachers, therapists or par-ents, to nominate children
Hold Play Group Try-Outs	• Invite different combinations of experts and novices to play together in play group setting
Extend Invitation to Players	• Invite peers to volunteer participation and commit to being a player for a specified period
Secure Permission Through Informed Consent	• Obtain signed permission from legal guardian • Give full disclosure of program and any potential benefits or risks to the child • Include request for permission to photograph/ videotape

Autism - Diversity Awareness

The children selected to be expert players often have had limited exposure to children with autism and related special needs. As a reflection of their social and cultural experience, many are likely to have preconceived or conflicting notions about people with differing abilities in general, and autism in particular. They may be curious, confused, anxious and even hostile in their initial encounters with children whose outward appearance offers no clues as to why they might behave in unusual or unexpected ways.

It is our intention to set a tone in Integrated Play Groups that extends beyond merely tolerating others' differences. Rather, we aspire to impart a sense of appreciation and acceptance of *all* people – including children on the autism spectrum who present distinct ways of playing, communicating and relating.

As a consideration to the children and families, we get explicit permission from families to make reference to autism, autism spectrum disorders, Asperger Syndrome or any other associated terms when preparing expert players to partic-ipate in Integrated Play Groups. We understand and respect that there are reasons why parents may not want a child's diagnosis exposed or shared with others. In such cases, we advocate using more general descriptors to raise awareness about children with diverse abilities and needs, such as referring to "children with differ-ing ways of playing, communicating and relating."

Both formal and informal approaches may be used to help expert players become more aware, receptive, in tune with and responsive to the novice players when they begin Integrated Play Groups. Raising awareness may be as simple as reading a book with children in the neighborhood or as elaborate as carrying out a large-scale program in a school. In all cases, our aim is to:

- Provide accurate information about children with autism/differing abilities

- Foster empathy and understanding for the unique ways in which children with autism/differing abilities play, communicate and relate

- Encourage discussion, inquiry and first-hand experience around issues facing children with autism/differing abilities

- Identify similarities and differences among children with diverse abilities and ways of playing, communicating and relating

- Enhance opportunities for building meaningful relationships and friendships among children with diverse abilities and ways of playing, communicating and relating

Awareness Programs

Many schools and community-based programs offer diversity awareness programs that include a focus on issues surrounding disability. Awareness programs are sometimes instituted as a major event featured on a particular day or over the course of a week or even a month. They are often conducted at the start of the new school year as a way for children within special and general education classes to get to know one another.

Some awareness programs present general information on a wide range of disabilities with specific reference to autism spectrum disorders. Others present information in more general terms about individuals with differing abilities and needs while attempting to avoid labels altogether. Still others focus exclusively on developing awareness about people with autism.

Autism awareness programs often include presentations, activities and resource materials geared to children and adults. When parents give us permission to refer to autism, we typically focus on the following topics:

Autism Awareness for Children – Discussion Topics

- What does autism mean?

- What are children with autism like? How do they act, play, communicate and relate to others? How are they the same as other children? How are they different from other children?

- Why do children with autism sometimes act, play, communicate and relate differently than other children? What causes autism?

- How do you think it might feel to be a child with autism who sometimes feels confused, afraid or overwhelmed? How do you think it feels to be left out by other children?

- What can you do to include a child with autism as a playmate and friend?

The Autism Society of America (1999) has developed a booklet, *Growing Up Together: A Booklet about Kids with Autism,* which offers a simple explanation of autism and features photographs of children engaging in everyday activities. Included in this booklet is a list of important tips for being a friend with a child with autism.

How Can I Be a Friend to Someone with Autism?

- Accept your friend's differences.
- Protect your friend from things that bother him or her.
- Talk in short sentences and use gestures.
- Use pictures or write down what you want to say to help your friend understand.
- Join your friend in activities that interest him or her.
- Be patient – understand your friend doesn't mean to bother you or others.
- Invite your friend to play with you and join group activities.
- Sit near your friend whenever you can, and help him or her do things if they want you to.
- Help other kids learn about autism by telling them about your special friend.

(Autism Society of America, 1999)

An especially noteworthy program is "Friend 2 Friend," which was developed by Heather McCracken (2002), a parent of a child with autism in Vancouver, B.C., Canada. Using life-sized puppets, performances are tailored for different age groups to teach friendship skills and educate peers about autism from a child's perspective (see Resources in Appendix C).

Awareness Activities

The following are some awareness activities that may be helpful in promoting an understanding of children with diverse ways of relating, communicating and playing.

Interactive discussion. Taking the time to discuss and address issues, questions and concerns are important ways to teach children about diversity and acceptance. Discussion topics may vary according to children's ages and level of understanding. With younger children, the focus might be on similarities and differences in the ways children relate, communicate and play with one another. With older children, discussion topics might be extended to deal with the same concepts, but on a more abstract and sophisticated level as well as cover more factual information about autism spectrum disorders and related conditions. Sample discussion topics might include:

**Diversity Awareness – Discussion Topics
on Play and Friendships**

- How are we alike? How are we different from one another?
- What do you like to play? What do you not like to play?
- What is easy for you to play? What is hard for you to play?
- What are some ways you play with friends?
- How do you communicate to your friends to let them know you want to invite them or join them in play?
- Have you ever felt left out by your friends during play? How does it feel to be left out?
- How might you include someone who is playing by him or herself?

Books and videotapes. Books and videotapes are wonderful ways to introduce peers and siblings to children with diverse backgrounds, abilities and needs. There are a number of books for children about children with autism (some biographical) that are geared to different age groups. Some of these include discussion questions and activities. Films and videos offer another means to raise awareness about children with autism and related special needs. They may be used to stimulate discussion about diversity and inclusion (see Resources in Appendix C).

Simulation games. Simulating challenges that children with autism encounter in social interaction, communication, imagination and play offers peers and siblings opportunities to experience the world from their perspective. The following is a sample simulation game:

Simulation Game – "Not So Simple Simon Says"

Lead the children in a game of "Simon Says."

First, play the game in the ordinary way. Ask the children to imitate you as you perform simple one-step actions – "Simon Says touch your nose, Simon Says clap you hands."

Tell the children, "You are all such wonderful players. Look at what experts you all are playing this game."

Next, make the game difficult for the children. Ask the children to imitate you as you perform complex actions with multiple steps at a rapid rate. To make the task even more difficult, you might speak in gibberish so the children cannot understand the direction – "Simon Says blah-blah-blah, Simon Says ya-da-ya-da."

When it becomes too difficult for the children to perform the actions accurately, ask the children, "What's the matter? Don't you know how to play anymore?"

The children will likely tell you that it just got too difficult and give you reasons why – You went too fast; it was hard to understand what you were saying, etc. …

Ask the children how it felt not to be able to play, probing for such responses as feeling frustrated, confused and overwhelmed.

Lead the children to understand that this is often how children with autism/special needs feel, not only when they are playing but also in many everyday situations. Point out how important it is to be patient, considerate and understanding.

Role-playing. Role-playing provides a way to engage peers and siblings in real-life social situations that are often a struggle for children with autism. Through first-hand experience, children may learn to problem solve ways to understand, accept and include others despite their differences. One way in which to set up a role-play is to select a small group of children to act out different roles on cards as in the following examples:

Sample Role-Play Scenario #1

Role 1: Pretend that you don't know how to play with other children. At recess you wander around the other children, but you don't join them.

Roles 2-4: Pretend to play ring-around-the rosy and London Bridge with each other. What can you do to include the child who is not joining in?

(Hint: Think of ways to invite the child to join you and ways you can join the child)

Sample Role-Play Scenario #2

Role 1: Pretend that you are interested in talking about only one topic – your favorite topic focuses on the planets and solar system.

Roles 2-4: Pretend to talk with your friends about Halloween. You may talk about your costumes, trick-or-treating, etc. ... What can you do to include everyone in the conversation?

(Hint: Think of ways to bring the two different topics of conversation together)

Story-telling, puppet and theater performances. Story-telling, puppet and theater performances offer a means to bring to life real or imagined characters with differing abilities and ways of playing, relating and communicating. It is possible to create your own performances or stage productions that involve parents, professionals and children as storytellers, actors or puppeteers. Some communities have established storytellers, puppet or theater troupes that would be willing to collaborate with knowledgeable parents and professionals to produce and put on a performance for children. Libraries are often a good resource for getting in touch with storytellers, whereas performing art centers may be a resource for puppeteers and theater groups.

Similar to the "Friend 2 Friend" program is a local resource known as "Kids on the Block," which features life-size "Muppet-like" puppets representing a range of visible and invisible disabilities, including autism. The children always have loads of questions and by the end of the performance they are better able to appreciate what it must be like to experience the world in a different way than they had ever imagined.

Art activities. Art is another wonderful medium to engage peers and siblings in developing awareness and sensitivity for children with diverse abilities and needs. Art activities may be used to stimulate discussion as well as to culminate other awareness activities. Children may engage in individual or group projects as a way to express their newly forming awareness. For instance, you might ask the children to draw or paint pictures of the different play activities that they could invite a child with special needs to join.

A popular group activity is to create a mural with all of the children's handprints to show that they are all alike in that they all have hands with five fingers, but that they are all different in that their hands are different sizes and shapes. A more sophisticated art activity for older children might be to create a large mosaic or quilt made up of individually designed tile or fabric pieces focused on something unique about each individual. Embracing diversity in all its forms would be the dominant theme in this type of activity.

Create personalized books, slide shows and videos. Creating your own books, slide shows and videos about real-life children offers a very personalized approach to raising awareness. A beautiful example of a personalized book is "Hearts and Hands" developed by Rebecca Berry of Developmental Pathways for Kids with the children of Redeemer School in Redwood City, California (Berry et al., unpublished book). The book was created with one little girl in mind who attended the school while also participating in Integrated Play Groups with classmates. Focusing on ways in which the children are all alike and different, the book includes a montage of their drawings, quotations and photographs.

Play Group Orientation

An important step prior to conducting the first play session is to orient both the expert and the novice players so they are as fully prepared as possible to participate in Integrated Play Groups. All of the children will need to anticipate, at least on some level, what they are to expect when the play groups begin.

What the Children Need to Know

Prior to the first play session it may be helpful to plan an introductory meeting to present vital information and answer "what," "why," "who," "where" and "when" questions about Integrated Play Groups. In some cases it might be appropriate to meet individually with each novice and expert player. In other cases you might choose to meet with the children as a group. The following is a presentation that can be tailored to children of various ages and abilities.

INTEGRATED PLAY GROUPS ORIENTATION PRESENTATION	
WHAT	**What is a play group?** A play group consists of a small group of children who meet regularly to play together. **What kinds of things will you play?** You will have the opportunity to play in all sorts of ways – pretending, constructing, making things and interactive games. The play area will have lots of wonderful toys and materials, such as a play kitchen and store, cars and trucks, blocks, art materials. You may help us choose or even make new things that you think would be fun to play with.
WHY	**What is the purpose of a play group?** The purpose of a play group is to have fun and make friends while learning how to play together in some special ways. We will all learn how to communicate, cooperate and use our imagination. We will also learn how to make an extra effort to help each other out so that everyone is included and no one is left out. This is important because some of you may be very good at playing in some ways but still learning how to play in other ways.
WHO	**Who will be participating in the play group?** The children participating in your play group will be (names). **Who will be leading the play group?** The grown-up(s) leading your play group will be (names).
WHEN	**When will the play group take place?** Your play group will take place on (days, times, periods).
WHERE	**Where will the play group take place?** Your play group will mainly take place in (physical location). There might be some times when the play group will go to other locations, such as to play outside. **How will you get to the play group?** Example – A teacher will pick you up for your play group.

Adaptations for Novice Players

It is important to keep in mind that for many novice players the information presented above may be too abstract and difficult to grasp without actually having had the experience. In such cases it may be helpful to use visual supports and even tangible experiences to introduce the concept of a play group at a level the children are able to comprehend.

Provide visual supports. Many children with autism benefit from some sort of visual cue or graphic representation to help them anticipate what their play group might be like. At a very basic level, you might introduce some sort of simple cue or visual icon that the child may learn to associate with play groups – such as a photograph of the players in the play area, line drawing of toys, or a miniature toy (see Figure 4.1). These may be used as a transitional device when the play groups begin. In some cases it may be appropriate to incorporate the cue as a part of a child's independent schedule, such as those used in programs that use the TEACCH method (Schopler & Mesibov, 1986) or PECS – Picture Exchange Communication System (Frost & Bondy, 1994). In Chapter 6 we will provide examples of how to create personalized schedules for children.

Figure 4.1. Examples of visual supports to represent Integrated Play Groups.

The Picture Communication Symbols © 1981-2003, used with permission from Mayer-Johnson Inc., P.O. Box 1579, Solana Beach, CA 92075. 800/588-4548 (phone), 858/550-0449 (fax) and www.mayer-johnson.com.

The concept of a play group might also be introduced to children through a picture story sequence that is personalized to the child. In some cases, it might be appropriate to relay information through a Social Story or Comic Book Conversation as developed by Carol Gray (1995). This might be especially helpful to children at a higher level who experience anxiety when there are changes in the routine or they are introduced to new social situations.

Allow the child to spend time in the play area. Some novice players need to gradually adjust to play groups as a new routine in their schedule. For these children, it may be appropriate to begin taking them to the play area at designated times and slowly increase the amount of time they are expected to stay. The idea is to make this a very positive experience so that the child will regularly look forward to this event. At first you might only spend a few minutes in the play area allowing the child to freely explore the space and play materials that he or she will expect to find at each play session. You might increase the time by engaging the child in motivating and stimulating activities that you might later introduce to the group.

Show a live or videotaped play group session. It may also be helpful for some children to view a play group or a videotape of a play group session in progress. If you do not have an actual play group to use as a model, you might create a mock group by bringing together a small group of children to play in the area where you will be holding your play groups. If the children are not going to be the actual participants in the group, it is important to clarify for more literalminded observers that this is merely an example of a play group – not the actual group they will be joining.

Chapter Summary

This chapter focused on gathering and preparing novice and expert players to participate in Integrated Play Groups. A number of factors must be taken into account when forming groups. The players are carefully selected on the basis of compatibility with consideration of numerous variables that may afford differing benefits and experiences. We offer tips on how to recruit players from within natural peer social networks. Once permission is secured and the selection process is complete, the players need to be prepared to participate in Integrated Play Groups. Autism or diversity awareness programs and activities may be helpful in preparing expert players to understand and accept children with differing abilities and needs. Orientation should be provided to both novice and expert players so that they become familiar with and anticipate Integrated Play Groups at their level of understanding. In the next chapter we will focus on preparing the play environment.

CHAPTER 5

Preparing the Play Setting

Chapter Highlights

This chapter focuses on preparing the play setting for Integrated Play Groups. The following topics will be highlighted:

► Choosing a Suitable Venue

► Designing Play Areas

► Selecting Play Materials

Playhouse ... we made our house of rock, and each room
would be divided off with little rows of rocks. In the kitchen
another rock would be a stove and maybe we would have a table
made of a board over four sticks driven in the ground.
And our dishes and pans would be anything that we could salvage,
say a pork-and-bean can ... a bed would be a doll bed ... made of leaves
in a pile with some kind of an old rag over it ...
We used to make telephones to talk inside of our playhouse.

– Helen Nichols, *Reminiscences from Appalachia*
(Page & Smith, 1985)

Integrated Play Groups are carried out in specially designed play settings that offer optimal opportunities for peer socialization and play. Thoughtful preparation goes into creating safe, familiar, predictable and highly motivating settings within which children feel a sense of comfort, belonging and ownership. A number of important environmental features must be considered, including the physical ecology of the play area and the play materials.

Choosing a Suitable Venue

Natural Integrated Setting

Integrated Play Groups take place in natural integrated settings. We define a natural setting as a location where, given the opportunity, children would naturally play. An integrated setting refers to a social setting where children with diverse abilities come together, with a higher proportion of children who are typically developing than children who require extensive social support. Suitable locations for setting up and implementing Integrated Play Groups may be found within school, community, therapy and home environments, as presented in Table 5.1.

Consistent Play Area

The availability of a permanent space and its regular use over an extended period of time are important factors in choosing a suitable venue for Integrated Play Groups. Integrated Play Groups sessions always begin and end in the same play area. Play areas may be used for other purposes when Integrated Play Groups are not in session as long as they remain intact. Allowing children access to the play area at alternative times may be especially helpful in promoting generalization of the newly acquired skills in Integrated Play Groups.

Depending upon the venue, play areas may be set up in any number of possible locations. In a school, they may be located in a corner of a classroom, therapy room or in other neutral places that may be accessed by children for

Table 5.1

Suitable Venues for Integrated Play Groups

Venue	Examples of Natural Integrated Settings
Schools	• Inclusive classrooms • Integrated classrooms • Special day classes with reverse mainstreaming (i.e., general education students join special education class)
Community	• After-school programs • Childcare programs • Recreation centers • Neighborhood park programs • Summer camp programs • Secular and religious affiliated programs
Therapy	• Child development centers • Pediatric clinics
Home	• Novice player's home • Expert player's home

other purposes at different times of the day. At home, play areas may be set up in a child's bedroom, a corner of a living room or den, a separate playroom or an outdoor playhouse. In other settings, play areas may be established in just about any room that has available space.

Since children with autism are best served in environments that offer high degrees of predictability (Rutter, 1978), we cannot stress enough how critical a consistent play area is to the success of Integrated Play Groups. A permanent play area offers a level of external structure that better equips children for play. In our experience, Integrated Play Group programs that rely on make-shift or nomadic play areas tend to be disorienting for the children, as well as frustrating for play guides to facilitate.

From a pragmatic standpoint, however, we are fully aware of the many obstacles to finding a permanent play space. We recognize that space is often at a premium and that itinerant professionals are especially restricted in their capacity to find a space to call their own. While we are wholly sympathetic to these issues, we are also steadfast in our belief that it is in the best interest of the children to have a consistent play area.

Other Play Spaces

Although Integrated Play Groups always begin and end in the same play area, the children are not necessarily confined to that area for the duration of each session. In the early phases of the program it is often best for the children to stay within the confines of the play area. But once children acclimate to the routine and one another, it may be appropriate to move the group to other spaces that afford opportunities for different types of play activities and experiences. For instance, the group might move to a large indoor space or sensory-motor room to engage in large-motor activities – such as playing with a parachute, hula hoops or jumbo balls. It may also be appropriate to set up play activities in outdoor spaces that lend themselves to particular themes – such as creating a make-believe campground in a grassy area or a roadway and gas station on an asphalt playground. You may also wish to take advantage of the elements and build leaf houses in the autumn and snow forts in the winter, or set up water play activities on a hot summer day.

Designing Play Areas

The physical ecology of the play setting has a tremendous impact on how children play and socialize with one another (Phyfe-Perkins, 1980; Smith & Connolly, 1980; van der Beek, Buck, & Rufenachm, 2001). Acoustics, lighting, colors, placement of furniture and materials and the overall aesthetics of space all affect how children feel, move, explore, interrelate and organize themselves for play. These and other important variables known to specifically impact on the behavior of children with autism are considered in the design of play areas for Integrated Play Groups. For instance, children who tend to wander in social situations are more likely to do so in wide open play spaces than smaller confined play spaces. Children who are easily distracted and have difficulties with planning and self-regulation are more likely to become lost and overwhelmed in a disordered as opposed to a highly organized play space. The following guidelines for designing play areas will accommodate children's differing abilities and needs.

Size Restrictions and Spatial Density

Play areas are purposely restricted in size with a comfortable amount of space to accommodate a small group of children and their play materials. There is just enough space for the children to move about freely, but not so much space that they wander off or segregate themselves into different parts of the area. We suggest avoiding large open spaces since they tend to inhibit social interaction and small overcrowded spaces since they often intensify interpersonal conflict.

Clearly Defined Boundaries

Play areas also have clearly defined boundaries with partitions on at least three sides. For example, a corner is very effective with two walls as boundaries. Stable shelves are practical partitions as they can be used to store play materials. Sturdy child-size play kitchen sets consisting of a stove, refrigerator and sink are also useful as dividers.

Explicit Organization

Arranging the play space in a highly systematic fashion helps children to better initiate, plan and organize their play, as well as makes it easier to clean up after play sessions. Play areas are explicitly organized so that materials are accessible, visible, clearly labeled and logically arranged around activities and themes. Shelves and containers are labeled with photographs, pictures, written words or some other marker that children can easily identify.

Many of our programs label their play areas with visual icons that are familiar to and consistently used with the child across therapy and educational environments, such as The Picture Communication Symbols ©1981-2002 developed by Mayer-Johnson, Inc., and adopted for use by TEACCH (Schopler & Mesibov, 1986) and PECS (Frost & Bondy, 1994). A clever way to organize play materials was developed for early childhood programs by High/Scope Education Research Foundation (Hohman & Weikart, 1995). Paper cutouts that match the shape and color of a prop are laminated and attached to a shelf to indicate where the prop belongs; for instance, a red cooking pot may be matched to a red cutout placed on a cupboard shelf in the play kitchen.

Limited Distractions

To help children focus and attend while playing with peers, it is important to limit distractions within the play environment in sensible ways. One way to address this consideration is to create and maintain explicit organization as described above. Another way to limit distractions is to consider how and how much is visually displayed. Avoid overcrowding the play area with too much clutter and excess by being very selective about what furniture and play materials you choose to have out on permanent display.

While we encourage children to choose from a large selection of play materials and activities that are easily accessible, everything does not need to be out in the open at all times. It is useful to place curtains over shelves where materials are stored so they can be easily opened and closed at appropriate times. It may also be helpful to limit toys that contain multiple pieces as these tend to get thrown about and clutter up the play area. In some cases, it may be appropriate to store certain play materials outside of the play area and make them available upon request.

Consider also the functionality of the space. For instance, while a table and chairs serve many functions as a gathering place for children to pretend and make things, a second set would usually be superfluous while taking up additional space.

Activity- and Theme-Based Arrangements

Play areas are logically arranged around activities and themes for Integrated Play Groups. Figure 5.1 provides a visual example of the layout of a play area. Depending upon the age, development and interests of the players, there may be different variations of the types of activities and themes that will be most prominent and how they will be arranged. The play area may be thought of as similar to a center-based program in a condensed form; that is, furniture and play materials are grouped in sections around specific activities and themes within a single space.

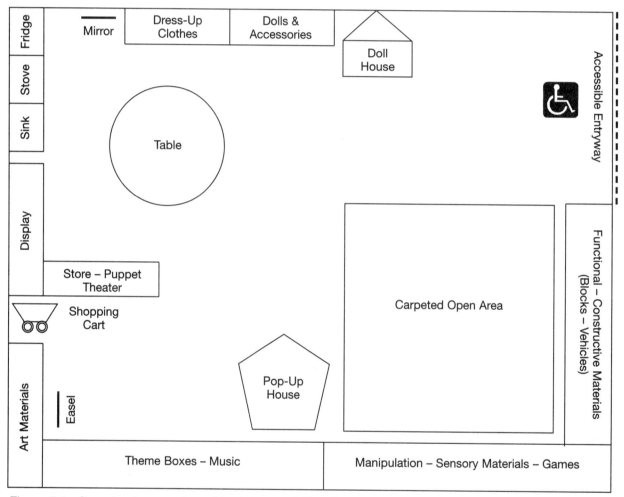

Figure 5.1. Sample play area layout for Integrated Play Groups.

In general, play areas are arranged around sociodramatic, functional-constructive and manipulation-sensory play materials while also including space for art, music, games and sets of theme-based materials (see Selecting Play Materials below and suggested play materials in Tables 5.2, 5.3, and 5.4). The children are by no means restricted to playing with specific materials in a designated section of the play area. Rather, they are encouraged to flexibly explore, experiment and combine materials in novel ways.

A sociodramatic section of the play area might feature a housekeeping theme to include a play kitchen, table and chairs, dolls and accessories. This might be juxtaposed to an area set up as a store so play materials can be transferred back and forth. In the case of older children, the sociodramatic section might feature an elaborate self-made store, sophisticated puppet theater or stage set for putting on performances. A construction section might be situated around a carpeted area to include building blocks, vehicles and miniature figures that children may combine to create a bustling city. Older children might have an actual workbench with realistic constructive materials that they may use to create a more elaborate construction. A manipulative section might also be situated near the carpeted area to include a wide assortment of materials that children may explore and use in any number of ways.

Considerations for Designing Play Areas for Integrated Play Groups

Variables known to influence the social and play behavior of children on the autism spectrum are considered in the design of play areas:

- Size restrictions and spatial density
- Clearly defined boundaries
- Explicit organization
- Limited distractions
- Activity and theme-based arrangements

Selecting Play Materials

To accommodate novice and expert players' diverse interests, abilities and needs, a wide range of play materials are made available to children in Integrated Play Groups (see Suggested Play Materials below and Tables 5.2, 5.3, and 5.4). Since the interactive potential (Beckman & Kohl, 1984), structure (Dewey, Lord, & Magil, 1988) and complexity (Ferrara & Hill, 1980) of toys and props, as well as the selection of preferred activities (Koegel, Dyer, & Bell, 1987), have been found to impact on the play of children with autism, these are among the factors considered in the selection process.

High Motivational Value

Motivational value is an especially important factor in selecting play materials. Thus, a part of the assessment process includes determining the play preferences of both novice and the expert players (see Chapter 7). We want to be sure to include materials that are especially attractive and inviting to novice players. At the same time, we want to be sure to include play materials that are equally stimulating for the expert players. A part of the selection process includes determining what is popular in the play culture of children at a particular point in time.

Developmentally and Age Appropriate

Consideration of how play materials are matched to children's developmental level as well as chronological age is also a critical part of the selection process. This involves choosing toys and props that are acceptable to children within a particular age range, and are also appealing to children with differing abilities. There is generally a discrepancy between the age and development of novice players in terms of how they play. Therefore, we are careful to choose materials that are perceived by peers as age-appropriate as well as attractive to the novice player from a developmental perspective. It is especially important that the materials do not stigmatize children in any way. For instance, we would not give a baby rattle to a 5-year-old novice player who likes to shake things. Instead, we might include age-appropriate play materials that provide the same feedback – such as musical instruments (e.g., maracas, rain sticks) or pretend props (e.g., cooking pot with raw beans, cereal box filled with beads).

It is important to point out here that many toys that are commercially sanctioned or traditionally available in schools are not necessarily developmentally or age-appropriate. For instance, many board games that are labeled by manufacturers as appropriate for younger children are in fact far too difficult for young children to play without adult direction.

It is also a myth (largely perpetuated by schools) that older children prefer games with rules to the exclusion of pretend play. In reality, many of the props traditionally available for younger children hold just as much interest and enjoyment for older children. What differs is what children of differing ages and development choose to do with the materials. The key is to find materials that are relatively generic and even ageless in their form and function.

High Social Potential

Play materials with high potential for eliciting socially interactive play as opposed to solitary play are preferred in Integrated Play Groups (see Tables 5.2, 5.3, and 5.4). For instance, play dough, building blocks and dress-up clothes are more conducive to social engagement than puzzles, books and computer or videogames, which tend to be geared to independent play. Board games are generally recommended for older children for whom they are developmentally and age-appropriate. Although board games are considered to be social by nature, they can be very competitive and frustrating for less able youngsters.

High Imaginative Potential

Play materials with high potential for creative or imaginative play are also desirable in Integrated Play Groups. The realism and structure of toys and props will influence how children will use them and therefore need to be taken into consideration. *Realism* refers to the degree to which a toy resembles its real-life counterpart while *structure* refers to the extent to which toys have specific uses. High-realism toys are generally highly structured. For example, a realistic replica of a fire truck is meant to be played with as a fire truck while a less realistic toy such as a block with four wheels can represent any kind of a vehicle. High-realism and structured toys may enhance emerging representational skills while less realistic toys may foster more advanced forms of symbolic pretend play.

Representing Diversity

Integrated Play Groups include children from all cultures, ethnic backgrounds, socioeconomic levels, etc., so we are thoughtful in choosing toys that represent people in the same way. Many commercial toys are beginning to include dolls and puppets that reflect diverse cultures, ethnicities, gender roles and abilities. Toys that are overtly racist, sexist, or disrespectful toward any group of people are purposefully excluded.

Nonviolent

Although it is possible for children to create imaginary weapons using whatever materials are available (e.g., using a block to represent a gun), we prefer not to include realistic replicas of weapons or war-related toys that may potentially lead to violent acts. At the same time, we recognize and respect that there may be different views on this issue depending upon the culture and community in which one lives. For instance, hunting may be a very natural part of a child's upbringing in Alaska, so it may be natural to give children replicas of hunting rifles for play. In such cases it is important that rules be established that reflect real-life uses of such objects (e.g., never point the toy at a person).

Safe and Durable

Safety and durability are naturally important to consider when purchasing or making toys. We recommend discretion in choosing items with mechanical or electrical features as well as with sharp points, edges, small parts, or long strings or cords, as these may be potentially harmful. It is also important to check toys periodically for wear and tear and to replace items when they cannot be properly repaired. Be sure to check that self-made, second-hand or imported toys are non-toxic, use flame-retardant fabrics and have the U.L.-approved seal if electrical. (For more information on toy safety, contact: Toy Industry Association, Inc., 1115 Broadway, Suite 400, New York, NY 10010; www.toy-tia.org.)

Considerations for Selecting Play Materials for Integrated Play Groups

A wide range of sensory-motor, exploratory, constructive and sociodramatic play props and toys are selected on the following basis:

- High motivational value

- Developmentally/age appropriate

- High social potential

- High imaginative potential

- Reflecting diversity of culture, ethnicity, gender roles, abilities

- Nonviolent

- Safe and durable

Suggested Play Materials

Tables 5.2, 5.3, and 5.4 list play materials that we have found children of a variety of ages and abilities to enjoy while playing in Integrated Play Groups. The basic set of play materials are meant to be permanently incorporated and maintained within the play area (see Table 5.2). The theme-based sets are collections of props that may be gathered in boxes or kits for either permanent display or intermittent use in the play area (see Tables 5.3 and 5.4). Table 5.3 notes themes we have observed to be especially popular among a wide range of children. These suggestions are by no means exhaustive; there is room for revision and expansion as needed. The most important thing to keep in mind is that the children are the ones who define what play materials and themes are appropriate and popular with respect to their peer play culture.

Table 5.2

Basic Play Materials for Integrated Play Groups

MANIPULATION – SENSORY PLAY	FUNCTIONAL – CONSTRUCTIVE
Beanbags	Building blocks (wooden/cardboard)
Balls	Snap-together blocks
Bubbles	Duplos, Legos
Child-safe shaving cream	Tinker Toys
Water, rice, sand buckets/tables	Tools and workbench
Wind-up toys	Train and connecting track
Spinning tops	Vehicles (cars, trucks, airplanes)
Marble run and mazes	Roads
Play dough, cookie cutters, rolling pins	Ramps
Boxes of all sizes	Tunnels
Bed sheets, blankets, spandex	Bridges
Parachute	Garage
Rope, therabands (elastic bands)	Road signs
Hoola hoops	

SOCIODRAMATIC PLAY	ART
Child Size:	Paper
Stove	Paints, pencils, pens, crayons, markers
Refrigerator	Sidewalk chalk
Sink	Stamps, stencils
Kitchen set – dishes, pots, utensils	Tape, glue
Play food	Scissors
Telephones (at least 2)	Easel – chalkboard, whiteboard

SOCIODRAMATIC PLAY (cont.)	MUSIC
Household accessories – vacuum, iron	Musical instruments
Dress-up clothes and accessories	Musical toys
Make-up and hairbrushes	Rain sticks
Mirror (shatter-proof)	Rhythm sticks
Cash register, shopping carts	Microphone
Puppets (people and animals)	Sound machines
Stuffed animals	Junk band – pots, pans, rubber bands

SOCIODRAMATIC PLAY (cont.)	MISC. GAMES (Older Children)
Dolls – babies, boys, girls, families	Board Games – *Sorry, Parcheesi*
Doll beds, carriages	Chess
Puppet theater/store front	Checkers
Pop-up tent/house/bus	*Mouse Trap*
	Operation
Miniatures:	*Hang-Man*
Dollhouse	*Boggle/Scrabble Junior*
Dollhouse furniture	*Stratego*
Dollhouse accessories (dishes, blankets, phones)	*Bingo*
Doll families	Playing cards (*Uno, Old Maid, Go Fish*)
"Barbie/Ken"-size dolls	Pick-up-Sticks
"Barbie/Ken"-size clothes, accessories	Jacks
Action figures (nonviolent)	Strings
Zoo and farm animals	*Jenga*
	Twister

Table 5.3

Popular Play Themes in Integrated Play Groups

Household Themes	Community Themes

Caring for babies
Cleaning/housekeeping
Cooking – meals
Daily rituals – bedtime, waking up
Dress-up/make-up
Family
Household pets
Tea party
	Construction – building:
	  Bridges
	  Cities
	  Forts
	  Towers
	Eating out:
	  Drive-thru
	  Fast food
	  Ice cream parlor
	  Pizza parlor
	  Sit-down restaurant

Social Event Themes	**Emergency helpers:**
	  Ambulance
	  Firefighters
	  Police (cops and robbers)
	  Rescue workers

"Academy Awards"
Amusement park/fair
Birthday party
Bowling alley
Circus
Dance/ball
Fiesta
Magic show
New year party
Olympics
Orchestra/band
Parade
Puppet/theater performances
Slumber party
Talent show
Wedding
	Health care:
	  Dentist
	  Doctor
	  Hospital
	  Nurse
	  Veterinarian (animal hospital)
	School:
	  Cafeteria
	  Library
	  School bus
	  Teacher – students
	Shopping:
	  Clothing store
	  Grocery store
	  Toy store
	  Video store

Outdoor – Nature Themes	**Television:**
	  Cartoons
	  Commercials
	  Shows
	  Weather reporter

Beach
Camping
Cave exploration
Fishing
Gardening
Hiking in the forest
Jungle
Mountain climbing
Ocean
Picnic
Rodeo
Treasure hunt
Zoo
	Travel:
	  Airport
	  Boats
	  Buses
	  Cars
	  Gas station
	  Taxi driver

Fantasy Themes	**Other:**
	  Computer programmer
	  Hairdresser – beauty salon
	  Office workers

Dinosaurs Disney Fairy tales Imaginary societies Movie stars Olden days Outer space Pioneers Pirates Video rock stars	

Table 5.4

Examples of Theme-Based Sets of Play Materials for Integrated Play Groups

HOUSEHOLD THEMES

PLAY THEME: Cooking – Meals

Materials-Props:
- Play kitchen set (stove, sink, fridge)
- Pots and pans
- Large utensils
- Play food/real food* (e.g., raw beans)
- Play dough
- Aprons
- Chef hats
- Table and chairs
- Plates/cups/small utensils
- Placemats/table cloth

*If using real food, please be aware of any food allergies.

PLAY THEME: Caring for Babies

Materials-Props:
- Baby dolls
- Baby diapers/clothes
- Baby bottles/food
- Highchair
- Crib
- Stroller/snuggly
- Blanket
- Bathing tub
- Bubble bath/lotion/powder
- Towels

PLAY THEME: Housekeeping

Materials-Props:
- Feather dusters
- Broom
- Play vacuum cleaner
- Sponges/rags
- Aprons
- Play washing machine
- Miscellaneous clothing
- Ironing board

PLAY THEME: Dress-Up

Materials-Props:
- Clothing
- Hats
- Shoes
- Accessories – scarves, ties, jewelry
- Purses
- Make-up
- Hairbrushes/combs
- Mirror

COMMUNITY THEMES

PLAY THEME: Grocery Store

Materials-Props:
- Grocery boxes/cans
- Fruits and vegetables
- Shopping carts/baskets
- Shopping bags
- Cash register
- Play money/credit cards
- Wallets/purses
- Store front/counter
- Telephones

PLAY THEME: Restaurant

Materials-Props:
- Cooking/meals theme-based set (see above)
- Menus (pictures/icons)
- Writing pad/pencil
- Cash register
- Play money/credit cards
- Wallets/purses
- Telephones

PLAY THEME: Doctor-Nurse-Hospital

Materials-Props:
- Doctor kit
- Stethoscope
- Blood pressure pump
- Reflex mallet
- Tongue depressors
- Syringe
- Thermometer
- Bandages – plaster/gauze/ace
- Medicine bottles
- Medical jacket/hospital scrubs

PLAY THEME: Hairdresser

Materials-Props:
- Combs/brushes
- Hairdryer
- Blunt play scissors
- Curlers
- Hair clips
- Play sink/buckets
- Smocks
- Towels
- Dolls/mannequins with hair
- Shampoo (for dolls)

Table 5.4 (continued)

SOCIAL EVENT THEMES

PLAY THEME: Birthday Party

Materials-Props:
- Wrapping paper/tape
- Small toys (to wrap as presents)
- Pretend cake (e.g., play dough)
- Candles
- Party hats
- Streamers/balloons/noise-makers
- Table and chairs
- Plates/cups/small utensils
- Placemats/table cloth
- Party games (e.g., piñata, pin/tape-the-tale on the donkey)

PLAY THEME: Circus in Miniature

Materials-Props:
- Animal figures/puppets
- Clown/performer figures/puppets
- Hoola hoops (represent circus ring)
- Blanket (circus tent)
- Blocks (climbing towers)
- Rope (tight rope/swings)
- Vehicles
- Assorted shapes (to perform stunts)

OUTDOOR – NATURE THEMES

PLAY THEME: Camping

Materials-Props:
- Pop-up or self-made tent
- Blankets
- Backpacks
- Pots and pans
- Sticks/cooking utensils
- Play food/tin cans
- Pretend firewood/fire
- Flashlights
- Ghost stories
- Stuffed animals

PLAY THEME: Beach

Materials-Props:
- Blanket/towels
- Sun glasses
- Sun hats
- Beach umbrella
- Beach balls
- Flippers
- Goggles
- Buckets with sand
- Blue paper to represent water/waves
- Play fish/sea creatures

FANTASY THEMES

PLAY THEME: Fairy Tale - *Three Little Pigs*

Materials-Props:
- Boxes – 3 child size/3 doll size
- 3 pig dolls – stuffed or self-made
- 3 pig noses/masks
- 1 wolf doll – stuffed or self-made
- 1 wolf nose/mask
- Paper strips to represent straw
- Play dough to represent mud
- Blocks to represent bricks
- Paint to decorate boxes
- *Three Little Pigs* story-book/cassette

PLAY THEME: Outer-Space Travel

Materials-Props:
- Space suits
- Helmets
- Large box (space craft)
- Box (control panel)
- Plate (steering wheel)
- Space travel food
- Paper towel rolls (telescopes)
- Sleeping bags
- Styrofoam balls/balloons (planets)
- Streamers
- Star shapes

Most of the materials suggested for Integrated Play Groups tend to be very plain and simple. Our preference is for European-style toys that have the appearance of being hand-crafted and are made of natural or painted wood and some durable plastics. We try to avoid toys made of cheap plastic. Although larger items can be costly, it is possible to acquire many of the materials for little or no money. For instance, gathering empty grocery boxes from home is a cost-free way to stock a pretend supermarket. Used clothing, hats and shoes may be collected for dress-up and doll play.

With a little ingenuity, it is also possible to hand-make many of the suggested play materials. Creating play materials with the children can be a fun activity in and of itself. Many discarded consumer items may come in handy for creating sensory-based, constructive and pretend play materials as well as games. For instance, large boxes are especially useful for creating child-size kitchen sets, store fronts, puppet theaters, road vehicles and trains.

It is important to keep in mind that ongoing assessments will help to determine what is appropriate for a particular child or group of children at different points in time (see the Play Preference Inventory in Chapter 7). As a general rule, it is best to begin with too few rather than too many play materials – just enough to allow children to make choices without being overwhelmed. Over time, you may gradually add to your collection. You may also find that some materials may need to be temporarily set aside as your collection grows since what seems enticing to children in the early stages of a play group may lose its motivational value after repeated and extended use. At the same time, it is helpful to retain materials since children may wish to revisit themes that they abandoned at an earlier phase.

Chapter Summary

This chapter focused on preparing the play setting for Integrated Play Groups. Play groups may be carried out in home, school, therapy and community environments that afford natural opportunities for peer socialization and play. Within these environments, play areas are designed with close consideration of a number of important environmental features. The physical ecology of the play area is carefully constructed in order to optimize children's motivational and developmental potential. In addition, play materials are also selected on this basis as a way to maximize opportunities for social interaction, communication, play and imagination.

CHAPTER 6

Structuring the Play Session

Chapter Highlights

This chapter focuses on how to structure the play session in Integrated Play Groups. The following topics will be highlighted:

► Establishing a Schedule

► Play Group Rules

► Opening and Closing Rituals

► Fostering a Group Identity

In the sun that is young once only,
Time let me play and be
Gold in the mercy of his means

– Dylan Thomas

Once you have taken steps to plan the program, gather and prepare the players and set up the play environment, it is time to consider how you will structure the play session for Integrated Play Groups. Play sessions are structured in a number of ways through the use of visual supports, routines and rituals. These external supports are used to establish continuity across sessions.

It is important to keep in mind that consistency, order and predictability are critical components of the initial structure that children with autism need to optimally succeed in an intervention program (Rutter, 1978). The idea therefore is to provide children with a high degree of structure in the beginning stages so that they may more easily acclimate to Integrated Play Groups. Over time, as the children demonstrate a greater sense of internal order and control, these external supports may be gradually altered and even withdrawn. Ultimately, this will help children develop greater flexibility and adaptability so that they are better equipped to negotiate their social and imaginary worlds.

Establishing a Schedule

Meeting Times

Each Integrated Play Group consists of the same children, who meet on a regular basis over an extended period of time. Play group sessions may run for as little as 30 minutes or up to one hour, two or more times per week. Whenever possible, the time of day that groups meet should reflect natural play times during which novices are likely to be alert and focused. Integrated Play Groups are generally carried out over the course of a school year or an equivalent time frame. Our research suggests that six months is a minimally adequate length of time in which to implement Integrated Play Groups. Many children begin to show significant change after about three months, and continue to progress thereafter.

The frequency of play group meetings and the length of sessions will vary for individual children depending upon a number of factors. Some children need the minimum while others need longer times, more frequent meetings or a combination of both. The decision may be influenced by the children's age, development and experience as well as pragmatic factors. The important variable is for children to have ample opportunity to become familiar and comfortable with one another in play through consistent and repeated exposure (Lord & McGill, 1989). This will ultimately allow children to practice and appropriate skills within their "zone of proximal development" (Vygotsky, 1978).

Personalized Visual Schedules

Once you have established meeting times for Integrated Play Groups, it is important to develop a system of communicating this information to the children involved. One way is to augment or create a personalized visual schedule that depicts when, where and with whom the Integrated Play Groups are to take place. By introducing and referring to the schedule on a regular basis, children will better anticipate and prepare for each meeting. The use of a visual schedule may also help to alleviate any anxiety that may occur as a result of introducing a new routine or changes to an existing routine.

It is likely that most children already have a schedule or visual system within which times for Integrated Play Groups may be incorporated. (See for example, visual schedules developed using the TEACCH model; Schopler & Mesibov, 1986.) It is also possible to create a personalized visual schedule for children who do not yet have a schedule system in place.

Visual schedules are tailored to the individual based on the child's communication and learning style (ranging from concrete to abstract systems). Visual systems may incorporate objects, photographs, line drawings or written words to depict times (e.g., days of the week or times within a day) when play groups will be taking place.

We suggest that when you are developing these materials you make them adaptable (e.g., using Velcro strips) so that the visual symbol may be removed or replaced in the event of changes to the schedule. We also suggest that you display the schedule in a handy location so that you may refer to it at the start and close of each play session. Figure 6.1 gives an example of a personalized visual schedule using line drawings (adapted from The Picture Communication Symbols ©1981-2003 developed by Mayer-Johnson, Inc. See Appendix C, Resources).

Figure 6.1. Example of a personalized visual schedule.

Play Group Rules

It is immensely important to establish a set of rules for the children to follow while participating in Integrated Play Groups. The idea is to develop rules that the children can easily comprehend and adhere to. Play group rules may be established with the children during the first session when appropriate.

Each set of rules should include statements that are worded in the positive, indicating what the children are expected to do (e.g., Be nice to your friends) rather than what they are not expected to do (e.g., Don't be mean to your friends). Rules typically incorporate at least one statement that focuses on the overall goal of the group – to include one another in play.

It is generally most effective to use a visual format that both novice and expert players are able to understand. Depending upon the players, written words/phrases, line drawings and/or photographs may be used to spell out the rules on a poster. The poster should be displayed at the children's eye level in a prominent place in the play area. In this way, the play guide can make reference to the rules as needed.

The following are typical rules for younger and older children that may be adapted for use within Integrated Play Groups.

Example of Play Group Rules for Younger Children	Example of Play Group Rules for Older Children
• Be nice to your friends • Be nice to the toys • Stay in the play area • Ask for help • Play together	• Treat each other with respect • Treat the materials with respect • Stay with the group • Take turns being first • Ask if you want or need something • Include everybody and cooperate

Opening and Closing Rituals

Opening and closing rituals offer another important means for structuring the play session (see Table 6.1). The idea is to mark the play session so that there is a clear beginning, middle and end. Opening and closing rituals are carried out at the start and end of each and every play session. Particularly in the early stages, these rituals will help children acclimate more quickly to participating in Integrated Play Groups as a part of their weekly routine. Opening and closing rituals also provide temporal boundaries that support children in regulating their own behavior so that they may be freed up to pursue play in more spontaneous and flexible ways.

A variety of opening and closing rituals may be incorporated in play sessions, based on the children's ages, development, ability and interests. In all cases, rituals should be carried out in a fairly swift and succinct manner to avoid taking too much time away from the play. For younger and more involved children, opening and closing rituals tend to be very brief, while for older and more advanced children they tend to be a bit longer.

Table 6.1
Opening and Closing Rituals for Integrated Play Groups

Opening Ritual	Closing Ritual
Gather in same play space – sit with children in circle on rug, carpet squares, chairs around table	**Refer to visual sequence of play session** – help children transition to end their play (e.g., give one-minute warning to clean up)
Present visual sequence of play session – let children know order of events (see Figure 6.2)	**Clean up** – help children put play materials away in their proper place
Express greeting – engage children in activity/song that is motivating and easy to follow	**Gather in same play space** – sit with children in circle on rug, carpet squares, chairs around table
Review rules – give quick overview of rules using appropriate visual supports (e.g., poster of rules)	**Review** – have each child share something special about the play session (use visual supports as appropriate)
Recap – briefly discuss what the children played last session (use visual supports as appropriate)	**Plan for next session** – have each child suggest something to play next time they meet (use visual supports as appropriate)
Highlight strategies – introduce and reinforce key social-communication strategies that the children will practice within the session (see Chapter 10)	**Share a snack/special treat** – offer children or have children offer to each other popcorn, raisins, stickers, stamps, etc.
Make a plan to get started in play – help novice and expert players choose and connect desired play activities/themes (use visual supports as appropriate)	**Say good-bye** – engage children in activity/song that is motivating and easy to follow; remind children when they will meet again

Opening Rituals

Gather in the same play space.
A first step for virtually all children is to get in the habit of gathering in the same play space within the play area at the start of each session. This may entail sitting on chairs around a table or on stools, carpet squares or a floor rug.

Present visual sequence of play session. It is at this juncture that many play guides introduce a simple visual sequence of the play session to let the children know the order of events. This may also be posted for the children to review during the play session. Figure 6.2 gives an example of a visual sequence of the play session using line drawings. Alternatively, photographs and other visuals may be used.

Figure 6.2. Sample visual sequence of play session.

The Picture Communication Symbols © 1981-2003, used with permission from Mayer-Johnson Inc., P.O. Box 1579, Solana Beach, CA 92075. 800/588-4548 (phone), 858/550-0449 (fax) and www.mayer-johnson.com.

Express greeting. Each play session starts with a ritual whereby children greet one another. Ritual greetings typically incorporate some sort of activity or song that is motivating and easy for the children to follow. Many groups kick off their play session with a special signal, password, chant or cheer initiated by the children (see Fostering a Group Identity at the end of this chapter).

Ritual greetings might be as simple as having the players say hello, reach out and shake hands or give a high-five to one another. In addition, the players might place a photograph of each other on a chart to signify who is present for the day.

Numerous songs may also be appropriate, many of which incorporate children's names as well as focus on play and friendship themes. Songs that involve finger play and props (such as puppets) are especially motivating and engaging for younger children. Many songs are available on tape as well as on sheet music. Some readers may recall from their own childhoods the following popular songs that have caught on in many of our play groups.

Playmate

Say, say, oh playmate,
Come out and play with me
And bring your dollies three
Climb up my apple tree

Slide down my rainbow
Into my cellar door
And we'll be jolly friends
Forever more …

The More We Get Together

Oh, the more we get together,
Together, together,
Oh, the more we get together,
The happier we'll be.

For your friends are my friends,
And my friends are your friends.
Oh, the more we get together,
The happier we'll be!

Review rules. Providing a quick overview of the play group rules (using the appropriate visual supports) is especially important in the early phases of the program. Once the children are well acquainted with the rules, it is no longer necessary to repeat them each session. However, it is sometimes helpful to review the rules from time to time to be sure that the children have retained an understanding of what is expected of them.

Recap. To establish continuity from session to session, it is also helpful to quickly recap what the children played together in their last play session. Visuals that represent the different activities, such as photographs, line drawings and written words, can be displayed as a reminder. More able children may be encouraged to share some thoughts about their last play session in order to apply what they learned to the present session. Questions might focus on what was fun, successful or challenging for them.

Highlight strategies. Once the children are settled, it is time to introduce and reinforce key strategies that they will practice within the context of their play group session. The major emphasis is on social-communication strategies, which will be covered in significant detail in Chapter 10. The focus will differ from child to child and from group to group. In some cases only a single simple strategy will be introduced and reinforced later while the children are playing. In other cases, the children will learn more sophisticated strategies that they may initially discuss or role-play and later practice within the session.

Make a plan to get started in play. Next the children are asked to make a simple plan of what they'd like to play that session. This is merely a way to help children get started playing; they are not bound to stick to their original choices. They are free to alter their choices and the course of the session as befits the true nature of play. There are different ways to help children initiate choices or construct a plan; all need to be tailored to the individual and the group.

Choosing desired play activities/themes. Younger and more involved children are often encouraged to swiftly choose play activities and themes in order to maintain focus and motivation. This may be as simple as asking children what they would like to play and encouraging them to choose from among the materials present in the play area. Since the materials will be laid out in a visually organized fashion, this is often an efficient way for novice players to let us know what they most desire to play. It is from this starting place that we are able to guide novice and expert players to find ways to coordinate their play interests in a mutually satisfying manner.

Some novice players may benefit from using a visual choice board that displays an array of pictures or photographs depicting preferred play materials, activities and themes as determined by a thorough assessment (see Chapter 7). This is especially helpful for children who tend to gravitate to the same play things when given the freedom to choose from among the materials directly within the play area, as it helps diversify and expand their repertoire of preferred play activities. Expert players may be encouraged to use the same visual choice board as a way to find common ground with the novice player. It is immensely important to keep in mind that a visual choice board must be continually updated in order to expand the range of options available to children.

Co-constructing plans. Older and more capable children may be able to participate in a discussion that focuses on co-constructing a plan for play. For example, each child may be given the opportunity to suggest a play activity or play theme. The group must then come up with a plan to coordinate activities so that everyone is involved in playing with someone else. This may mean playing together as one large group in a single activity, or breaking up into dyads and triads into different activities. For children who can read and write, it is often helpful to write out the children's suggestions and plans so that they may refer back to them throughout the session and in future sessions.

Closing Rituals

Refer to visual sequence of play session. To help transition the children to end their play, play guides should refer to the next event depicted in the visual sequence of the play session (see Figure 6.2).

Clean up. It goes without saying that clean-up is an ongoing ritual that is instituted at the close of each and every play session. It is best to give children adequate notice that the play session will be coming to a close since abruptly ending the play can be very disconcerting for many children. A few gentle reminders, such as "three minutes, two minutes, one minute until clean-up," help bring the children out of their "play reality" into the reality of what is coming next.

Different activities and songs may accompany clean-up, especially for young children. Many children are familiar with the ever-so-popular clean-up song from the children's show "Barney." It may be helpful to assign a child the task of being the clean-up supervisor. That child might carry a special sign or wear a special hat that signifies clean-up.

Cleaning up is in itself a critical part of the closing ritual. A strong sense of security comes from knowing that each time the children arrive in the play area, they will find every item in the place where it was left the last time they met. All of the players should participate in some way in putting items back where they belong.

Gather in the same play space. After the play area has been cleaned and organized, the children gather once again in the same play space as at the start of the session.

Review. After the children have gathered, it is time to review the session's events. Each child is now given the opportunity to share, in some way, something played or experienced during the session. It is important to reinforce the use of visuals and augmentative forms of communication so that every child may contribute at his level of ability. Some children might simply touch or pick up a toy they played with during the session. Others might point to a picture or a written word or phrase. Others might repeat a simple word or phrase. And still others might talk about what they played in a whole sentence or an elaborate narrative. A popular way to motivate verbal children to share is by passing around a microphone, such as those used with tape recorders or karaoke machines.

The following statements/questions may be tailored to the group to stimulate discussion:

- Show/tell us what you played today.
- Show/tell us who you played with today.
- Show/tell us what your favorite thing was that you played today.
- Show/tell us what was fun to play today.
- Show/tell us what was not so fun – what would make it more fun next time.

Plan for next session. As appropriate, ask the players to think about and discuss what they would like to play the next time they meet for play groups. Some players may need support in communicating their interests. This might involve making suggestions on behalf of a child, based on a particular play preference the child exhibited in the present session.

Share a snack or special treat. At the close of the session it is nice to share a snack or special treat with all of the children. Quick and healthy snacks include a handful of popcorn or a few raisins. Popular treats include stickers or stamps. Our colleagues at Developmental Pathways for Kids (Fuge & Berry, in preparation) created an especially motivating way to treat the children. Each play group receives a star after each play session. After the group has accumulated a certain number of stars, each child gets to retrieve a prize from a "treasure chest" filled with trinkets. Some of our older play groups have a similar system where they fill in pretend pepperonis on a pizza after every session. Once the blank spaces are filled, the group gets to have a real pizza party.

Say good-bye. At the very end of a session, it is important that the children acknowledge one another in some way before they depart. Younger children may sing a special good-bye song, whereas older children might simply wave, shake hands, or say good-bye to one another. As a final note, it is important to remind the children when they will see each other again for play groups by referring to their personalized calendar or schedule.

Fostering a Group Identity

Another important way to structure the play session is to incorporate rituals and routines that foster a sense of group identity among the players. The idea is to help children develop a sense of belonging as members of a common social group that they regard as meaningful and valuable. One of the very first play sessions may be devoted to carrying out activities that focus on developing a group identity. Group identity rituals and routines may be reinforced thereafter in subsequent play sessions. The following are examples of ways to foster a group identity that may be adapted for children of different ages and abilities.

Play Group Names

Coming up with a group or club name is a simple way children can begin to identify with one another as members of the same play group. In many cases, play group names reflect a special interest of the novice players as a way to motivate them. The trick is to entice the expert players into taking ownership of the name as well. This is often easily accomplished if the novice player's interest is fairly conventional. For instance, many children with autism are enamored with Thomas the Tank Engine, a character who is also popular among preschool children. Incorporating this interest, a play group name might be literal – "Thomas the Tank Engine Group" – or some variation, such as "Choo-Choo Club."

If a novice player has a fairly unconventional interest, however, it may take a bit of effort to shape the interest into a play group name that everyone can agree upon. For instance, if an older novice player is fixated on eye glasses, an interest generally not shared by elementary-aged peers, it may be possible to come up with names that incorporate some aspect of the interest; for example, "The Eye-Spy Club." The following are examples of names for Integrated Play Groups generated by and with children.

- Barbie Play Group
- Best Buds
- Friends Together
- Choo-Choo Club
- Clifford's Friends
- Cool Cats
- D. W. Friends Group (character from Arthur the Aardvark books/videos)
- Eye-Spy Club
- Flying Angels
- Harry Potter Club
- Lion Club
- Loma Vista Video Club
- Luigi Lobsters
- Lucky Lunch Bunch
- Mickey Mouse Club
- Pee Wee Playhouse
- Playmania
- Play Pals
- Pokémon Group
- Power Puffs
- Special Friends
- Super Heroes
- Teddy Bear Friends Club
- Tele-Tubbies
- Thomas the Tank Engine Group
- Wee Pals

Posters - Logos

In addition to coming up with a play group name, children may be able to create some kind of visual that corresponds to the group's name. As a group, the children might first decorate a poster that incorporates the group's name and images that represent the name. The poster might be displayed each time the play group meets.

A specific symbol or logo that represents the group theme might also be developed. Older children might be able to come up with a specific logo by designing their own, while a logo might also be derived from younger children's creations. Logos may also be taken from photos in magazines, computer clip art or other prefabricated means. Once defined, logos may be displayed on any number of items, including buttons, t-shirts or hats. Arts and crafts stores supply kits for transferring images on these various items. It is also possible to hand-make them with the children.

Signals, Passwords, Chants and Cheers

Another way to foster a group identity is to come up with some kind of ceremonial ritual that the players carry out each time they meet. This might include a signal, password, chant or cheer that becomes a part of the opening or closing ritual. For instance, the children might come up with a special handshake when they greet one another, a special chant that they shout out each time the session begins or a top-secret word that they must reveal upon entering the play area. In Tara Tuchel's play groups, the children begin their session with the ritual of placing their hands in the middle, one on top of the other, and then shouting "Woo!" while lifting their hands above their heads all at once. Rituals may also correspond to the special interests of players that are reflected in the play group name as in the following case vignette.

> ## CASE VIGNETTE
> ## Kato – Fostering a Group Identity
>
> As introduced in Chapter 1, Kato is a 10-year-old boy with Asperger Syndrome who has a fascination with the airline industry. Twice a week for 30 minutes Kato participates in an Integrated Play Group with four of his classmates. The group is facilitated by his speech and language therapist.
>
> Initial play sessions focus on helping Kato and his peers establish a group identity. The children discuss different possible club names. After generating a list of choices, the children take a vote and settle on Kato's suggestion to name the group the "Flying Angels."
>
> Next the children design a group poster to be displayed at each meeting. They draw a large airplane and strategically place themselves in different parts of it. Kato eagerly draws himself in the cockpit. A peer attempts to draw a picture of himself beside Kato's, which Kato initially resists. When the play guide suggests that the two boys be co-pilots, Kato agrees as long as he is the lead pilot, which seems to resolve the matter.
>
> As the children continue to draw, the play guide stimulates a discussion about travel. An expert player shares an experience of traveling to China with his family. Kato chimes in by reciting facts about the country. The discussion leads to an idea of designing "passports" when they meet again.
>
> In the following session the play guide brings along her passport to use as a model. The children cut out cardboard and paper to size and staple them together to simulate a passport. Then they spend some time drawing pictures and writing pertinent information as depicted in a real passport. Once the passports are completed, the children establish a ritual of taking turns stamping each other's passports each time they enter the play area to begin a play group session.

Play Group Story Books

Another way to help children establish a group identity is to create picture story books that are personalized to the players in the group. The idea is to portray the children's experiences while having fun playing together. The books must be tailored to the novice players' level of comprehension. Books might include photographs of all the players while depicting their play group experiences in story form. A book for younger and more involved children might follow a simple story line of what the children do when they are together in play groups. A more advanced book might focus on a particular play theme the children carried out together.

Story books should be readily available for the players to share when they are together in play groups. Additional copies might also be provided for members to take with them. In this way, they can share their books with other children, their family members as well as their teachers. The following is narrative from a story book that Tara Tuchel put together with photographs of the children enacting a favorite theme.

Playing Police

Alex is the robber.
He steals money from Marcy the cashier

Tom and Carla are the police – They chase the robber.
Catch him! Catch him!

Tom catches the robber and puts him in jail.

Now, Tom is the robber!
He steals money from Marcy.

Alex and Carla try to catch Tom.
Tom runs from the police.

Uh-oh! They catch Tom and put him jail for stealing money.

Cooperative Activities

For more sophisticated play groups that include older, more advanced children, a number of cooperative activities may help foster a group identity. The aim of such activities is to help children discover the advantages of collaboration and joining together as a unified group to overcome obstacles and challenges. The idea is to build a sense of mutual understanding and trust as children learn how to collaborate with others who may behave in unexpected ways or need extra assistance and encouragement to participate.

It is important to keep in mind the unique needs and sensitivities of novice players when carrying out activities that involve close physical contact with others. One popular trust-building activity involves pairing off children so that one is blindfolded while the other acts as a guide, who leads the child through an obstacle course. The following is a cooperative game that is followed by a group discussion.

Cooperative Game: "Keep the Ball Rolling"

- Have the children make a circle holding the edges of a parachute or large bed sheet so it is held taut.

- Place a ball in the middle of the fabric and ask the children to make it roll around in a circle without falling off.

- Once the ball gets going, instruct one child to let go and the others to stay in their places (the object being to disrupt the rhythm and cause the ball to stop or fall off).

- When this happens, ask the children to give you reasons why it happened. Lead the children in a discussion about the importance of cooperation among all members of a group if the group is to succeed. Point out that this is a major aspect of Integrated Play Groups – to cooperate by supporting one another, making sure that everyone is included and no one is left out.

Sample Follow-Up Discussion Topics for Advanced Children

Why are we together for play groups?

- To have fun together
- To develop creativity and imagination
- To learn how to get along with others
- To learn how to communicate
- To learn how to cooperate
- To learn about friendship

What is a friendship – what does it mean to be a friend?

- Friends share common interests – have fun together – are creative together
- Friends communicate well with each other – they know how to communicate with and without words (e.g., facial expressions, body language)
- Friends play well together – they know how to take turns and share their favorite things; they know how to cooperate
- Friends are compassionate/empathetic – they care about the other person's feelings; they support each other when they need help
- Friends are honest and trust each other – they are good sports

Let's think of some fun, creative, imaginative ways you can play together as friends.

Chapter Summary

This chapter focused on structuring the play session for Integrated Play Groups in a number of ways, including visual supports, routines and rituals. External supports are created by establishing a consistent schedule with regular and ongoing meeting times, developing a set of rules that the children can easily comprehend and follow, and carrying out opening and closing rituals that mark the start and close of each session. Another way to structure the play session is to incorporate routines and rituals that help to foster a sense of group identity. This concludes Phase II – Setting the Stage for Play – which emphasized program and environmental design. After the following hands-on activities, turn to Phase III – Observing Children at Play – with a focus on assessment techniques.

Phase II Hands-On Activities

(See Phase II Tools and Field Exercises)

IPG Action Plan

Formulate an Integrated Play Groups action plan for a child you wish to support in a peer play program.

IPG Field Exercises

Conduct the following field exercises that correspond to the IPG action plan and Phase II – Setting the Stage for Play: IPG Program and Environmental Design:

- Field Exercise 1 – Autism – Diversity Awareness

- Field Exercise 2 – Play Group Orientation

- Field Exercise 3 – Selecting Basic Play Materials

- Field Exercise 4 – Selecting Theme-Based Play Materials

- Field Exercise 5 – Designing a Play Area

- Field Exercise 6 – Designing a Personalized Schedule

- Field Exercise 7 – Establishing Play Group Rules

- Field Exercise 8 – Developing Opening and Closing Rituals

- Field Exercise 9 – Fostering a Group Identity

IPG Program and Environmental Design Evaluation

As you begin implementing Integrated Play Groups, reflect on your practice by conducting an IPG Program and Environmental Design Evaluation.

Phase II Tools and Field Exercises

IPG Program and Environmental Design Tools

- IPG Action Plan
- IPG Program and Environmental Design Evaluation

INTEGRATED PLAY GROUPS DESIGN TOOL
Integrated Play Groups Action Plan

Formulate an IPG action plan for a child you wish to support in Integrated Play Groups. With members of your team, conduct the corresponding field exercises.

Integrated Play Groups Team	
Form a team; designate roles and primary responsibilities • Play Guide • Assistant Guide • Key Consultants • IPG Coordinator	
Set up regular team meetings/task force	
Gathering and Preparing the Players	
Determine how you will recruit the players and secure permission	
Choose novice players 1. 2.	Choose expert players 1. 2. 3. 4. Alternates
Design and implement awareness and orientation activities to prepare the players (Field Exercises 1-2)	
Preparing the Play Setting	
Choose a venue	
Decide where to set up the play area	
Select and gather basic and theme-based play materials (Field Exercises 3-4)	
Design and set up the play area (Field Exercise 5)	
Structuring the Play Session	
Establish meeting times for play groups	
Design a personalized play group schedule (Field Exercise 6)	
Establish play group rules (Field Exercise 7)	
Design opening and closing rituals (Field Exercise 8)	
Design activities to foster a group identity (Field Exercise 9)	
Other Planning Issues	
Securing administrative support	
Soliciting and raising funds	
Conducting awareness programs	
Recruiting staff, interns, volunteers	

Wolfberg, P. J. (2003). *Peer play and the autism spectrum: The art of guiding children's socialization and imagination.* Shawnee Mission, KS: Autism Asperger Publishing Company.

INTEGRATED PLAY GROUPS DESIGN TOOL
IPG Program and Environmental Design Evaluation (Part I)

Play Guide:

Novice Player(s):

Date of Evaluation:

Reflect on how you are addressing the following while customizing Integrated Play Groups for each novice player.

Design Component	Considerations	Comments
Play Group Composition	• Group size: 3 to 5 players • Ratio of expert to novice players	
Compatible Players	• Gender • Age • Development and ability • Temperament, play, social style • Play interests • Primary language • Siblings	
Recruitment of Players	• Contact peers within natural social network • Get to know players • Solicit recommendations • Hold try-outs • Extend invitations • Obtain permission – informed consent	
Preparation of Players	• Autism – diversity awareness • Play group orientation	
Suitable Venue	• Natural integrated setting – school, community, therapy, home • Consistent play space • Other play spaces	
Play Area	• Size restriction/spatial density • Clearly defined boundaries • Explicit organization • Limited distractions • Activity/theme-based arrangements	
Selection of Play Materials	Wide range manipulation-sensory, functional-constructive, sociodramatic toys/props: • High motivational value • Developmentally/age-appropriate • High social potential • High imaginative potential • Representing diversity • Nonviolent • Safe and durable	

Wolfberg, P. J. (2003). *Peer play and the autism spectrum: The art of guiding children's socialization and imagination.* Shawnee Mission, KS: Autism Asperger Publishing Company.

IPG Program and Environmental Design Evaluation (Part II)

Play Guide:

Novice Player(s):

Date of Evaluation:

Reflect on how you are addressing the following while customizing Integrated Play Groups for each novice player.

Design Component	Considerations	Comments
Schedule	• Meeting times: 30- to 60-minute sessions/twice weekly • Personalized (visual) schedules	
Play Group Rules	• Worded in positive terms • Understood by players • Clearly displayed	
Opening Rituals	• Gather in same play space • Present visual sequence of play session • Express greeting • Review rules • Recap • Highlight strategies • Make a plan to get started in play	
Closing Rituals	• Refer to visual sequence of play session • Clean up • Gather in same play space • Review • Plan for next session • Share a snack/special treat • Say good-bye	
Group Identity	• Play group name • Poster-logo • Signals, passwords, chants, cheers • Play group story books • Cooperative activities	

Wolfberg, P. J. (2003). *Peer play and the autism spectrum: The art of guiding children's socialization and imagination.* Shawnee Mission, KS: Autism Asperger Publishing Company.

Phase II Tools and Field Exercises

Field Exercises 1-9

1. Autism – Diversity Awareness
2. Play Group Orientation
3. Selecting Basic Play Materials
4. Selecting Theme-Based Play Materials
5. Designing a Play Area
6. Designing a Personalized Schedule
7. Establishing Play Group Rules
8. Developing Opening and Closing Rituals
9. Fostering a Group Identity

PREPARING THE PLAYERS
Field Exercise 1: Autism – Diversity Awareness

Design an awareness activity that will help the expert players develop empathy and understanding for children with autism spectrum disorders. Focus on the unique ways children socialize, communicate and play (please refer to Chapter 4).

_____

_____

_____

_____

_____

_____

_____

_____

_____

_____

_____

_____

_____

_____

_____

_____

_____

_____

_____

_____

Wolfberg, P. J. (2003). *Peer play and the autism spectrum: The art of guiding children's socialization and imagination.* Shawnee Mission, KS: Autism Asperger Publishing Company.

Field Exercise 2: Play Group Orientation

Design an orientation activity that will help novice and expert players become familiar with Integrated Play Groups (please refer to Chapter 4).

_____

_____

_____

_____

_____

_____

_____

_____

_____

_____

_____

_____

_____

_____

_____

_____

_____

_____

_____

_____

_____

Wolfberg, P. J. (2003). *Peer play and the autism spectrum: The art of guiding children's socialization and imagination.* Shawnee Mission, KS: Autism Asperger Publishing Company.

Field Exercise 3: Selecting Basic Play Materials

Create a wish list of basic play materials you would like to include in your play area; rate these in terms of high and low priority. Be sure to consider the children's play preferences (please refer to Chapter 5).

Wish List	High Priority	Low Priority
Manipulation – Sensory		
Functional – Constructive		
Sociodramatic		
Art – Music – Miscellaneous Games		

Wolfberg, P. J. (2003). *Peer play and the autism spectrum: The art of guiding children's socialization and imagination.* Shawnee Mission, KS: Autism Asperger Publishing Company.

Field Exercise 4: Select Theme-Based Play Materials

Brainstorm familiar and motivating play themes; list corresponding play materials to form theme-based sets of play materials. (Please refer to Table 5.3 for a list of popular play themes and Table 5.4 for examples of theme-based play materials for Integrated Play Groups.)

PLAY THEME:	PLAY THEME:
Materials-Props:	Materials-Props:

PLAY THEME:	PLAY THEME:
Materials-Props:	Materials-Props:

PLAY THEME:	PLAY THEME:
Materials-Props:	Materials-Props:

Wolfberg, P. J. (2003). *Peer play and the autism spectrum: The art of guiding children's socialization and imagination.* Shawnee Mission, KS: Autism Asperger Publishing Company.

PREPARING THE PLAY SETTING
Field Exercise 5: Designing a Play Area

Draw a sample play area, keeping the following in mind (please refer to Chapter 5):
- Physical boundaries
- Density of space
- Organization of space
- Arrangement of play materials around activities/themes

Play Area Layout

Wolfberg, P. J. (2003). *Peer play and the autism spectrum: The art of guiding children's socialization and imagination.*
Shawnee Mission, KS: Autism Asperger Publishing Company.

Field Exercise 6: Design a Personalized Schedule

Design a personalized play group schedule or calendar appropriate to the novice players' ability and style of learning (please refer to Chapter 6).

Personalized Schedule

Wolfberg, P. J. (2003). *Peer play and the autism spectrum: The art of guiding children's socialization and imagination.* Shawnee Mission, KS: Autism Asperger Publishing Company.

Field Exercise 7: Establishing Play Group Rules

Develop a set of play group rules that may be introduced in the first session. Be sure to present them in a way that may be easily understood by both novice and expert players using appropriate visual supports (please refer to Chapter 6).

Play Group Rules

Wolfberg, P. J. (2003). *Peer play and the autism spectrum: The art of guiding children's socialization and imagination.* Shawnee Mission, KS: Autism Asperger Publishing Company.

Field Exercise 8: Developing Opening and Closing Rituals

Develop specific activities that may be routinely carried out at the beginning and end of each play group session as opening and closing rituals (please refer to Chapter 6). Create a visual sequence of the play session depicting the order of events (see Figure 6.2).

Opening Ritual

Closing Ritual

Visual Sequence of Play Session

Wolfberg, P. J. (2003). *Peer play and the autism spectrum: The art of guiding children's socialization and imagination.* Shawnee Mission, KS: Autism Asperger Publishing Company.

STRUCTURING THE PLAY SESSION
Field Exercise 9: Fostering a Group Identity

Design activities that will help foster a group identity among novice and expert players – such as helping the players come up with a play group name, signal, code, password, poster, logo, story book based on a shared interest or motivating theme (please refer to Chapter 6).

Wolfberg, P. J. (2003). *Peer play and the autism spectrum: The art of guiding children's socialization and imagination.* Shawnee Mission, KS: Autism Asperger Publishing Company.

PHASE III
Observing Children at Play
Integrated Play Groups Assessment

Imagination is more important
than knowledge . . .

- Albert Einstein

CHAPTER 7

Conducting Quality Assessments

Chapter Highlights

This chapter presents tools and techniques for conducting quality assessments in Integrated Play Groups. The following will be highlighted:

► Key Elements of the IPG Assessment Approach

► IPG Observation Framework

► IPG Assessments

"Knowing where the child is,
is more important than where the child is."

– Adriana Schuler (personal communication)

The art of guiding children in Integrated Play Groups hinges on conducting quality assessments based on astute observations of children at play. Play guides must be well versed in the assessment tools and techniques specifically developed for use with this model. This is key to understanding, interpreting and guiding children's social interaction, communication and play with peers. The IPG assessment process is ongoing and essential for:

• Setting realistic and meaningful goals

• Guiding decisions on how best to intervene on behalf of the novice players

• Systematically documenting and analyzing the children's progress

Our assessments are designed to offer a window onto the unique abilities and challenges of children on the autism spectrum while navigating the world of play with peers. They allow us to qualify and quantify observations of what children do and say in a purposeful and holistic fashion.

Key Elements of the IPG Assessment Approach

Knowledge Base – Understanding Play and the Autism Spectrum

Acquiring a knowledge base grounded in current theory and practice pertaining to the play of children on the autism spectrum is essential to sound assessment. It is especially important to be familiar with the complex challenges children with autism spectrum disorders experience in peer socialization and play in relation to characteristic problems in social interaction, communication, imagination, theory of mind development and sensory processing. In addition, it is essential to be cognizant of patterns of play development in typical children compared to noted variations among children on the autism spectrum.

The first phase of this book offered a brief introduction to the nature of autism spectrum disorders and play development in both typical and atypical populations. This is merely the bare bones of what play guides need to know to conduct quality assessments. To expand and refine your knowledge in this area, we urge you to delve deeper into the literature. *Play and Imagination in Children with Autism* (Wolfberg, 1999), which is a prelude to this book, offers a comprehensive literature review along with detailed discussions of related theory and practice. We additionally refer you to the list of selected readings (see Appendix C – Resources).

Naturalistic Observation - "Jane Goodall Approach"

Play guides must hone their observation skills to effectively understand, interpret and guide children's participation in Integrated Play Groups. In our experience, the most effective way to gain an accurate picture of each child within his play culture is to adopt the "Jane Goodall approach" to naturalistic observation. Jane Goodall is famous for her patient, unobtrusive and meticulous observations of chimpanzees living in social groups within their natural habitat (Goodall, 1971/1988). Our assessment approach follows a similar direction by requiring the observer to periodically stand back, watch and reflect on the natural play lives of children with the least amount of intrusion. While the temptation to jump in and prompt or interact with the children may be great, by resisting this temptation you will gain invaluable insight into how children spontaneously socialize and play without adult guidance.

Our assessments are also designed to be carried out across a variety of natural social play settings. For example, prior to beginning Integrated Play Groups, it helpful to observe and gather information about the child within the home, school and community (i.e., to establish a baseline). Once Integrated Play Groups begin, the focus continues within the context of the child's particular group. As the child progresses, it is important to periodically assess how well the child is generalizing his newly acquired skills across other natural social play contexts.

Methodical Documentation -
Multiple Sources and Perspectives

Another aspect of our assessment approach involves methodical and scrupulous documentation of each child's social and symbolic growth drawing from multiple sources and perspectives. This is achieved through extensive and repeated practice using the assessment tools developed for Integrated Play Groups.

We have found videotaping to be one of the most valuable and effective means of recording naturalistic observations of children at play. Videotapes provide a lasting documentation of each child's progress over time, which may be analyzed in many different ways from various perspectives and therefore allow us to detect patterns of development and behavior that might otherwise go unnoticed. For instance, we discovered through videotapes that many novice players, whom we assumed were unengaged in earlier play sessions, spontaneously exhibited delayed imitation of play routines that were carried out by expert players during those sessions.

In addition to documenting naturalistic observations, it is helpful to gather supplemental information from key individuals who have insight into the child's play development. In particular, interviews and discussions with parents and professionals who have substantial contact with a child may prove to be invaluable sources of information. It is important to check in with these key individuals to substantiate or validate our own observations, perceptions and interpretations of a child's experience.

Insightful Interpretation – Uncovering Each Child's Potential

Another fundamental aspect of the Integrated Play Groups assessment approach involves insightful interpretation that taps into the unique developmental potential of each child. Our assessments are especially sensitive to the qualities rather than deficiencies observed in the play of children on the autism spectrum. We are not concerned with determining what is missing or wrong with the way children socialize or play, but are intent on uncovering present and emerging abilities. This is in contrast to assessments that delineate play skills within a normative framework. While identifying play skills typical of different ages and developmental stages may be useful for targeting specific deficits as a frame of reference, these types of assessments may fail to take into account individual variations in play. Based on the assumption that play develops as a linear process involving the accumulation of discrete behaviors and skills, such assessments do not easily translate into interventions for children who exhibit discontinuities in development.

Our assessments are descriptive, rather than hierarchical, based on the premise that children's play transforms over time without necessarily following a series of successive stages. This is consistent with Vygotsky's (1978) conceptualization of childhood development:

> ... a complex dialectical process characterized by periodicity, unevenness in the development of different functions, metamorphosis or qualitative transformation of one form into another, intertwining of external and internal factors, and adaptive processes which overcome impediments that the child encounters. (p. 73)

Although our primary aim is to help each child progress beyond her current capabilities, we purposely avoid classifying child behavior as fitting into developmental slots. This allows us to alter our perceptions of normalcy when we observe children at play. Essentially, we always see the glass as half full rather than half empty. We interpret all behavior, even subtle, obscure or unconventional expressions in play, as purposeful and adaptive – as meaningful attempts to initiate independent and social play activities. Thus, observations of child initiations in play, even in unusual forms, may serve as indices of present and emerging abilities in play.

IPG Observation Framework

An initial step to carrying out quality assessments is to become familiar with the Integrated Play Groups Observation Framework. The IPG Observation Framework is intended to be used in conjunction with a corresponding set of assessment tools specifically designed for this model (see Phase III Tools and Field Exercises). When recording observations of children, the framework is used as a reference for identifying characteristics associated with various aspects of play behavior. The IPG Observation Framework encompasses the following areas, which are highlighted in Tables 7.1 through 7.4 and described below:

- Social Play Style
- Symbolic and Social Dimensions (Developmental Play Patterns)
- Communicative Functions and Means (Social Communication)
- Play Preferences – Diversity of Play

Social Play Styles

Table 7.1 presents characteristics that reflect social play styles that may be evident when observing novice players in the company of peers. As described in Chapter 1, children on the autism spectrum present patterns of play with peers that include the following social play styles (adapted from Wing & Gould, 1979):

- Aloof
- Passive
- Active-odd
- Other

Some children present a distinct social play style that is consistent over time. Others present social play styles that change over time. Still others present overlapping characteristics that may shift according to the social play context. To fully understand a child's present and emerging capacities, it is helpful to document the child's social play style, and how it might change over time as well as across social contexts.

Symbolic Dimension of Play

Table 7.2 delineates developmental play patterns associated with the symbolic dimension of play (adapted from Leslie, 1987; McCune-Nicholich, 1981; Piaget, 1962; Sigman & Ungerer, 1981; Smilansky, 1968; Westby, 2000).The symbolic dimension refers to play acts that the child directs toward objects, self or others, and that signify events. They range from simple to more complex and imaginative play schemes. Within the symbolic dimension of play, observations of a child may include:

- Not engaged (no apparent play act)
- Manipulation-sensory (exploratory or sensory motor forms of play)
- Functional (conventional play with objects and simple scripts)
- Symbolic-pretend (imaginary forms of play and complex scripts)

Table 7.1

Framework for Observing Children's Social Play Styles in Integrated Play Groups

Social Play Style	Characteristic Patterns of Play with Peers
Aloof	• Child withdraws or avoids peers • Child wanders among peers, but does not take notice of them • Child is unresponsive to peer initiations • Child may approach peers to fulfill simple wants and needs as she would an adult
Passive	• Child appears indifferent toward peers • Child is easily led into play with peers • Child is generally compliant toward peers • Child shows little or no self-initiation with peers
Active-Odd	• Child shows an active interest in playing with peers • Child approaches peers in socially awkward or idiosyncratic ways • Child carries on a one-sided conversation focused on a personal fascination or obsessive interest • Child's attempts to initiate or join peers for play are poorly timed
Other	• Child's behavior patterns do not reflect a distinct social play style • Child's behavior patterns reflect a combination of social play styles

(Adapted from Wing & Gould, 1979)

Social Dimension of Play

Table 7.2 also delineates developmental play patterns associated with the social dimension of play (adapted from Parten, 1932). The social dimension of play focuses on different ways in which a child might behave in the company of one or more children. These include behaviors that follow a progression from a total lack of social engagement to active social engagement with peers. Within the social dimension of play, observations of a child may include:

- Isolate (playing alone)
- Orientation-onlooker (watching peers)
- Parallel-proximity (playing beside peers)
- Common focus (playing with peers in a reciprocal fashion)
- Common goal (collaborating with peers in an organized fashion)

Table 7.2

Framework for Observing Children's Developmental Play Patterns (Symbolic and Social Dimensions) in Integrated Play Groups

Symbolic Dimension of Play	Social Dimension of Play
Not Engaged Child does not touch objects or toys or act out roles in play. Child may enact self-stimulatory behavior that does not involve play materials (e.g., gazes at own hand; rocks body; waves or flaps arms and hands; glances at toys). **Manipulation-Sensory** Child explores and manipulates objects or toys, but does not use them in conventional ways. There is an apparent motivation to obtain sensory input and exert control over the physical world. Play schemes include: 1. Simple actions with single objects (e.g., mouth, gaze, shake, bang, drop) 2. Simple action sequences combining objects (e.g., line up, fill and dump, twist and turn) 3. Performing difficult feats with objects (e.g., balance a coin, spin a plate) **Functional** Child demonstrates conventional use of an object or association of two or more objects. Child responds to logically related physical properties of objects. There is a quality of delayed imitation that may reflect simple pretense. Play schemes include: 1. Uses object/toy as intended (e.g., roll car on floor, press buttons on cash register) 2. Combines two or more related objects (e.g., stack blocks, connect train track, place cup on saucer) 3. Follows simple scripts/familiar routines with realistic props directed to self, dolls or peers (e.g., hold telephone to ear, place bottle in doll's mouth, brush peer's hair) **Symbolic-Pretend** Child acts as if doing something or being someone else with an intent that is representational. Play scripts vary in complexity and cohesion. Play schemes include: 1. Object substitutions, using one object to represent another (e.g., hold banana to ear as if it were a telephone) 2. Attribution of absent or false properties (e.g., hold teapot over cup, make slurping sounds while drinking from empty cup) 3. Imaginary objects as present (e.g., move hand to mouth as if holding a cup) 4. Role-playing scripts (real or invented) with dolls, self, peers and/or imaginary characters (e.g., tea party with teddy bears; telephone conversation with make-believe person; acting out bedtime sequence with doll in reciprocal roles of mother and baby; acting out space fantasy with peers and invented creatures)	**Isolate** Child appears to be oblivious or unaware of others. May wander without looking at peers, occupy self by watching anything of momentary interest, play with own body or play alone (e.g., lies on floor, gets on and off chair, sits quietly gazing into space, plays with back to peers) **Orientation-Onlooker** Child shows an awareness of the other children by looking at them or in the direction of their play materials and activities. Child does not enter into play with peers (e.g., quietly watches peers, turns body to face peers, peripherally gazes at peers, imitates peers while watching from distance) **Parallel-Proximity** Child plays independently beside rather than with other children. There is simultaneous use of the same play space or similar materials as peers. Child may occasionally imitate, show objects, or alternate actions with peers (e.g., child plays beside peers at water table; child pushes a truck beside a peer who builds a roadway; child lines up animal figures next to peer who lines up animal figures; child brushes a doll's hair near a child pushing a doll carriage) **Common Focus** Child plays by interacting with one or more peers. There is joint attention on the play as child and peer engage in joint action, mutual imitation or reciprocal social exchanges. The play may include: taking turns, giving and receiving assistance and directives, active sharing of materials, sharing of emotional expression (e.g., child and peer exchange blocks, take turns brushing a doll's hair, pretend to talk to each other on telephone, engage in peek-a-boo, talk and laugh with one another) **Common Goal** The child engages in play with peers, which is structured for the purpose of attaining a common goal or making a product. Child and peers explicitly plan and carry out a common agenda by defining specific rules and roles, negotiating behavior exchanges and compromising around divergent interests. The efforts of one child supplement those of another. There is a sense of cooperation and belonging to a group (e.g., child and peers plan and build a block tower to a specified height, plan and act out restaurant each with an assigned role, plan in advance to take turns being first to play a game)

(Adapted from Leslie, 1987; McCune-Nicholich, 1981; Parten, 1932; Piaget, 1962; Sigman & Ungerer, 1981; Smilansky, 1968; Westby, 2000)

Communicative Functions and Means

Table 7.3 presents a framework for observing children's social communication (communicative functions and means) within the context of peer play activities (adapted from Peck, Schuler, Tomlinson, Theimer, & Haring, 1984). *Communicative functions* describe the purpose for which the child is communicating:

- No clear communicative intent
- Request for objects
- Request for peer action/assistance
- Request for peer interaction
- Request for affection
- Declaration/comment
- Protest

The functions of communication may be accomplished through a variety of verbal and nonverbal *communicative means*:

- Facial expression
- Eye gaze
- Physical proximity
- Touching
- Showing-giving-taking object
- Enactment
- Gaze shift
- Gesture
- Intonation
- Vocalization
- Nonfocused echolalia
- Focused echolalia
- Simple speech-sign-written words
- Complex speech-sign-written words

Each child's communicative attempt (as expressed through any one or a combination of communicative functions and means) is recognized as a potential initiation to play with someone or something, even when expressed in a subtle or obscure form.

Table 7.3

Framework for Observing Children's Social Communication (Communicative Functions and Means) in Integrated Play Groups

Communicative Functions *What the child intends to convey*	Communicative Means *How the child conveys intentions*
No Clear Communicative Intent No clear evidence or indication that child is communicating in play with peers **Request for Object** Acts to obtain play materials or engage in a desired activity **Request for Peer Action/Assistance** Acts that direct peer to attend to child's wants and needs including to help, do or get something for the child **Request for Peer Interaction** Acts to elicit a peer's response to establish joint attention and engage in reciprocal social exchanges – may be initiated by child or in response to peer initiation **Request for Affection** Acts to show fondness or desire for shared emotional expression and/or physical contact with peers **Declaration/Comment** Acts to elicit a peer's attention for the purpose of sharing information, interests or feelings **Protest** Acts to demonstrate rejection or dissatisfaction	**Facial Expression** Affective-emotional states (e.g., smiles, frowns, wrinkles forehead, winces, pouts, shows surprise) **Eye Gaze** Eye contact without an attempt to direct a peer's gaze elsewhere **Physical Proximity** Positioning oneself close to peers or desired objects **Touching** Physical contact with peers (e.g., patting, pushing, pulling; grasping peer's hand; moving or manipulating peer's hand, face or body) **Showing-Giving-Taking Object** Holding up object facing peer; handing object to peer; taking object from peer **Enactment** Recreating partial or entire behavior sequence associated with past experience (e.g., hides in box to recreate hide-n-seek; runs, looks back at peer to recreate chase) **Gaze Shift** Attempts to direct or guide the attention of others by shifting gaze from the person to the focus object and back again **Gesture** Conventional movements such as pointing, waving, nodding head, shrugging shoulders **Intonation** Non-speech use of vocal mechanisms or noise **Vocalization** Variations in vocal or speech pitch, volume or duration **Nonfocused Echolalia** Exact or partial repetition of speech that is reproduced directly after being heard (immediate) or at a later time (delayed); no association with play context **Focused Echolalia** Exact or partial repetition of speech that may be reproduced directly after being heard (immediate) or at a later point in time (delayed); directly related to play context **Simple Speech-Sign-Written Words** One or two words/short phrases spoken, signed or expressed through augmentative communication systems **Complex Speech-Sign-Written Words** Conventional language spoken, signed or expressed through augmentative communication systems

(Adapted from Peck, Schuler, Tomlinson, Theimer, & Haring, 1984)

Play Preferences – Diversity of Play

Table 7.4 offers a framework for recognizing novice players' play preferences and diversity of play. Play preferences refer to that which the child spontaneously chooses for free play given a variety of materials, activities and themes. A child's play preferences may be either conventional or unconventional – obsessions, obscure interest, rituals and hobbies. Play preferences include a child's fascinations, attractions to and interactions with toys or props, choice of play activities and themes and preferred playmates. The number and range of play preferences exhibited by the child provides a basis for determining diversity of play.

Documenting the play preferences of novice players offers a means of selecting motivating play materials, activities and themes that may be connected to the play interests of expert players. Determining diversity of play provides a basis for setting forth a plan to expand upon the child's repertoire of play interests that may be pursued both as independent and social activity.

IPG Assessments

Corresponding to the observation framework are the following specific assessment tools designed for Integrated Play Groups, which are provided at the end of this section (see Phase III Tools and Field Exercises).

- Play Questionnaire
- Play Preference Inventory
- Integrated Play Groups Observation
- Profile of Individual Play Development
- Record of Monthly Progress in IPG
- Integrated Play Groups Summative Report

These tools are used to record observations and document children's ongoing progress. A suggested timeline for carrying out assessment activities using each of these tools is provided in Table 7.5. Each Integrated Play Groups assessment tool is described and illustrated in the following sections.

Table 7.4

Framework for Observing Children's Play Preferences – Diversity of Play in Integrated Play Groups

Play Preferences	Observations	Examples
Play Fascinations	How does the child mostly prefer to pass the time?	• Wanders • Balances sticks on fingertips • Sorts letter and number shapes • Measures the furniture • Collects train schedules • Reads books • Draws pictures
Play Materials	What types of toys or props are most attractive to the child?	• Wind-up toys • Marble maze • Shiny objects • Blankets and boxes • Action figures • Realistic props (plastic fruits and vegetables, doctor kit)
Actions with Materials	How does the child prefer to engage with toys or props?	• Smells and mouths toys • Gazes at toys • Spins toys • Sifts objects through fingers • Fills and dumps objects • Hoards objects • Lines up toys • Conventional actions
Play Activities	What play activities does the child prefer?	• Physical (rough-housing, hide-n-seek, dancing) • Sensory exploration (sand and water play, play dough) • Constructive (building blocks, trains) • Sociodramatic (dress-up, dollhouse, grocery store) • Art (painting, drawing) • Music (singing, playing instruments) • Social games (duck-duck-goose, London Bridge) • Board games/cards *(Sorry, Uno)*
Play Themes	What play themes does the child prefer?	• Familiar life routines (shopping, birthday party, doctor) • Fantasy play (Harry Potter, classic fairy tales, Britney Spears) • Invented stories (monsters, space travel, land of the lost kitty cats)
Play with Others	With whom does the child prefer to play?	• No one in particular • One or more specific peers • One or more specific adults

Table 7.5
Sample Timeline for Conducting Assessment Activities for Integrated Play Groups

| | | BASELINE | | | | Month 2 | | | | Month 3 | | | | Month 4 | | | | Month 5 | | | | FOLLOW-UP | | | | |
| | | Month 1 | | | | | | | | | | | | | | | | | | | | Month 6 | | | | |
Sessions per month	Pre	1/2	3/4	5/6	7/8	9/10	11/12	13/14	15/16	17/18	19/20	21/22	23/24	25/26	27/28	29/30	31/32	33/34	35/36	37/38	39/40	41/42	43/44	45/46	47/48	Post
Play Questionnaire	X																									X
Play Preference Inventory	X				X								X								X					X
IPG Observation		X	X	X		X		X		X		X G		X		X		X		X G		X		X		G
Profile of Individual Play Development					X				X				X				X				X					X
Record of Monthly Progress in IPG					X				X				X				X				X					X
Integrated Play Groups Summative Report																										X

Key: **X** Carry out IPG assessment activity   **G** Probe for generalization in related play contexts

Play Questionnaire

The Play Questionnaire provides comprehensive information about a child's play experiences and development based on observations made by significant others (e.g., parents, teachers, therapists) in a variety of natural play contexts (e.g., home, neighborhood, school, community). The Play Questionnaire is divided into the following parts:

I.   Background – Play Experience

II. Play Preferences – Diversity of Play

III. Peer Relations – Social Play Style

IV. Developmental Play Patterns

The questionnaire may be given to an individual to fill out or be presented in an interview format. Respondents are encouraged to share examples, comments and questions when completing the questionnaire. Although it is not necessary to have formal training to fill out this questionnaire, in some cases it is necessary to explain terminology to individuals who are unfamiliar with its content.

The Play Questionnaire is most useful when completed prior to beginning Integrated Play Groups as a way to gather preliminary information about a child, and then again at the end of a term as a way to evaluate a child's progress (see Table 7.5).

Play Preference Inventory

The Play Preference Inventory corresponds directly to the IPG Observation Framework illustrated in Table 7.4. The Play Preference Inventory is used to record the (a) play preferences of a novice player and (b) play connections with expert players. This tool also generates information for determining diversity of play, which is recorded in the Profile of Individual Play Development (see page 135).

This assessment is initially carried out in the early (baseline) phases of the program, and periodically updated thereafter (see Table 7.5). To complete the inventory, information about the play preferences of each novice player is gathered through a variety of sources (i.e., direct observation, Play Questionnaire and interviews with significant others). Play preferences should reflect what the child spontaneously chooses for free play given a variety of materials, activities and themes.

Once you have produced a list of the novice player's play preferences, the next step is to generate a list of ideas that connect the novice's play interests with the interests of the expert players. This typically involves holding a discussion or brainstorming with the children at the start of a play group session.

In our experience, it is not difficult to entice and motivate the expert players to find creative ways to connect their play interests with those of the novice players. When novice players have conventional interests that correspond to what is popular within children's mainstream culture, it is easy to find common ground. For instance, many of our novice players share an interest with expert players in popular characters from games, books and films, such as Thomas the Tank Engine, Pokémon and Harry Potter. When novice players have more obscure fascinations or interests, however, the play guide must probe deeper to make connections with expert players. Figure 7.1 gives an example of a Play Preference Inventory for Laura, who has a relatively obscure interest, as noted in the following case vignette.

CASE VIGNETTE
Laura – Play Preference Inventory

Laura is a 9-year-old girl with autism, who has a unique fascination with hair. She enjoys stroking other people's hair, particularly when it is long and flowing. She appears entranced as she gazes at others when they brush their hair. Laura also has an attraction to dolls with long hair. She will shake them and watch as the doll's hair flings from side to side. At the same time, Laura repeats the word "hair" over and over in a melodic fashion.

Laura's parents noted their daughter's interests in Part II of the Play Questionnaire. Laura's teacher, as play guide, recorded this information as well as her own observations in the Play Preference Inventory. To complete this assessment, she held a discussion with all of the children at the start of the next Integrated Play Groups session. Each of the players was asked to mention one thing they enjoyed playing. When it was Laura's turn, she was prompted to share her joy of hair and flowing things. The children were next asked to brainstorm some fun activities and themes that would incorporate this fascination. The children generated a long list of creative ideas connecting Laura's play interests with those of the expert players.

INTEGRATED PLAY GROUPS ASSESSMENT TOOL
Play Preference Inventory (Example)

Novice Player: Laura
Observer(s): Play Guide, Parents
Date: 10-14-01

Play Preference	Novice Player	Play Connections with Expert Players
Play Fascinations How does the child mostly prefer to pass the time? (e.g., may include obsessive interests, rituals, hobbies)	Anything to do with hair	• Hair dresser – styling one another's hair • Hair dresser – styling doll's hair • Hair dresser – styling wigs • Dressing up wearing different types of wigs • Making wigs out of different materials such as yarn, string and ribbon
Play Materials What types of toys or props are most attractive to the child? (e.g., wind-up toys, shiny objects, action figures, realistic props)	Dolls with long hair Wigs Hairbrushes Ribbons	• Grooming toy horses with long manes and tails • Making pretend horses out of mops • Grooming toy dogs – holding a dog show
Actions with Materials How does the child prefer to engage with toys or props? (e.g., spin, sift, fill-dump, hoard, line up, conventional actions)	Stroking hair Shaking dolls Flinging hair from side to side Gazing at hair when brushed	
Play Activities What play activities does the child prefer? (e.g., physical, sensory exploration, constructive, sociodramatic, art, music, games)	Sensory exploration – touching and watching anything that resembles hair as it flows	• Attaching ribbons to the end of a stick to wave in a parade • Making ribbons flow in the air while performing rhythmic gymnastics for the Olympics
Play Themes What play themes does the child prefer? (e.g., familiar routines, fantasy, invented)	Familiar routines – brushing and combing hair	• Decorating with streamers for a birthday party
Play with Others With whom does the child prefer to play? (e.g., no one in particular, one or more specific adults, one or more specific peers)	Adults and peers with long hair	

Figure 7.1. Example of completed Play Preference Inventory.

Integrated Play Groups Observation

The Integrated Play Groups Observation corresponds directly to the Integrated Play Groups Observation Framework illustrated in Tables 7.2 and 7.3. This assessment tool offers a format for recording naturalistic observations of a child specifically within the context of Integrated Play Groups. The form may also be used to record supplemental information about a child within other natural peer play contexts (e.g., to establish baseline and generalization).

To conduct this assessment, observations are systematically carried out, either live or via videotape, over the course of the planned program (see Table 7.5). It is important that the assessor spend time observing the child with minimal adult intervention (e.g., by stepping out and observing from the sidelines, à la Jane Goodall). This is a practice that should be heavily emphasized in the early (baseline) phases (e.g., one observation per week) and instituted regularly thereafter (e.g., one observation every other week). As a rule of thumb, 10 minutes out of a play session is a minimally sufficient amount of time in which to record observations using this assessment tool.

The protocol is divided into play schemes, within which the child's symbolic dimension of play, social dimension of play and communicative functions and means are recorded. A *play scheme* is defined as a distinct period with a beginning, middle and end that involves a change from one activity, theme and/or behavior to another. This may also include a distinct period of inactivity, such as passively gazing or wandering. Over the course of a session, a child may engage in many brief play schemes or a few extended play schemes. Each play scheme is identified by a heading. The duration may also be recorded.

While observing a child, the recorder checks off the boxes and briefly notes the dominant behavior exhibited by the child within each play scheme. A more detailed description of the social play context should also be included to give a more complete picture of the child's experience. Figure 7.2 gives an example of a 10-minute observation using the Integrated Play Groups Observation assessment tool for Teresa (refer to Wolfberg, 1999, for a complete case portrait of Teresa, who participated in Integrated Play Groups for two years).

INTEGRATED PLAY GROUPS ASSESSMENT TOOL

Integrated Play Groups Observation

Child's Name: Teresa
Date of Birth: 3-16-78
IPG Setting: Special day class
Play Guide: Teacher

Observer: Teacher
Date: 10-3-87
Start time: 2:40 P.M.
End time: 2:50 P.M.

PLAY SCHEME: Initiates dollhouse play with peer
Duration: 5 minutes

Play Scenario

Teresa initiates dollhouse play with Sook (expert player) while Ronny and Keila (expert players) organize materials to play grocery store. Standing beside Sook, Teresa touches and picks up the dollhouse. Sook momentarily watches her.

Symbolic Dimension		Social Dimension		Description
Not engaged	X	Isolate	X	Teresa attempts to initiate dollhouse play with Sook, who does not respond. Teresa fails to use conventional communicative means (e.g., facing peer, looking at peer, directing question to peer) to establish joint attention with peer. Unable to repair communicative breakdown, Teresa ends up isolated and not engaged in any particular play activity. She launches into repetitive verbalizations (echolalia) focused on the dollhouse.
Manipulation-Sensory		Orientation-Onlooker		
Functional		Parallel-Proximity		
Symbolic-Pretend		Common Focus		
		Common Goal		
Communicative Functions/Means				
Requests peer interaction – initiates playing dollhouse with peer		Physical proximity – positions self close to object with back to peer		
		Complex speech – "Play in dollhouse … play in dollhouse, Sook?"		
		Focused echolalia – "This is a dollhouse."		

Teresa: (Facing dollhouse) Play in dollhouse, play in dollhouse. (Briefly looks at Sook) Play in dollhouse, Sook?

Sook: (Does not respond – she walks away and joins the other children)

Teresa: (Facing dollhouse) This is a doll-house. Do not play in the dollhouse, do not play in the dollhouse. This is a dollhouse. (Points to picture-word label on shelf) Says dollhouse. This is a dollhouse, dollhouse.

Figure 7.2. Example of completed Integrated Play Groups Observation. *(Page 1 of 3)*

INTEGRATED PLAY GROUPS ASSESSMENT TOOL
Integrated Play Groups Observation

Observer: Teacher
Date: 10-3-87
Start time: 2:40 P.M.
End time: 2:50 P.M.

Child's Name: Teresa
Date of Birth: 3-16-78
IPG Setting: Special day class
Play Guide: Teacher

PLAY SCHEME: Enters Grocery Store Play
Duration: 2 minutes

Play Scenario

Teresa next attempts to join Sook, Ronny, and Keila, who now have established roles of cashier and shoppers. While watching Keila talk on the telephone from behind the cash register, Teresa repeats lines from a commercial for a grocery store chain.

Teresa: Easy check-out, please, hello, call the telephone (Writes numbers with finger in air while saying them) ... 67097 ... Easy check-out, please

Keila: You be the supermarket lady (Leaves to join Sook and Ronny in another part of the play area)

Teresa I'll be the supermarket lady (Takes Keila's place behind the cash register)

Symbolic Dimension	
Not engaged	
Manipulation–Sensory	
Functional	X
Symbolic–Pretend	

Social Dimension	
Isolate	
Orientation–Onlooker	
Parallel–Proximity	
Common Focus	X
Common Goal	

Communicative Functions/Means

Requests peer interaction – initiates playing super-market

Focused (delayed) echolalia – repeats commercial related to play (Easy check-out)

Complex speech – responds to peer

Description

Teresa initiates joining supermarket play by repeating commercial "Easy check-out." This time Keila understands and responds by inviting her to take her place as "supermarket lady." Teresa accepts by standing behind cash register and saying, "I'll be the supermarket tool!" She apparently does not understand concept of "supermarket lady" but gets the gist of what to do. This was a brief, albeit, positive social exchange

Figure 7.2. Example of completed Integrated Play Groups Observation. (Page 2 of 3)

INTEGRATED PLAY GROUPS ASSESSMENT TOOL

Integrated Play Groups Observation

Child's Name: Teresa
Date of Birth: 3-16-78
IPG Setting: Special day class
Play Guide: Teacher

Observer: Teacher
Date: 10-3-87
Start time: 2:40 P.M.
End time: 2:50 P.M.

PLAY SCHEME: Initiates dollhouse play with peer
Duration: 5 minutes

Symbolic Dimension		Social Dimension		Description
Not engaged		Isolate	X	Teresa imitates Keila, who earlier pretended to talk on the telephone ("echo-playlia"). She engages in functional as opposed to pretend play since she does not clearly understand her role. She launches into repetitive verbalizations (echolalia) that relate to the grocery store play based on a commercial. In the midst of her monologue she calls out to Sook, who does not respond. Teresa continues to remain isolated.
Manipulation-Sensory		Orientation-Onlooker		
Functional	X	Parallel-Proximity		
Symbolic-Pretend		Common Focus		
		Common Goal		

Communicative Functions/Means

Requests peer interaction – initiates playing super-market

Declaration/comment – directed to Sook

Focused (delayed) echolalia – repeats commercial related to play (Easy check-out)

Complex speech – "Sook, say hello"

Play Scenario

Imitating Keila, Teresa picks up and holds the telephone to her ear. She talks, looking at no one in particular.

Teresa: Stop, you hear me? I want to call 74897 … Easy check-out, easy check-out please, easy check-out … Ok … bye, bye. Hello, speak register please, hello. Sook, say hello.

Sook: (Looks at Teresa confused – ignores her)

Teresa: Easy check-out, please? Easy check-out. Ok, ok. Easy check-out, please, easy check-out, please. Stop, you hear me?

Figure 7.2. Example of completed Integrated Play Groups Observation. *(Page 3 of 3)*

Profile of Individual Play Development

The Profile of Individual Play Development draws on all of the previously mentioned assessment tools and other relevant sources as a way to evaluate the ongoing progress of novice players in Integrated Play Groups. As a rule of thumb, the Profile of Individual Play Development is completed on a monthly basis (see Table 7.5). This evaluation tool involves systematically compiling and analyzing information pertaining to each child's prevailing and emerging developmental characteristics in the following play domains:

- Social Play Style
- Symbolic Dimension of Play
- Social Dimension of Play
- Communication (rate and quality of social initiation and responsiveness)
- Play Preferences – Diversity of Play

Figure 7.3 gives an example of a Profile of Individual Play Development conducted over a six-month period.

CASE VIGNETTE
Felix – Profile of Individual Play Development

As introduced in Chapter 1, Felix is a 7-year-old boy with autism, who spends much of his time exploring letter and number shapes apart from his peers during free play. Felix participates in an Integrated Play Group with another novice player from his special day class and three expert players from a second-grade general education class. The play groups meet two times per week for 30 minutes each during the last half of a lunch-recess hour. Sessions are led by his special education teacher with assistance from his speech and language therapist and occupational therapist, who alternate sessions.

INTEGRATED PLAY GROUPS ASSESSMENT TOOL
Profile of Individual Play Development

Child's Name: Felix
Date of Birth: 9/25/95
IPG Setting: Special Day Class

Play Group Guide: Marta Ruiz, teacher
Assessor: Marta Ruiz/JJ Hill, SLP/Tom Lu, OT
Start/End Date: 9/30/00–2/31/01

Play Domains	Monthly Progress						Key Observations
	1	2	3	4	5	6	
Social Play Style							• Typically ignores, avoids, withdraws from peers
Active-Odd					E	X	• Tolerates proximity to peers
Passive							• Shows some interest in peers
Aloof	X	X	X	X	X		• Actively seeks out peers
Other (describe)							
Symbolic Dimension of Play							• Shows no interest in activities
Symbolic-Pretend							• Hoards letter shapes
Functional				E	X	X	• Fills and dumps – starting to construct with letter blocks
Manipulation-Sensory		E	X	X			• Constructs block towers
Not Engaged	X	X					• Pushes vehicles on roadways
Social Dimension of Play							• Tries to escape play area
Common Goal							• Wanders away from peers
Common Focus					E	X	• Plays alone – peeks over at peers
Parallel-Proximity				X	X		• Plays beside peers
Orientation-Onlooker			E				• Starts to give and take toys
Isolate	X	X	X				• Engages in brief exchanges with peers
Communication – Functions/Means							• Makes no initiations to peers
Rate of Social Initiation – Responsiveness							• Generally ignores peer initiations
High							• Makes subtle initiations by watching, touching toys, proximity to peers
Moderate					X	X	• Makes more overt initiations by approaching peers/taking toys
Low	X	X	X	X			• More responsive by accepting toys from peers
Quality of Social Initiation – Responsiveness							
Clear Intent					E	X	
Unclear Intent	X	X	X	X	X		
Play Preferences – Diversity of Play							• Initially uninterested in activities
Range of Play Interests							• Hoards letter shapes
Highly Diverse							• Fills and dumps shapes in containers – sorts letters by color
Moderately Diverse					X	X	• Interested in letter blocks
Limited – Restricted	X	X	X	X			• Constructs with different blocks
Number of Play Interests	0	1	2	5	8	10	• Enjoys vehicles, roads, bridges

COMMENTS:
Felix has made steady progress over the past six months while participating in Integrated Play Groups. He was slow to warm up, but is now comfortable with the routine. He expresses excitement and joy when his peers arrive for play sessions. Some of what he has learned appears to be generalizing to his independent play, as he now explores a larger variety of materials during independent free play. He is also spontaneously seeking out familiar peers on the playground during recess. By the same token, Felix's playmates have grown fond of him, and are making more of an effort to include him during lunch and recess.

Key: **X** Prevailing characteristic   **E** Emerging characteristic

Figure 7.3. Example of a completed Profile of Individual Play Development conducted over a six-month period.

Record of Monthly Progress in IPG

The Record of Monthly Progress in IPG is used to chart each novice player's ongoing progress on a specific set of goals while participating in Integrated Play Groups. IPG goals are individualized for each novice player for the purpose of maximizing the child's competence and spontaneous development in play with peers. Goals are carefully crafted based on a thorough and ongoing analysis of the assessments.

After gathering preliminary assessments within an initial baseline period (see Table 7.5), goals are targeted for novice players that correspond to one or more of the following play domains as needed.

- Symbolic Dimension

- Social Dimension

- Communication – Language

- Play Preferences – Diversity of Play

- Generalization (e.g., Does child exhibit newly acquired skills across settings, peers, activities?)

- Other

Sample goals for Integrated Play Groups are provided in Table 7.6. Please note that this is in no way an exhaustive list. Moreover, these examples are meant to be used merely as a reference, not as a "recipe" for assigning goals to children in any prescribed fashion.

Based on a monthly analysis of accumulated assessments, progress on each goal is recorded in the Record of Monthly Progress in IPG form. A mark indicating progress (i.e., o No change, + Noticeable improvement, – Noticeable regression, ✓ Projected goal attained) is placed within the box corresponding to a supporting document that provides evidence of the child's progress (i.e., Play Questionnaire, Play Preference Inventory, Play Observation, Profile of Individual Play Development, Other Documentation).

When evaluating goals, it is important to keep in mind that children develop at different rates and to varying degrees, and that many factors are influencing this. It is therefore essential to follow trends when charting a child's progress to determine whether or not a goal continues to be realistic and meaningful. As a rule of thumb, if there is no evidence of progress within a three-month period, it is likely that the goal needs to be adjusted or changed so that the child may realistically achieve the goal within a reasonable timeframe (e.g., six months). By the same token, if a child quickly achieves a targeted goal shortly after it is established, it is important to adjust or change that goal so that the child continues to be challenged.

Figure 7.4 gives an example of a Record of Monthly Progress in Integrated Play Groups conducted over a six-month period.

Table 7.6
Sample Goals for Integrated Play Groups

Play Domain	Sample Goals for Integrated Play Groups
Symbolic Dimension	General Aim: *To maximize child's development in representational play.* Child will demonstrate manipulation play by: • exploring physical features of objects/toys • enacting simple actions with single objects/toys • enacting simple actions with two or more objects/toys Child will demonstrate functional play by: • enacting conventional use of objects/toys • associating two or more related objects/toys • enacting simple scripts/familiar routines with realistic props directed to self, dolls or peers Child will demonstrate symbolic-pretend play by: • substituting one object to represent another • attributing absent or false properties to objects • inventing imaginary objects as if they were present • role playing scripts (real or invented) with dolls, self, peers and/or imaginary characters
Social Dimension	General Aim: *To maximize child's development in social play with peers.* Child will demonstrate an interest and awareness of peers (orientation-onlooker) by: • physically orienting self toward peers and their play activities • directly watching peers and their play activities • imitating peer actions while watching from a distance Child will demonstrate parallel play with peers by: • engaging in play activities beside peer in same play space • engaging in play activities with similar play materials as peer • imitating peer actions while playing beside peer Child will demonstrate a common focus in play with peers by: • establishing joint attention with peer • engaging in joint action with peer • engaging in mutual imitation with peer • engaging in reciprocal social exchanges with peer Child will demonstrate common goals in play with peers by: • engaging in cooperative play activities with peer • jointly planning and carrying out a common agenda with peer • negotiating and compromising with peer around divergent interests
Communi-cation – Language	General Aim: *To maximize child's social-communicative competence in play with peers.* Using one or more verbal and/or nonverbal means (refer to Table 7.3), child will direct social initiations to peers by: • requesting objects/toys from peer • requesting peer action/assistance • requesting peer interaction • requesting affection from peers • making declarations or comment to peer • entering peer group and joining established play event

Communication – Language *(continued)*	Using one or more verbal and/or nonverbal means (refer to Table 7.3), child will <u>respond</u> to peer social bids by: • attending to peer • receiving objects/toys from peer • accepting peer assistance • accepting affection from peer • imitating peer • following peer's lead Using one or more verbal and/or nonverbal means (refer to Table 7.3), child will demonstrate <u>social reciprocity</u> with peers by: • sustaining joint attention with peer • establishing joint action with peer • giving and receiving peer assistance • exchanging objects/toys with peers • mutually imitating peer • taking turns/alternating actions with peer • carrying on a conversation with peer • acting out a sociodramatic play script with peer Child will <u>expand language</u> expression in play with peers by: • asking peer questions • making declarations/comments to peer • carrying on a conversation with peer • narrating pretend play scripts • negotiating rules and roles in play with peer
Play Preferences-Diversity	General Aim: *To expand and diversify child's repertoire of spontaneous play preferences/interests.* Child will demonstrate an increased number of self-selected play interests. Child will demonstrate a wider range/variety of self-selected play interests. (refer to Table 7.1 for examples of play preferences)
Generalization	General Aim: *To maximize child's social, communicative and play development across natural contexts.* Child will demonstrate social, communicative and play abilities acquired in Integrated Play Groups across diverse play settings and peer/sibling partners (see examples below): <u>Home/Community</u> • free play with peers at home • free play with siblings at home • independent play at home • free play in a community playground • other home and community-based social activities (e.g., birthday parties, soccer club) <u>School</u> • free play with peers on the playground at school • free play with peers in the classroom at school • independent play at school • other socially integrated activities in school (e.g., lunch, assemblies, field trips)

INTEGRATED PLAY GROUPS ASSESSMENT TOOL
Record of Monthly Progress in IPG

Child's Name: Maya
Date of Birth: 3/27/98
IPG Setting: Preschool

Play Guide: Liza Jaffe – Shadow Aide
Assessor: Ming Wu – Program Coordinator
Start/End Date: January–June 2001

Play Domain	Integrated Play Group Goal	1	2	3	4	5	6	Supporting Documents
Symbolic Dimension	Maya will demonstrate functional play by enacting simple scripts/familiar routines with realistic props directed to self, dolls or peers.	o					+	Play Questionnaire
								Play Preference Inventory
		o	o	+	+	+	+	IPG Observation Form
		o	o	+	+	+	+	Profile of Individual Play Development
								Other Documentation
Social Dimension	Maya will demonstrate a common focus in play with peers by establishing joint attention in preferred activities.	o					✓	Play Questionnaire
								Play Preference Inventory
		o	o	+	+	+	✓	IPG Observation Form
		o	o	+	+	+	✓	Profile of Individual Play Development
								Other Documentation
Communication-Language	Maya will direct social initiations to peers by facing peer and saying: "Let's play" – "Play with me."	o					✓	Play Questionnaire
								Play Preference Inventory
		o	o	+	+	+	✓	IPG Observation Form
		o	o	+	+	+	✓	Profile of Individual Play Development
								Other Documentation
Play Preferences-Diversity	Maya will demonstrate a wider range/variety of self-selected play interests that extend beyond her current interest in books/videos.	o					+	Play Questionnaire
		o	o	–	o	+	+	Play Preference Inventory
								IPG Observation Form
		o	o	–	o	+	+	Profile of Individual Play Development
								Other Documentation
Generalization	Maya will demonstrate social, communicative and play abilities acquired in Integrated Play Groups during free play at home with playdates and her sister.	o					+	Play Questionnaire
								Play Preference Inventory
								IPG Observation Form
		o	o	o	o	+	+	Profile of Individual Play Development
								Other Documentation
Other	Maya will demonstrate social, communicative and play abilities acquired in Integrated Play Groups during free play at school with her classmates.	.					+	Play Questionnaire
								Play Preference Inventory
		o	o	o	o	+	+	IPG Observation Form
		o	o	o	o	+	+	Profile of Individual Play Development
								Other Documentation

Key: o No change + Noticeable improvement – Noticeable regression ✓ Projected goal attained

Figure 7.4. Example of completed Record of Monthly Progress in Integrated Play Groups.

CASE VIGNETTE
Maya - Record of Monthly Progress in Integrated Play Groups

As introduced in Chapter 1, Maya is a 4-year-old girl with pervasive developmental disorder, who tends to wander but will also play beside peers while engaged with figures featured in popular books and videos. Maya participates in an Integrated Play Group for 20 minutes each morning in her preschool with two expert players from her class. The play groups are facilitated by her shadow aide (who also works as a therapist in the home) in collaboration with a specialist, who coordinates Maya's preschool and home-based program.

Integrated Play Groups Summative Report

The Integrated Play Groups Summative Report offers a format for writing an evaluation summary of a child's participation in Integrated Play Groups at the end of a term. The report is developed based on documentation gathered throughout the assessment process. A synopsis of the following is included in the report:

- Child's peer socialization and play needs prior to participation in Integrated Play Groups
- Methods used to address child's peer socialization and play needs
- Child's progress in play domains and on stated goals
- Recommendations to address child's peer socialization and play needs in the future

Chapter Summary

Quality assessments involving astute observation are key to understanding, interpreting and guiding children in Integrated Play Groups. The assessment tools presented here are designed to tap into the unique challenges and capacities children on the autism spectrum experience in play with peers, allowing us to qualify and quantify observations from multiple sources and perspectives in a purposeful and holistic fashion. The assessment process is not only essential for targeting realistic and meaningful goals and evaluating children's ongoing progress, but also for guiding decisions on how best to intervene on behalf of the novice players. We now turn our attention to crafting a system of support in Integrated Play Groups by applying the practices of guided participation.

Phase III Hands-On Activities

Field Exercises

Conduct the following field exercises that correspond to Phase III – Observing Children at Play: IPG Assessment.

- Field Exercise 10 – Naturalistic Observation of Typical Children at Play with Peers

- Field Exercise 11 – Practice Assessment

Phase III Tools and Field Exercises

Assessment Tools

- Play Questionnaire
- Play Preference Inventory
- Integrated Play Groups Observation
- Profile of Individual Play Development
- Record of Monthly Progress in IPG
- Integrated Play Groups Summative Report

Play Questionnaire

Child's Name:	Name of Person Completing Questionnaire:
Gender:	Relationship to Child:
Date of Birth:	IPG Setting:
Diagnosis:	Date:

PART I: BACKGROUND – PLAY EXPERIENCE

How often does child have regular opportunities for play? (choose one)			
Less than one hour		*More than one hour*	
Every day		Every day	
3 to 5 days a week		3 to 5 days a week	
1 to 2 days a week		1 to 2 days a week	
Not a part of child's schedule			
Where does child regularly play? (check all that apply)			
Home			
School			
Community			
Therapy			
Other (describe)			
In which situations does child regularly play? (check all that apply)			
Free play without adult support		*Adult-directed play*	
Independently		Independently	
With one or more siblings		With one or more adults	
With one peer		With one or more siblings	
Small group of 2 to 5 peers		With one peer	
Large group of 5 or more peers		Small group of 2 to 5 peers	
Outdoors		Large group of 5 or more peers	
Indoors		Outdoors	
		Indoors	
Please feel free to comment:			

PART II: PLAY PREFERENCES – DIVERSITY OF PLAY

Whom does child spontaneously seek out for play? (check all that apply)			
Younger sibling		Parent	
Older sibling		Other adult family member	
Twin		Teacher	
Same-aged peers		Therapist	
Older peers		Other adult	
Younger peers		No one	
Please feel free to comment:			

Wolfberg, P. J. (2003). *Peer play and the autism spectrum: The art of guiding children's socialization and imagination.* Shawnee Mission, KS: Autism Asperger Publishing Company.

PART II: PLAY PREFERENCES – DIVERSITY OF PLAY (continued)

What kinds of activities does child spontaneously seek out for play? (check all that apply)	
Face-to-face interactions (e.g., peek-a-boo, tickles, rough-housing)	
Physical activity (e.g., swinging, running, jumping, riding a bike)	
Sensory (e.g., water, sand, play dough)	
Construction (e.g., building blocks, Legos, train and track)	
Realistic props (e.g., dolls, animal figures, dress-up clothes)	
Pretend (e.g., invents and role-plays stories, has imaginary companion)	
Art (e.g., drawing, painting)	
Music (e.g., singing, playing instruments)	
Puzzles and games	

Please list child's preferred play activities, materials, themes, special interests, unique fascinations:

What best describes child's repertoire of play interests? (choose one)	
Highly diverse – enjoys many different types of play activities	
Moderately diverse – enjoys more than a few different types of activities	
Limited restricted – enjoys one or only a few different types of activities	

Does child exhibit any of the following characteristics in play? (check all that apply)	
Rituals	
Repetitive routines	
Stereotyped behaviors	
Unusual fascinations, obsessions	
Repetitive themes	
Aggression toward others	
Destructive – mistreats toys	
Other	

Please describe and give examples:

Wolfberg, P. J. (2003). *Peer play and the autism spectrum: The art of guiding children's socialization and imagination.* Shawnee Mission, KS: Autism Asperger Publishing Company.

PART III: PEER RELATIONS – SOCIAL PLAY STYLE

Does child have a mutual friendship with another child? (check all that apply)	
No mutual friends	
One mutual friend	
More than one mutual friend	
Friend is same age	
Friend is younger	
Friend is older	
Friend is of the same gender	
Friend is of a different gender	
Friend is identified as typically developing	
Friend is identified as having special needs	

Please describe the nature of this friendship – how they know each other, when they first met, what they do together, what makes each desire to be friends with the other.

Which best describes child's social style with peers? (choose one category)		
Aloof	Generally withdrawn in company of peers	
	Actively avoids contact with peers	
	Unresponsive to peer initiations	
	Approaches peers to fulfill wants and needs in same way as adults	
Passive	Appears indifferent toward peers	
	Generally compliant toward peers	
	Easily led into play and follows along with peers	
	Shows little or no self-initiation in play with peers	
Active-Odd	Shows active interest in playing with peers	
	Approaches peers in socially awkward or idiosyncratic ways	
	Carries on a one-sided conversation focused on own interests	
	Attempts to initiate or join peers, but has poor sense of timing	
Other	Social play style does not fit any of the above	
	Social play style reflects a combination of the above	
	Social play style is comparable to that of typical children	

What is child's primary mode of communication with peers? (check all that apply)	
Complex speech/sign/written language	
Simple speech/sign/written language – one or two words, short phrases	
Echolalia – repeats words and phrases of others	
Picture communication – photographs, line drawings	
Vocalization – makes sounds	
Gestures (e.g., points, nods head, waves)	
Physical touch (e.g., leads peer by hand)	
Augmentative (e.g., computer voice output device)	
Other	

Please feel free to comment:

Wolfberg, P. J. (2003). *Peer play and the autism spectrum: The art of guiding children's socialization and imagination.* Shawnee Mission, KS: Autism Asperger Publishing Company.

PART IV – DEVELOPMENTAL PLAY PATTERNS

Which best describes child's social play patterns?
(choose one category)

Isolate	Wanders without looking at peers	
	Briefly occupies self with anything of interest apart from adults	
	Plays alone apart from peers	
Orientation-Onlooker	Watches peers play	
	Orients body in direction of peers or their play activities	
	Imitates peer actions while watching them from distance	
Parallel-Proximity	Plays independently beside peers in same play space	
	Plays with similar play materials as peers	
	Imitates peers' actions while playing beside them	
Common Focus	Engages in reciprocal play with one or more peers	
	Takes turns in activities/shares materials with peers	
	Imitates/shares emotions (smiles, laughs) with peers	
Common Goal	Engages in cooperative play with one or more peers	
	Explicitly plans and carries out a common agenda with peers	
	Negotiates and compromises around divergent interests	

Which best describes child's representational play patterns?
(choose one category)

Manipulation-Sensory	Explores single objects (e.g., mouths, bangs, shakes)	
	Explores combined objects (e.g., lines up, fills and dumps)	
	Performs difficult feats with objects (e.g., balances, spins, lasso)	
Functional	Uses objects as intended (e.g., rolls car on floor, stacks blocks)	
	Associates related objects (e.g., puts teacup on saucer)	
	Simple scripts with realistic props (e.g., holds telephone to ear)	
Symbolic-Pretend	Uses one object to represent another (e.g., banana as telephone)	
	Attributes absent or false properties (e.g., wipes table as if wet)	
	Invents imaginary objects (e.g., motions with hand as if stirring pot)	
	Role plays characters/scripts with dolls and peers (e.g., tea party)	
Other	Does not display dominance in any one play level	
	Shows dominance in two or more play levels	

Please feel free to comment:

Do you have anything else to share or questions you'd like to ask about this child's play and peer relations?

THANK YOU FOR TAKING THE TIME TO FILL OUT THIS QUESTIONNAIRE!

Wolfberg, P. J. (2003). *Peer play and the autism spectrum: The art of guiding children's socialization and imagination.* Shawnee Mission, KS: Autism Asperger Publishing Company.

INTEGRATED PLAY GROUPS ASSESSMENT TOOL
Play Preference Inventory

Novice Player:
Evaluator:
Date:

Play Preference	Novice Player	List Play Connections with Expert Players
Play Fascinations How does the child mostly prefer to pass the time? (e.g., may include obsessive interests, rituals, hobbies)		
Play Materials What types of toys or props are most attractive to the child? (e.g., wind-up toys, shiny objects, action figures, realistic props)		
Actions with Materials How does the child prefer to engage with toys or props? (e.g., spin, sift, fill-dump, hoard, line up, conventional actions)		
Play Activities What play activities does the child prefer? (e.g., physical, sensory exploration, constructive, sociodramatic, art, music, games)		
Play Themes What play themes does the child prefer? (e.g., familiar routines, fantasy, invented)		
Play with Others With whom does the child prefer to play? (e.g., no one in particular, one or more specific adults, one or more specific peers)		

Wolfberg. P. J. (2003). *Peer play and the autism spectrum: The art of guiding children's socialization and imagination.* Shawnee Mission, KS: Autism Asperger Publishing Company.

INTEGRATED PLAY GROUPS ASSESSMENT TOOL
Integrated Play Groups Observation

Child's Name: Observer:

Date of Birth: Date:

IPG Setting: Start Time:

Play Guide: End Time:

PLAY SCHEME: **DURATION:**

Symbolic Dimension		Social Dimension		Description
Not Engaged		Isolate		
Manipulation-Sensory		Orientation-Onlooker		
Functional		Parallel-Proximity		
Symbolic-Pretend		Common Focus		
		Common Goal		
Communicative Functions/Means				

PLAY SCHEME: **DURATION:**

Symbolic Dimension		Social Dimension		Description
Not Engaged		Isolate		
Manipulation-Sensory		Orientation-Onlooker		
Functional		Parallel-Proximity		
Symbolic-Pretend		Common Focus		
		Common Goal		
Communicative Functions/Means				

PLAY SCHEME: **DURATION:**

Symbolic Dimension		Social Dimension		Description
Not Engaged		Isolate		
Manipulation-Sensory		Orientation-Onlooker		
Functional		Parallel-Proximity		
Symbolic-Pretend		Common Focus		
		Common Goal		
Communicative Functions/Means				

Wolfberg, P. J. (2003). *Peer play and the autism spectrum: The art of guiding children's socialization and imagination.*
Shawnee Mission, KS: Autism Asperger Publishing Company.

INTEGRATED PLAY GROUPS ASSESSMENT TOOL
Profile of Individual Play Development

Child's Name: Play Guide:

Date of Birth: Assessor:

IPG Setting: Start/End Date:

Play Domains	Monthly Progress						Key Observations
	1	2	3	4	5	6	
SOCIAL PLAY STYLE							
Active-Odd							
Passive							
Aloof							
Other (describe)							
SYMBOLIC DIMENSION OF PLAY							
Symbolic-Pretend							
Functional							
Manipulation-Sensory							
Not Engaged							
SOCIAL DIMENSION OF PLAY							
Common Goal							
Common Focus							
Parallel-Proximity							
Orientation-Onlooker							
Isolate							
COMMUNICATION – FUNCTIONS/MEANS							
Rate of Social Initiation – Responsiveness							
High							
Moderate							
Low							
Quality of Social Initiation – Responsiveness							
Clear intent							
Unclear intent							
PLAY PREFERENCES – DIVERSITY OF PLAY							
Range of Play Interests							
Highly Diverse							
Moderately Diverse							
Limited – Restricted							
Number of Play Interests							

COMMENTS:

Key: **X** Prevailing characteristic   **E** Emerging characteristic

Wolfberg, P. J. (2003). *Peer play and the autism spectrum: The art of guiding children's socialization and imagination.* Shawnee Mission, KS: Autism Asperger Publishing Company.

INTEGRATED PLAY GROUPS ASSESSMENT TOOL
Record of Monthly Progress in IPG

Child's Name: Play Guide:
Date of Birth: Assessor:
IPG Setting: Start/End Date:

Play Domain	IPG Goal	Monthly Progress						Supporting Documents
Symbolic Dimension								Play Questionnaire / Play Preference Inventory / IPG Observation Form / Profile of Individual Play Development / Other Documentation
Social Dimension								Play Questionnaire / Play Preference Inventory / IPG Observation Form / Profile of Individual Play Development / Other Documentation
Communication-Language								Play Questionnaire / Play Preference Inventory / IPG Observation Form / Profile of Individual Play Development / Other Documentation
Play Preferences-Diversity								Play Questionnaire / Play Preference Inventory / IPG Observation Form / Profile of Individual Play Development / Other Documentation
Generalization								Play Questionnaire / Play Preference Inventory / IPG Observation Form / Profile of Individual Play Development / Other Documentation
Other								Play Questionnaire / Play Preference Inventory / IPG Observation Form / Profile of Individual Play Development / Other Documentation

Key: o No change   + Noticeable improvement   − Noticeable regression   ✓ Projected goal attained

Wolfberg, P. J. (2003). *Peer play and the autism spectrum: The art of guiding children's socialization and imagination.* Shawnee Mission, KS: Autism Asperger Publishing Company.

Integrated Play Groups Summative Report

Child's Name: Play Guide:

Date of Birth: Assessor:

IPG Setting: Start/End Date:

Child's peer socialization and play needs prior to participation in Integrated Play Groups.

Methods used to address child's peer socialization and play needs.

Wolfberg, P. J. (2003). *Peer play and the autism spectrum: The art of guiding children's socialization and imagination.* Shawnee Mission, KS: Autism Asperger Publishing Company.

Child's progress in play domains and on stated goals.

Recommendations to address child's peer socialization and play needs in the future.

Wolfberg, P. J. (2003). *Peer play and the autism spectrum: The art of guiding children's socialization and imagination.* Shawnee Mission, KS: Autism Asperger Publishing Company.

Phase III Tools and Field Exercises

Field Exercises 10-11

- 10 – Naturalistic Observation of Typical Children at Play with Peers
- 11 – Practice Play Assessment

OBSERVING CHILDREN AT PLAY
Field Exercise 10: Naturalistic Observation of
Typical Children at Play with Peers

Spend some time observing typically developing children at play with peers in natural settings such as in a home, community park or school yard. Write field notes describing the children's social interaction and play (please refer to Chapter 7).

_____

_____

_____

_____

_____

_____

_____

_____

_____

_____

_____

_____

_____

_____

_____

_____

_____

_____

_____

Wolfberg, P. J. (2003). _Peer play and the autism spectrum: The art of guiding children's socialization and imagination._ Shawnee Mission, KS: Autism Asperger Publishing Company.

Field Exercise 11: Practice Play Assessment

Based on what you currently know about the novice player, practice filling out a Profile of Individual Play Development – record prevailing and emerging characteristics across play domains noting preliminary observations (please refer to Chapter 7).

Novice Player:
Evaluator:

Play Domains		Preliminary Observations
SOCIAL PLAY STYLE		
Active-Odd		
Passive		
Aloof		
Other (describe)		
SYMBOLIC DIMENSION OF PLAY		
Symbolic-Pretend		
Functional		
Manipulation-Sensory		
Not Engaged		
SOCIAL DIMENSION OF PLAY		
Common Goal		
Common Focus		
Parallel-Proximity		
Orientation-Onlooker		
Isolate		
COMMUNICATION – FUNCTIONS/MEANS		
Rate of Social Initiation – Responsiveness		
High		
Moderate		
Low		
Quality of Social Initiation – Responsiveness		
Clear Intent		
Unclear Intent		
PLAY PREFERENCES – DIVERSITY OF PLAY		
Range of Play Interests		
Highly Diverse		
Moderately Diverse		
Limited – Restricted		
Number of Play Interests		

Key: **X** Prevailing characteristic   **E** Emerging characteristic

Wolfberg, P. J. (2003). *Peer play and the autism spectrum: The art of guiding children's socialization and imagination.* Shawnee Mission, KS: Autism Asperger Publishing Company.

PHASE IV
Guided Participation in Play
Integrated Play Groups Intervention

The training of children is a profession,
where we must know how to waste time
in order to save it.

- Jean Jacques Rousseau

CHAPTER 8

Monitoring Play Initiations

Chapter Highlights

This chapter introduces the Integrated Play Groups intervention (guided participation) focusing on the practice of monitoring play initiations. The following topics will be highlighted:

► Stepping into the Role of Play Guide

► Recognizing Play Initiations

► Interpreting Play Initiations

► Responding to Play Initiations

Important Things I Learned While Guiding Children in Integrated Play Groups

... I've had time to reflect over the past year and think about how rewarding the play groups have been for me and my students ...

Relax and Be a Good Observer

One of the things I learned from my first year doing Integrated Play Groups is that I needed to relax (especially at first) and be a good observer. By observing closely, and not intervening, I was able to pick up on the level that each of my students was at. It was important for me to take good baseline data.

Let the Children Lead the Way

Sometimes I had great ideas for play schemes or themes to use, but the children decided to play something else. This is OKAY! Be ready to watch the "planned stuff" flop, and watch the kids come up with their own ideas!

Repeat and Expand on Favorite Activities

It is okay (even encouraged) to repeat favorite activities. I had one student who learned to act out a "police chase" with his play group. They all loved playing police chase and switching roles (which was a new step for my student). I allowed them to do it for the last three months of school. At first it was just the actual police chase (police chased and caught the robber), but then we expanded on that and had a whole story about it. The police would sit at a table and eat doughnuts (ha-ha), and the robber would steal money from the video store clerk (we at first played video store for a while). Then the video store clerk called 911 and the police chased, caught, and put the robber in jail. The place of the robbery could change to any number of places, but we continued to keep the police chase as part of the play because the kids just LOVED acting it out each time.

Use Visuals

This is something I really worked on at the end of the school year. I added tags to hang like a necklace that had a picture and word on it for different roles (cashier, doctor, janitor, etc. ...) so the kids could switch roles visually and physically. I also took digital pictures of all of the toys or toy sets in my playroom and attached them to a foam board with Velcro. This way students could pick what they wanted to do if they were too overwhelmed by looking around the room to decide.

Also, I had one student [Randy] who wouldn't share any of the dolls in the dollhouse. He hoarded them all every time we entered the play room. I had an idea to help facilitate sharing, but I didn't have much faith that it would work. I took a digital picture of each and every doll in the dollhouse. I used Velcro to attach them to a piece of laminated paper and brought it to the next play group. I showed it to my student and I said, "I'm going to play with the baby. Who are you going to play with?" Randy chose one, and then I said, "Now who do you think Bonny is going to choose?" He watched as Bonny picked a picture of a doll and reached and held the corresponding doll from the dollhouse. It was the moment of truth, and it worked! From then on, Randy let the other children play with dolls with him (though he did have his favorite doll that we always let him choose).

Build in Routines and Rituals

I always end play groups with a group handshake, and then I let all of the kids play on the sensory equipment (swings, trampoline, etc. ...) for 5-7 minutes. Then, they all pick a Starburst, and are on their way. They seem to like this routine.

Meet Regularly with the Players

One thing that I want to add for the 2001-2002 school year is to have ongoing meetings with the expert players to discuss problems/successes/ideas to help support the novice player. One meeting at the beginning of the year is just not enough.

Have Fun!

Sometimes if you get in there and play, it can help to get things going. If you act goofy, the kids will respond. Then, you can slowly downplay your part, and fade out. This is a good way to add a spark to a low-energy day.

It has been a joy to implement Integrated Play Groups into my program at school. The benefits to all involved are numerous. Be flexible, and mostly ... enjoy.

Tara Tuchel – Apprentice Play Guide

We earlier introduced Tara Tuchel as an exceptional practitioner, who successfully carried out Integrated Play Groups with students in her school. The preceding excerpt speaks to Tara's insightful reflection on her own practice. It highlights many of the key elements of guided participation and sheds light on the experience of facilitating Integrated Play Groups.

In Chapter 2 we introduced the concept of guided participation as applied to the Integrated Play Groups intervention. From a theoretical perspective, guided participation refers to the process through which children develop while actively participating in a culturally valued activity with the guidance, support and challenge of social partners who vary in skill and status (Rogoff, 1990; Vygotsky, 1966, 1978). In Integrated Play Groups, children with autism (novice players) participate in shared play experiences with socially competent peers/siblings (expert players) and the guidance of a skilled adult (play guide).

Guided participation translates into a carefully tailored system of support that is sufficiently intensive and responsive to each child's underlying difference and unique developmental potential. In practical terms, play guides facilitate Integrated Play Groups by applying a key set of practices:

- monitoring play initiations
- scaffolding play
- social-communication guidance
- play guidance

Figure 8.1 provides an overview of the practices of guided participation in Integrated Play Groups as discussed in the following chapters.

Figure 8.1. Overview of intervention practices.

Stepping into the Role of Play Guide

As mentioned in Chapter 3, our research and clinical experience has given us insight into the ways in which play guides experience their roles at various stages of facilitating Integrated Play Groups (see also qualities of effective and meaningful practice in Chapter 2). When stepping into the role of play guide, it may be helpful to keep in mind the following considerations.

Expect to Wear Many Hats

Play guides invariably take on a variety of roles while facilitating Integrated Play Groups, including model, coach, spectator, interpreter, peacemaker, theater director, entertainer and housekeeper. In other words, expect to wear many hats to effectively support the children.

Go with the Flow

Being neither too intrusive nor laissez-faire, play guides need to go with the flow when facilitating play groups. They must be extremely flexible and willing to follow the children's lead. This means being able to let go of control as opposed to imposing a rigid agenda of prescribed activities.

Set the Tone for the Group

Play guides can influence how the players treat one another without effectively taking over. It is important to set the tone for the group by modeling behavior that is respectful and inclusive of all the children. For instance, when giving an expert player a tip about a novice player, include the novice player in the discussion. Address the novice player even if she seems unable to comprehend. This will set a tone in which all of the children are seen as competent and contributing members of the group.

Distribute Attention Among the Players

To ensure that every child is maximally included in the group, play guides need to distribute their attention and support among the different children. At times it may be appropriate to guide a pair of players. At other times it may be appropriate to guide the entire group. Novice players do not always need to be at center stage to receive their due share of assistance. In certain instances it may be beneficial for the novice player to be on the periphery as the play guide interacts with the expert players.

Grow into the Role

Some play guides may initially feel awkward and frustrated in their roles. The best advice we can give is not to be too hard on yourself. Realize that this is a process that does get easier. Recognize that play guides grow into their roles while gaining proficiency through extended and reflective practice.

Find a Personal Style

Each play guide must find his own personal style that is both effective and comfortable. Allow yourself the freedom to experiment through trial and error – to figure out not only what works best for the children, but also feels right for you.

Take Hold of the Moment

It is important to recognize that we all have good days and bad days. During those instances in which you feel you have reached an impasse, it can be immensely helpful to step back, breathe and take hold of the moment. You may be pleasantly surprised to discover that the situation resolves itself – that you must be doing something right after all! Keep in mind that all those little moments when things are going well add up over time.

Enjoy the Experience

As Tara articulated, perhaps one of the most vital things to keep in mind while facilitating play groups is to enjoy the experience and simply have fun. This is a lesson that we have learned from many practitioners and family members, who have shared immensely rich and amusing accounts of children's play and friendships.

Reflect on Your Practice

To evaluate the fidelity of the intervention approach it is important that play guides engage in an ongoing process of reflective practice. A part of the reflective process is introspective – contemplating one's own experience and effectiveness as a play guide. Play guides may also engage in reflective practice with others by sharing experiences and evaluating one another in a constructive light. We have found videotapes to be especially useful for viewing oneself and others in action. To support play guides through this process, we have developed two intervention tools: (a) Guided Participation Evaluation, and (b) Self-Reflection Log (see Phase IV Tools and Field Exercises).

MONITORING PLAY INITIATIONS
Gary's Story

A student of mine, Gary, is in 2nd grade. He has very little language and demonstrates echolalia. During his first play [group] session, he cried for 10 minutes, until we ended the session short. Since then, he has made steady progress. He was able to imitate his peers with play animals, but due to the "mother-hen" nature of the two expert players, it turned into a drill session. They would say "make the horse jump over the fence," he would, and they would say "good job!" This would continue for the whole session if I let it!!!! I decided that I needed to find Gary's true level of play that he would genuinely ENJOY. We found it. He needed sensory input, and he was at a level of play were he enjoyed games such as "ring-around-the-rosy" rather than toy play. So, I got all three kids and myself up on the trampoline (which Gary loves), and we played "ring-around-the-rosy" together. We all held hands, and jumped in a circle, and when it came time to "all fall down," we all fell down on the trampoline, which made us bounce all over. You would not believe the laugh that came from Gary's gut when we all fell down. At first he just stood there and laughed (which was great in itself), but then we taught him to fall down too, and he could not get up because he was laughing so hard. This was a treat for the expert players, who rarely hear him utter a word, let alone laugh uncontrollably. We were all so proud. The next time we entered the play room, Gary said clearly "RING AROUND ROSY"!!! How is that for motivating!!! Of course we played and played and played ring-around-the-rosy for a long time.

One year later ...

I wanted to tell you that Gary ... has shown much, much more interest in toys ... he entered the play room and chose toys over trampoline several times this year. This is unprecedented for him! I talked to his mom and she said that he has started "playing" with toys at home. I think it is very much due to his exposure to toys and watching his peers with toys last school year. I can't wait to get going with him!

Tara Tuchel – Apprentice Play Guide

Recognizing Play Initiations

Monitoring play initiations is an especially critical part of the intervention process as it involves recognizing, interpreting and responding to the novice player's spontaneous attempts to socialize and play. Play initiations are the foundation on which to build the child's social and symbolic play repertoire. They are the springboards for novice and expert players to find common ground in mutually engaging activities.

The process of monitoring play initiations begins with tuning into the infinite ways in which novice players may express their interests in play. The assessment process naturally corresponds to this practice. A child's social play style, developmental play patterns, communicative functions and means and play preferences are all determined, at least in part, by recognizing play initiations.

Play initiations may include virtually any act or display that indicates a child's interest or desire to play in the company of peers. They may be directed to objects (e.g., toys and props), others (e.g., peers and adults) or oneself. Play initiations may be expressed in numerous ways. Novice players may communicate their intentions through verbal and nonverbal social-communicative means as described in Chapter 7 (see Table 7.3). For example, they may use facial expressions, eye gaze, physical actions, gestures, vocalizations and speech to show that they are interested in playing with an object and/or peer. Play initiations may be conventional or unconventional in nature and conveyed through overt, subtle or obscure means. Even acts that reflect unusual fascinations, obsessions, rituals or idiosyncratic language are recognized as play initiations.

Interpreting Play Initiations

A child's play initiations are always interpreted as purposeful and adaptive – as meaningful attempts to participate in the play culture. Play initiations may be indicative of a child's attempt to invite a peer for play, join peers for play or participate in play activities, themes, roles or events. While monitoring play initiations, the play guide makes a conscious effort to interpret every attempt as offering the potential for connecting novice and expert players in play. This means seeking out and capitalizing on play initiations to create opportunities for more interactive and creative forms of play.

The play guide is responsible for translating for the expert players what the novice player means by his actions and/or words when initiating play. This information must be revealed or explained in a constructive and tactful manner. Expert players must come to understand that the novice players are indeed trying to interact and play in spite of what might appear to be ambiguous outward behavior. At the same time, the play guide must help the novice player find ways in which to initiate play in more conventional ways (see Chapter 10 – Social-Communication Cues). Interpreting play initiations in this way sets a tone in the group that novice players are competent and contributing members with valid interests worthy of pursuit.

Play Initiations

Recognize-Interpret-Respond

Uncover child's spontaneous attempts to socialize and play:

- Directed to objects, self and others
- Conveyed through verbal and nonverbal means
- Expressed in overt, subtle or obscure ways
- Reflecting unique fascinations, obsessions, rituals

Responding to Play Initiations

When monitoring play initiations, the main task is to be as vigilant as possible in responding to the novice player's attempts to initiate. The idea is to stimulate and nurture opportunities for peer interaction and play by building upon that which is intrinsically motivating and developmentally appropriate for the novice player. Play guides must continually search for activities and themes that allow every child, novice and expert, to experience a satisfying role in play.

Quite often expert players come up with ideas for how to incorporate the novice player's novel behavior and interests once they are made aware of the child's intentions. Play guides also need to be creative in coming up with ideas that will be well received by the group. In most cases, responding to play initiations happens in the moment, as demonstrated in the examples of monitoring play initiations in Table 8.1.

Table 8.1

Examples of Monitoring Play Initiations in Integrated Play Groups

Recognizing Play Initiations	Interpreting Play Initiations	Responding to Play Initiations
Case Vignette: Teresa Standing beside Sook (expert player), Teresa touches the dollhouse. Facing the dollhouse she says, "Play in dollhouse, play in dollhouse." Glancing at Sook, she then asks, "Play in dollhouse Sook?"	Teresa wants to play dollhouse with Sook	Ask Sook to figure out what Teresa is asking her. Let her know that Teresa is inviting her to play house. Help Teresa communicate her interest more effectively. Remind Teresa to stand close and look at her friends when she asks them to play (see Chapter 10).
Teresa walks over to the play grocery store where her peers are playing. Facing away from her peers, she repeats a phrase from a commercial for a grocery store chain, "Easy check-out, easy check-out, easy check-out, easy check-out. (Writes in air with finger) Easy check-out, you hear me? Easy check-out."	Teresa wants to play grocery store with her peers in possibly two different ways: 1. She wants to take the role of shopper so that she may line up at the check-out stand. 2. She wants to take the role of cashier so that she may check out the other shoppers.	Ask the players to figure out what Teresa means by saying "easy check-out." Let them know that she wants to join them in playing grocery store. Ask the players to figure out which role Teresa should take and what she should do in that role. Help Teresa communicate her interest more effectively. Teach Teresa to ask, "May I play with you?" (see Chapter 10).

Table 8.1

Examples of Monitoring Play Initiations in Integrated Play Groups (continued)

Recognizing Play Initiations	Interpreting Play Initiations	Responding to Play Initiations
Case Vignette: Freddy Freddy watches as three peers take turns hiding in the play refrigerator … A moment later, Freddy quietly squeezes into the refrigerator, closing the door on himself. Meanwhile, the others go off to play something else. Moments later Freddy pokes his head out of the refrigerator door.	Freddy wants to play hide-and-seek with his peers.	Ask the players if they know where Freddy is. Let them know that he is hiding and wants them to find him. Help the players come up with different ways of playing hide-and-seek (e.g., hide in big boxes). Help Freddy communicate his interest more effectively (e.g., Teach Freddy to say, "Come and find me!").
While being videotaped, Freddy imitates the videographer. Freddy goes to the toy shelf and pulls out the toy camera. He sits in front of the full-length mirror. Holding the camera over his eye, he presses the button as though taking a picture of himself. He continues to look at himself through the camera, fixes his hair, smiles and takes another picture.	Freddy wants to play with the toy camera in two different ways: 1. He wants to be in the role of photographer/videographer by taking the pictures. 2. He wants to have his picture taken.	Tell the other players to look at what Freddy is doing. Ask them if they can figure out what he wants to play. Suggest that they take turns taking each other's pictures. Teach the players to say "Smile" and "Say cheese!" Help the players come up with ideas of how to play photographer/videographer (e.g., pretend to make a movie). Help Freddy communicate his interest more effectively (e.g., Teach Freddy to take pictures of his peers and offer the camera to his peers).
Case Vignette: Jared Jared watches Misha, Carlos and Dina (expert players) as they roll around on the floor, tickling each other and shouting with laughter. Jared smiles, jumps, claps, flaps his arms, turns and jumps in circles. His excitement escalates as he runs up to the group and joins them on the floor. At this moment, Misha and Dina move and sit on the bench. Jared follows and sidles up close to them, smiles while covering his ears and moving his head from side to side.	Jared wants to join his peers in rough-and-tumble play.	Tell the other players to look at what Jared is doing. Ask them if they can figure out what he wants to play. Let them know that he wants to join them in rolling around and tickling. Suggest some sensory games that might offer a similar experience (e.g., rolling each other up in a blanket like pretend burritos). Help Jared communicate his interest more effectively (e.g., Teach Jared to tickle his peers).
Jared takes the shopping cart and pushes it beside the grocery store where Carlos, Ronny (expert players) and Freddy (novice player) are situated. He then picks up the telephone attached to the store, holds it to his ear, and smiles.	Jared wants to join his peers who are playing grocery store. He wants a peer to talk with him on the telephone.	Tell the other players to look at Jared. Let them know that he is waiting for one of them to answer the phone and talk with him. Help the players come up with ideas of a role for Jared in the grocery store (e.g., Answering phones beside the cashier at the check-out stand). Help Jared communicate his interest more effectively (e.g., Teach Jared to push the buttons on the telephone to make it ring).

Sometimes it is possible to plan activities in advance that are based on a child's play initiations as in the following case vignette.

MONITORING PLAY INITIATIONS
David's Story

First, I have a 3rd-grader named David. He loves to be with his friends, but has a very difficult time maintaining the topic of conversation with his friends. He constantly wants to talk about whatever he is obsessed about at the time. (Last school year it was movies.) Well, after trying to get him to play a number of different things during Integrated Play Groups (but him only talking about movies the whole time), I was unsure of what to do next. I spoke with Pamela [field supervisor], and she suggested making a "video store." What a WONDERFUL idea! Boy, did it work out successfully. David was so excited to start the video store. Our first step was collecting "check boxes" to use as movie cases. We e-mailed all the staff in our school, and the check boxes started coming our way. (David also emptied out all of his dad's check boxes that were in storage at home and brought them to school ... oops.) Then, the play group got together and started making covers for the check boxes. I had cut out white paper to fit on the box, and the kids used markers to make the title, cover picture, who was in the movie, rating, etc. ... They made movies for about eight consecutive sessions. They were having a lot of fun, and David was in his glory because it was now appropriate for him to ask everyone all about the movie they were making. For the rest of the school year, the kids played "video store." They had tags to wear indicating the role they were to be, and they made up rental slips for the cashier to fill out.

Nine months later ...

This summer, during vacation, David called and left a message for me and my kids. He said, "Hi, can you come over to my house and pick out a video from my video store?" I think it says a lot about how much fun he had. I also think it was his way of saying that he misses playing ... connecting socially with the other children ...

Tara Tuchel – Apprentice Play Guide

Chapter Summary

Providing a bridge from theory to practice, this chapter introduced the Integrated Play Groups intervention (guided participation). Play guides must adopt a flexible, yet comfortable style that is highly responsive to the children's interests, abilities and needs. Monitoring play initiations is an especially critical part of the intervention process. This practice involves recognizing, interpreting and responding to the novice player's spontaneous attempts to socialize and play. Play initiations are the cornerstone on which to build opportunities for more interactive and developmentally appropriate play. We now turn our attention to the practice of scaffolding play in Chapter 9.

Scaffolding Play

Chapter Highlights

This chapter focuses on the practice of scaffolding play. The following topics will be highlighted:

► Maximum Support – Directing and Modeling

► Intermediate Support – Verbal and Visual Cueing

► Minimum Support – Standing By

> ## Amusing Moments
>
> ### Spiderman's Accent
>
> While consulting with a preschool outside of London, I was asked to facilitate a play group of 4-year-olds. The experts (a girl and boy) busied themselves in the roles of Mummy and Nanny while pretending to play house. Meanwhile, Jackie (a boy with autism) needed help figuring out how to be the Daddy. I first asked, "What do daddies do?" He replied, "Daddy drives the car," and then proceeded to exit the play area. I next suggested he pretend to drive home, then announce his arrival by saying, "Mommy, Nanny, I'm home."
>
> Jackie returned to the play area and enthusiastically repeated exactly what I had said. The "Nanny" suddenly broke out into contagious giggles that quickly spread to the others. This was my cue to exit, so as to not ruin the moment for them.
>
> I later learned what the laughter was all about. Jackie's very accurate imitation of my American accent reminded them all of the "Spiderman" cartoons they watch on television.
>
> (Wolfberg, 2000, p. 14)

The practice of scaffolding play is central to effectively guiding children in Integrated Play Groups. By definition, scaffolding refers to the provision of adjustable and temporary support structures. Applied to Integrated Play Groups, scaffolding involves building on the child's play initiations by systematically adjusting assistance to match or slightly exceed the level at which the child is independently able to engage in play with peers – within the child's "zone of proximal development." The idea of scaffolding is to avoid being so lax that the play falls apart or so intrusive that it ruins the moment. The key is to find that ever so delicate balance of allowing the play to unfold in genuine ways while sustaining child engagement. That means knowing when to step in, when to step out and especially when to be quiet.

Depending upon the players' interests, abilities and needs, the play guide regulates the type and amount of support accordingly. Children who are unfamiliar or have little prior experience may require a higher degree of adult assistance in the early phases of a play group. As the players acclimate to one another and grow increasingly competent in their play, the adult may gradually withdraw support. In contrast, children with greater familiarity and experience may need a lesser degree of adult support from the start. There are also groups of children who simply show a natural proclivity to play together and thus require only minimal assistance. Still others are variable in their needs, and rely on the play guide to be especially flexible and quick to step in and out to support them from one moment to the next.

To illustrate the process of scaffolding play, we delineated a three-tiered system of support (see Table 9.1 for an overview of scaffolding play based on this system of support). Each tier includes strategies that reflect a different degree of intensity and type of support.

- maximum support – directing and modeling
- intermediate support – verbal and visual cueing
- minimal support – standing by

It is important to point out that these are not mutually exclusive levels that function in a hierarchical fashion or follow a predetermined protocol. Rather, scaffolding is a fluid process that relies entirely upon the adult's ability to respond to the children at any given point in time. In some cases it may be appropriate to provide maximum, intermediate or minimum support for an entire play session and even over several play sessions. In other cases it may be appropriate to vacillate among the three layers of support during a single play session.

Table 9.1
Overview of Scaffolding Play

Degree of Intensity	Type of Support	Play Guide Role	Strategies
Maximum Support	Directing and Modeling	Stage Director	• Setting out play materials • Identifying parts or roles in play • Partnering novice and expert players • Scripting actions and dialogue • Inserting ritual and drama
Intermediate Support	Verbal and Visual Cueing	Coach	• Offering suggestions • Posing leading questions • Commenting on the play • Reframing the play event
Minimum Support	Standing By	Secure Base	• Remaining on periphery of the group • Being ready to step in as needed

Maximum Support – Directing and Modeling (Stage Director)

Scaffolding play sometimes involves providing children with a high degree of support. The role of the play guide is akin to that of a stage director when the actors are first learning their parts. The play guide physically steps in and shows the children how to play together using directing and modeling techniques. These strategies may take different forms and incorporate physical, verbal, nonverbal and visual supports.

Arranging Play Materials

Similar to preparing a stage set, the play guide must ensure that the props are set up so the children can engage in play events. In some cases this involves arranging an activity in advance by laying out toys or props in a visually clear and inviting manner. For instance, a water table set out with sponges, squeeze bottles, baby dolls and bath towels will be instantly recognizable and attractive to youngsters. Play materials may also be arranged as a way to introduce the players to a new activity or theme. Laying out a chef's hat, apron, paper pad and pencil, menus and play food may help initiate a restaurant theme. In many cases the play guide will need to set out play materials that are fitting to the moment; for instance, handing the customers utensils so that they may pretend to eat (see examples of theme-based sets in Chapter 5).

Identifying Parts or Roles in the Play

Another way in which to offer maximum support is by helping the players identify parts or roles in a particular play event. In some cases this involves directing or modeling for the children what part to take in a play activity; for instance, showing a novice how to pour water over a baby doll at the water table. A visual symbol may also be used to reinforce the child's part (e.g., a photograph or line drawing of water play). The play guide may assign a word or phrase to the action to help the child recognize his part – "wash baby." It may even be appropriate to elaborate by assigning a pretend role – "daddy washes the baby."

Directing and modeling may also be used to help players identify their roles in a more complex play activity or theme, for instance, asking a group of players to choose the role of chef, waiter or customer to play restaurant. Visual supports may be especially useful in helping players to clearly identify their roles (see Figure 9.1). Written or graphic labels that depict a specific role may be incorporated into a costume or worn on a string around the neck.

Figure 9.1. Example of visual supports for identifying a part or role in play.

The Picture Communication Symbols © 1981-2003, used with permission from Mayer-Johnson Inc., P.O. Box 1579, Solana Beach, CA 92075. 800/588-4548 (phone), 858/550-0449 (fax) and www.mayer-johnson.com.

Partnering Novice and Expert Players

Forming partnerships between more and less experienced players is another way to offer the players maximum support. Even though experts typically serve as models for the novice players, it is best when partnerships between novice and expert players reflect a mutual alliance. Novice and expert players may be paired off based on shared interests and connections around play preferences. Partnerships may also naturally be formed within the context of a specific activity or theme that requires more than one player to be in the part or role. For instance, it takes at least two players to play a game of catch, and it is common for two customers to eat together in a restaurant.

Scripting Actions and Dialogue

Scripting actions and dialogue is another way to offer intensive support. Like a stage performance, the players may need direction for how to perform their parts or roles. Thus, the play guide may direct and model for the children what to do and what to say to enact a play event.

This might involve scripting actions and/or dialogue to carry out simple play sequences. For example, the adult might model and/or physically guide a child to soak up water with a sponge and squeeze it over the baby dolls at the water table. Simple dialogue might be added, such as, "Wash, wash, wash … wash the baby."

It is also possible to script actions and dialogue to carry out elaborate themes, such as playing restaurant. For example, the play guide might walk the players through their different parts by showing them what to do and telling them what to say (e.g., telling the waiter to walk up to the table and say, "May I take your order please;" showing the customers how to order from a menu by pointing to a picture and/or asking for the desired food item).

Inserting Ritual and Drama

Another way of offering intensive support is to direct and model ways in which the children may insert ritual and drama into play events. This elicits and sustains the children's attention on the play. The play guide uses repetition and exaggerated or animated facial expressions, gestures and sounds in a predictable and amusing fashion. The idea is for the players to emulate and infuse such behavior into their play scripts. As play scripts are repeatedly carried out, the players will anticipate the sequence of events and discover a rhythm in the play. To keep the play event going, the ritual and drama may be varied.

An example for younger children might involve repeatedly dunking the baby doll in and out of the water while exclaiming, "Woops!" After a few repetitions, the adult might hold back the eagerly anticipated "woops," at which point the children may insert their own phrase and take over the play event.

Ritual and drama may be naturally inserted into sociodramatic play scripts. For example, the play guide may direct the children to take on different personas when they are performing their roles.

Intermediate Support – Verbal and Visual Cueing (Coach)

As the children become more engaged, adult support becomes less intensive. Hence the role of the play guide shifts from that of director to coach. The adult essentially steps out and away from the group, offering verbal and/or visual cues from the sidelines. The emphasis is on redirecting the children to look to one another rather than the adult for directions and cues to carry out play scripts.

There are numerous ways in which the play guide may use verbal cues (spoken language – oral or signed) and/or visual cues (pictures – photographs, line drawings; and/or written words on posters or cue cards) to support the players. Since not all novice players will respond to verbal and visual cues in the same way, strategies need to be adapted for individual children. For instance, some novice players will require verbal cues to be paired down to very simple spoken or signed words or phrases. Other novice players will require visual cues to reinforce verbal cues. Still others may benefit from visual cues in lieu of verbal cues.

The following are examples of verbal cues that may be used to support novice and expert players, many of which may be paired with or translated into visual cues. We will give examples of visual social-communication cues in Chapter 10.

Offering Suggestions

A rather straightforward way to cue the players is to offer suggestions that will foster social interaction and play. Suggestions are often presented in the form of a question. For some novice players it may be appropriate to offer suggestions in a more straightforward and less ambiguous way (keeping in mind that it is still a suggestion, not a directive).

In the following example, a novice player initiates play by pushing a grocery cart in one part of the play area while the expert players set up a cash register and food on shelves in another part of the play area. While standing on the periphery of the group, the play guide may remark and offer one or more suggestions to the novice and expert players:

It looks like Sally [novice player] is ready to go shopping in Alice's [expert player] store.

To Expert Player:

Alice, why don't you invite Sally to shop in your store.
Maybe you can show her how to shop in your store.
Why don't you go shopping with Sally.
Maybe you and Sally can push the shopping cart together.
Why don't you take turns putting the groceries in the cart.

To Novice Player:

Sally, do you want to go shopping?
Look at Alice and Max in the store.
Push your shopping cart to the store.
Put some food in your cart with Alice.
Give your groceries to Max, the cashier.

Posing Leading Questions

Another way of verbally cueing the players is to pose questions that will lead the children to figure out what they should do and say. Continuing with the former example of playing grocery store, the play guide might pose the following leading questions:

Do you see what Sally is doing?
What do you think she wants to play right now?
What roles do all of you have?
Who is the cashier, shopper, bagger?
Sally, who do you want to be?
Alice, Max … who do you think Sally wants to be?
Can you think of ways to shop together in the store?

Commenting on the Play

Another way to cue the players is to comment on the play. The idea is to make remarks that are contextually relevant in order to keep the children focused on the play activity. In the following example, a group of children are pretending to go shopping. A novice player (in the role of shopper) pushes her cart away from the store without the others noticing. In this situation the play guide might direct one or more of the following comments to the group:

> The store is losing its shoppers.
> The shopper is leaving the store, but forgot to pay.
> The cashier is waiting for the shoppers to come to the check-out stand.
> The bagger is ready to bag the groceries.

Reframing the Play Event

Another way to verbally cue the players is to reframe the play event. This is essentially an extension of commenting on the play. The adult adds a novel element to the play script by extending and varying the theme. This will help keep the children stimulated and focused on the play. Following the above example, the play guide might throw out the following remarks to redirect the children and expand upon the shopping theme.

> The store is losing its shoppers – it must be time to close the store.
> Maybe the shopper wants to go home and cook a meal for his family.
> Where is the family – who is the mother, father, sister, brother?

> The shopper is leaving the store, but forgot to pay.
> Quick, call the police.

> The shopper ran away and is hiding out in the swamp with Shrek, the ogre.
> Send out the fairy tale creatures to find them.

Minimum Support – Standing By (Secure Base)

As the children become fully engaged in play activities, adult support is at a minimum. The play guide withdraws to the periphery of the group, remaining on "standby" ready to jump in on a moment's notice.

The role of the play guide shifts from that of either director or coach to that of "secure base" – someone the children may rely on for a sense of emotional well-being, someone they may check in with from time to time.

A good indication that only minimum support is necessary is that the players are so completely absorbed in the play that they are oblivious of the adult's existence. It is nevertheless essential that the play guide stay within close range to offer children assurance and assistance as needed.

It is not uncommon for adults to initially feel uneasy about holding back support (particularly for long periods). There is an element of anxiety that the adult will somehow lose control over the group – that the players will essentially run amok. The best advice we can give is to test the waters. Allow yourself to step out at moments when there is a tinge of discomfort, and wait to step back in until you have passed your threshold. It is during these moments that we have seen genuine play unfold. These moments would have been lost had we intervened too soon.

In Table 9.2 we offer an example of scaffolding play in action as Andrew (a play guide in training) facilitates an Integrated Play Group session.

Table 9.2

Example of Scaffolding Play in an Integrated Play Group Session

Play Scenario	Level of Scaffolding
Alex (novice player), Jay and Lizzy (expert players) began the [session] with "head-shoulders-knees-and-toes" [Alex's favorite activity]. Jay then decisively suggested that they play "Hermit Crabs," and eagerly threw himself on the floor to model the appropriate "crawl." [The others were] a bit tentative at first … so I threw out some suggestions.	
I placed the collapsible cloth house in the play area …	Maximum Support – Directing and Modeling
[I] said, this could be your "crab house." Jay invited Alex into the house and Alex climbed in!	Intermediate Support – Verbal/Visual Cueing
Lizzy was still standing and watching, so I gave her a bag of plastic balls …	Maximum Support – Directing and Modeling
[I] said, "Maybe the crabs in the house need some food." Lizzy immediately ran with this, and said she needed a delivery car.	Intermediate Support – Verbal/Visual Cueing
I gave her a square plastic scooter/dolly, which she began driving to the house. Jay and Lizzy were rolling, but seemed to need a bit of assistance to help Alex participate. I asked them to watch me, and grabbed some balls and went to the "house." I took turns (pretend) feeding and being fed by Alex with the balls, and they both watched attentively.	Maximum Support – Directing and Modeling
I then stepped out [momentarily]. Jay continued the back and forth with Alex. Lizzy then drove up to the "drive-thru window" with an order (the crab theme had now evolved to a drive-thru restaurant).	Minimum Support – Standing By
I threw in the plastic cash register for added props.	Maximum Support – Directing and Modeling
Lizzy and Jay began a "transaction," but Lizzy paused in the middle and said "wait – we have to include Alex!" (Lizzy is quickly showing herself to be a star expert.) Although they weren't quite sure what to do next to include him, Alex was repeatedly handing Jay icons [which included food items] from his talking book inside the house/restaurant.	Minimum Support – Standing By

(Field notes by Andrew – Play Guide in Training)

Chapter Summary

This chapter focused on the practice of scaffolding play. This involves building on the child's play initiations by systematically adjusting assistance to match or slightly exceed the level at which the child is independently able to engage in play with peers – within the child's "zone of proximal development." To illustrate the process of scaffolding play, we delineated a three-tiered system of support. Each tier includes strategies that reflect a different degree of intensity and type of support: Maximum Support – Directing and Modeling, Intermediate Support – Verbal and Visual Cueing, and Minimal Support – Standing By. We now turn to Chapter 10, which focuses on the practice of social-communication guidance.

Social-Communication Guidance

Chapter Highlights

This chapter focuses on the practice of social-communication guidance. The following topics will be highlighted:

► Social-Communication Cues

► Selecting Relevant Cues

► Customizing Visual Cue Cards and Posters

► Introducing Social-Communication Cues

► Reinforcing Social-Communication Cues

An Invitation to Play

Misha (expert player) walks over to Jared (novice player) and bends over to face him. She puts her face close to his and talks to him in a way that is familiar, the way an adult would approach a small child. Although I cannot hear Misha, she seems to extend an invitation to Jared to play. Jared moves his mouth in such a way that makes me think he is echoing her words. She stretches her hand out to Jared. Jared complies by standing up and taking Misha's hand. Hand in hand, they walk together through the play area to the grocery store. As he passes me, Jared looks up with a genuine smile, a sight so rarely seen on his often-emotion-less face. With a sense of delight, he spontaneously shouts, "Play!" (Wolfberg, 1999, p. 96)

Social-communication guidance is another fundamental practice of guided participation. The focus is on supporting novice and expert players to adopt the use of verbal and nonverbal strategies to elicit one another's attention and sustain mutual engagement in play. Directed to novice and expert players alike, these strategies foster and nurture attempts to:

- Initiate play with peers (including persisting in enlisting reluctant peers)
- Respond to peer social overtures to play
- Join or enter established play events with peers
- Maintain and expand reciprocal exchanges in play with peers

On the one hand, expert players learn how to recognize, interpret and respond to novice players' subtle or obscure social-communicative attempts. On the other hand, novice players learn how to communicate more effectively by initiating and responding in more conventional ways.

Social-Communication Cues

To carry out this practice, the play guide supports the players in adopting verbal and nonverbal strategies. These strategies are presented in the form of social-communication cues. Social-communication cues focus on what the players may do (WHAT TO DO) and say (WHAT TO SAY) to invite and join peers for play. Social-communication cues additionally focus on ways to reinforce one another by showing appreciation or affection (e.g., smile, hug, clap, high-five).

Social-communication cues are especially useful for guiding children to establish joint attention so they may begin an interaction. Social-communication cues may also be used to help children sustain an interaction. The intent is for children to naturally incorporate these strategies into their repertoire, so they no longer rely on the adult to verbally or visually present cues.

The examples in Table 10.1 reflect different types of social-communication cues that may be used to support novice and expert players in Integrated

Play Groups. It is important to point out that this is in no way an exhaustive list that is representative of what every player should be doing or saying. Social-communication cues may need to be varied or added to accommodate individual children.

Table 10.1

Examples of Social-Communication Cues

What to Do	What to Say
Look/watch	[Playmate's name]
Stand close	Let's play
Stand back	May I play (with you)?
Tap shoulder	What do you want to play?
Take hand	Do you want to play with [playmate's
Point	name]?
Touch	What are you playing/doing/making?
Pick up (toy)	How do you play?
Take (toy)	Whose turn is it?
Give (toy)	May I have a turn?
Show (toy)	Your turn – my turn
Follow	Look at/watch (me/playmate)
Copy/mirror	Follow (me/playmate)
Lead	Do what I am/playmate is doing
Wait	Let's pretend ...
Take turns	
Pretend	

Selecting Relevant Cues

Social-communication cues are selected based on observations and analyses of what is most relevant for particular novice and expert players. Some older and more advanced children may be capable of learning several or a series of related cues at once. Younger and more involved children may need to concentrate on learning one or a few related cues at a time. In some cases, novice and expert players will be learning the same social-communication cue (or parts of the same cue). In other cases, novice and expert players will need to concentrate on completely different cues. Finally, children will vary with respect to the type and amount of instruction they will need to effectively learn relevant social-communication cues.

Customizing Visual Cue Cards and Posters

Social-communication cues may be customized for novice and expert players in a number of ways. As we earlier described the process of scaffolding play, social-communication cues may take the form of verbal cues (spoken language – oral or signed) and/or visual cues (pictures – photographs, line drawings and/or written words). Visual supports, such as cue cards and posters, may be customized and adapted from the examples presented in Figures 10.1, 10.2, 10.3, and 10.4. In many circumstances it will make most sense to adapt materials by incorporating visual icons that are a part of a child's educational and/or therapy program.

Illustrated by Olga Norman (1992) and used by permission.

Figure 10.1. Example of a customized social-communication cue card.

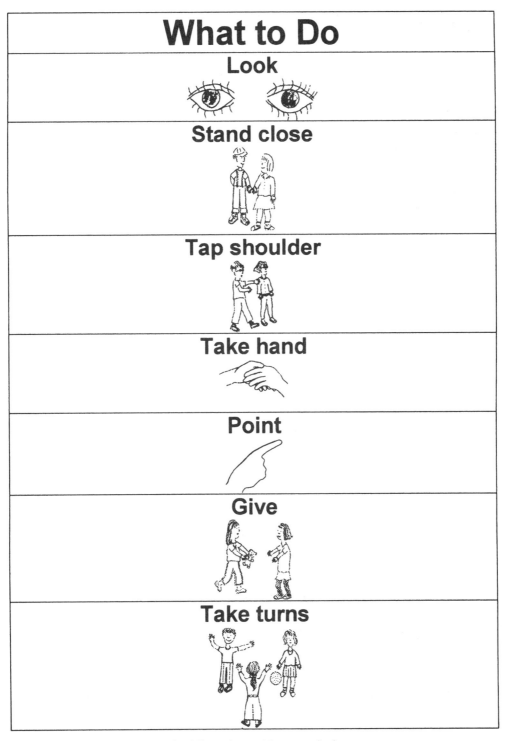

Illustrated by Olga Norman (1992) and used by permission.

Figure 10.2. Example of a customized poster of social-communication cues (what to do).

Illustrated by Olga Norman (1992) and used by permission.

Figure 10.3. Example of a customized poster of social-communication cues (what to say).

Illustrated by Olga Norman (1992) and used by permission.

Figure 10.4. Example of a customized poster of social-communication cues (showing our friends support).

Introducing Social-Communication Cues

Once relevant cues have been selected and customized as needed, the next step is to introduce the players to the strategy. Social-communication cues are typically presented in natural and logical sequences or series of steps. A natural time to introduce the social-communication cue is at the start of the play session during the opening ritual. Depending upon the ages and abilities of the players, cues may be introduced in different ways.

One way to introduce social-communication strategies to children and youth with ASD is through video models. Khalsa and Murdock (2003) have created *Joining In! A Program for Teaching Social Skills.* This three-volume videotaped set teaches children appropriate social behaviors such as listening, responding, understanding personal space and asking questions. The videotapes provide direct instruction and show children engaging in these behaviors with feedback.

Another way to introduce strategies to younger or more involved children is to demonstrate simple cues in a straightforward and engaging way (such as by role-playing with each other or with dolls or puppets). For instance, if a novice player is unlikely to respond when her name is called, it may be fitting to introduce cues to both the expert and the novice players that will elicit an appropriate response such as, "Tap shoulder" (to get a friend's attention), and "Look" (to respond to your friend). The play guide might display visual cue cards to represent the actions while introducing the strategies (see Figure 10.1). The following is an example of how a play guide might introduce basic social-communication cues.

Tap shoulder

Sample Introduction to Social-Communication Cues

Sometimes when you want to play with a friend, you call their name but they don't hear you or see you – they don't know that you want to play with them.
Can you think of a different way to get their attention?

One way might be to tap your friend on the shoulder, just like in the picture.

Let's try it with a partner – tap your friend on the shoulder.
(It may be necessary to provide guidance on how to tap appropriately, since many novice players have sensory issues.)

When you tap your friend on the shoulder, how do you know she is paying attention to you – how do you know that she is responding?
That's right, she "looks" at you, just like in the picture.

Let's try it with your partner – tap your friend on the shoulder – now look at your friend when he taps you on the shoulder.

Wonderful – now that you have your friend's attention, you can invite your friend to play with you – you can play together. Let's try this in our play groups.

Social-communication cues may be presented to older and more advanced children in more sophisticated ways. One way is to hold a formal discussion about the role of communication as in the following example:

Sample Discussion on Communication

What does communication mean?
How do people communicate with each other?
Do people communicate only by talking – or do people communicate in other ways?
Let's think of some other forms of communication.

Sign language, writing, pictures, facial expressions, body posture (turning toward and away from someone), proximity (standing close to or far from someone) and eye contact (looking at or away from someone) are all forms of communication.

How many people does it take to communicate?
It takes at least two people to communicate – one messenger who delivers the message and one receiver who receives and responds to the communicator.

What does it mean to be able to communicate well – to be a "good communicator"?
The messenger and receiver need to be able to understand each other.

There are some people who have difficulty communicating – they may have a hard time delivering clear messages. It is like they are communicating using "secret code" so you have to figure out what they mean.

Sometimes people have a hard time receiving and responding to the messages of others – so you have to try different ways of communicating a message so that they understand you better.

As the posters around the room show, there are different things you can do and different things you can say to communicate well with your friends in play groups. Let's try out some of these together.

Reinforcing Social-Communication Cues

Once the players are familiar with particular social-communication cues, they may practice them in their play sessions. The idea is to reinforce cues incidentally as natural circumstances arise. Typically the play guide gives gentle verbal and/or visual reminders by referring to the posters and cue cards. As children incorporate strategies into their repertoire, new social-communication cues may be introduced and practiced in ongoing sessions as needed.

Table 10.2 gives examples of different ways in which social-communication cues may be combined to support novice and expert players in Integrated Play Groups.

Table 10.2

Examples of Social-Communication Cue Combinations

	What to Do	**What to Say**
Initiate play with peers	Tap shoulder	Let's play.
	Show [doll] Give [doll]	Do you want to play dolls?
	Stand close Look [at playmate] Point [to game]	[Playmate's name], What are you doing? Let's play [game].
Respond to peer social overtures to play	Take [playmate's] hand Follow [playmate's lead]	Show/tell me what you want to play.
	Watch [playmate] Stand close	[Playmate's name], What are you doing?
	Pick up [blanket that play-mate touches] Show [shake blanket]	Do you want to play with the blanket?
Join/enter estab-lished play events with peers	Stand close [to playmate pushing shopping cart] Pick up [groceries]	Can I go shopping with you?
	Watch [playmates playing marbles] Stand close Wait [for break in play]	That looks cool! May I have a turn?
Maintain/expand reciprocal exchanges in play with peers	Watch [playmate] Copy [playmate]	Look at me. Follow me.
	Take turns [playing a game]	Whose turn is it? Your turn – my turn.
	Take turns [hide-n-seek]	Go hide. Count to 10. Ready or not, here I come to find you.
	Pretend to cook [beside playmate] Stir the pot Give spoon	What are you making? I'm making soup. Taste it. Yum-yum – delicious.

Chapter Summary

This chapter focused on applying the practice of social-communication guidance, which involves supporting the players in adopting selected verbal and nonverbal strategies to elicit one another's attention and sustain mutual engagement in play. Directed to novice and expert players alike, these strategies are presented in the form of social-communication cues. Social-communication cues focus on what the players may do (WHAT TO DO) and say (WHAT TO SAY) to invite and join peers for play. Relevant cues are introduced and reinforced with the aid of visual supports. We now turn to Chapter 11, which focuses on play guidance techniques.

Play Guidance

Chapter Highlights

This chapter focuses on play guidance. The following topics will be highlighted:

► Orienting

► Imitation-Mirroring

► Parallel Play

► Joint Focus

► Joint Action

► Role Enactment

► Role-Playing

Amusing Moments

Earthquake Rescue

Shortly after an earthquake in Northern California, five elementary-aged children re-enacted a drama in Integrated Play Groups. Using cardboard blocks, they built around one another a tower of blocks, then knocked it down, yelling "Earthquake!" "Rescue workers" rushed to the scene to dig out the "victims" and rebuild the tower. The highlight of the drama was when Cecilia, a novice player, pretended to give birth by pulling a baby doll out from beneath her shirt as the "paramedics" tended to her in the rubble.

Pop-Star Baby

In one play group, Randy, a 5-year-old novice player, pretended to be the pop-star Paula Abdul. He dressed in a fringed-mop wig and an oversized silky blue bathrobe. He played house with peers, who pretended to be his mother, father, sister and brother. Randy (a.k.a. Paula) complained that his "mother" had brought him the wrong milk for supper as she placed a cup before him. He stomped to the play kitchen, pulled a baby-bottle from the cupboard, brought it to the table and pretended to drink. A moment later, he announced, "I'm going to a party to dance the night away."

(Wolfberg, 2000, p. 14)

Guided participation also involves the practice of play guidance, which encompasses an array of techniques designed to enhance play within the child's "zone of proximal development" (Vygotsky, 1978; see Chapter 2). The idea is for novice players to be fully immersed in peer play experiences even if their participation is minimal. While participating in complex play events with more capable peers, these children may practice and appropriate new and emerging skills. The key is to know where the child is on the developmental continuum (i.e., the child's present and emerging capacities) in order to foster opportunities that propel development forward.

Play guidance techniques are to a large extent common-sense approaches that one may think of as tricks of the trade. Any number of these may be tailored to individual children and applied to a variety of social play situations. Table 11.1 presents an overview of such techniques.

Orienting

Orienting is a play guidance strategy that is generally aimed at novice players who are not spontaneously socially attending to peers. Some of these children may be at a place in their development at which they are not yet able to tolerate proximity to peers. Others may occupy themselves in the vicinity of peers, but appear to be unaware or uninterested in other children and their activities. Still others appear tentative or cautious around peers, clinging to adults while in the presence of other children. In all of these cases, an initial step involves orienting the novice player to socially attend to the other children and their play activities.

Table 11.1
Overview of Play Guidance Techniques

Type of Play Guidance	Strategies
Orienting	• Allow novices to stay close to adults while pointing out peers and activities • Entice novices to watch peers by giving them motivating materials and activities with which to play
Imitation-Mirroring	• Stimulate mutual imitation with duplicate materials • Engage children in mimicking or "copy-cat" games
Parallel Play	• Guide novices and experts to play beside one another • Set up similar materials in the same physical play space • Set out materials and activities that lend themselves to parallel play (e.g., water table)
Joint Focus	• Guide novices and experts to attend to different parts of the same play activity (e.g., dollhouse) • Guide novices and experts to show and share materials
Joint Action	• Guide novices and experts to take turns and coordinate actions with the same materials and activities • Set out materials and activities that lend themselves to turn-taking (e.g., train set) • Use turn-taking markers (e.g., pass the hat, arrow)
Role Enactment	• Guide novices to act out real-life activities within complex play themes/scripts supported by experts • Provide realistic props that are fitting to behavior
Role-Playing	• Guide novices and experts to take on imaginary roles within jointly constructed play themes/scripts • Set out a collection of theme-based props

One of the simplest and most logical ways to orient children to peers is to make sure that the peers are engaged in something that is of particular interest to the novice player. This might involve giving peers objects or play materials that are especially appealing to the novice player. If a child is fascinated with sparkly things, for example, peers might be given sparkly toys with which to play, sparkly stickers to wear on their clothes or even sparkly temporary tattoos to wear on their hands or faces. If a child is fascinated with train travel, the players might be given an assortment of related props with which to pretend to go on a train trip.

Novice players who are more likely to attend to adults than peers may need to take advantage of the adult as an attachment figure to make this transition. In such instances, the play guide gradually eases the novice player into the group while orienting him to the other players. Initially, the adult might encourage the child to hang on and stick close by to her. Younger children might sit on the adult's lap for a time. Other children might hold hands with the adult. And still others might simply maintain close physical proximity to the adult. During such instances, the play guide orients the novice player to peers by pointing out who they are and what they are doing in a manner that attracts the child to them. The play guide might repeat the names of peers and comment on their play activities using facial expressions, intonations and gestures that denote enthusiasm and encouragement. As the novice player grows increasingly comfortable and begins to take notice of the other players and their activities, the adult steadily withdraws.

Imitation-Mirroring

Fostering opportunities for mutual imitation and mirroring is a powerful tool for stimulating novice players to establish shared attention with peers in play. Typically developing children are quite naturally drawn to and responsive to peers who look and act like they do. Although many children on the autism spectrum may be at a place in their development where they possess similar attractions, they may not be intrinsically inclined or organized to socially connect with peers in this way. There are a number of ways in which play guides may unlock this potential.

Providing duplicate materials is one way to arouse novice players to spontaneously imitate or mirror peer behavior. Certain toys and props are logically made available in duplicate because of their function. For instance, two telephones would naturally stimulate a two-way interaction between children who are able to hold a feigned or actual conversation in play. Telephones may also be used in other ways than intended to promote spontaneous imitation. In one play group, an expert player pretended to call a novice player on the telephone and then proceeded to manipulate the receiver by lightly banging it on his head in a "clowning" manner. This immediately attracted the novice player's attention as he picked up a second telephone and mirrored the expert player's actions.

Duplicate materials that are highly motivating to a novice player may be especially effective in generating spontaneous imitation and mirroring. If a novice player delights in Spiderman, for example, it may be appropriate to include at least two sets of Spiderman action figures and costumes for dress-up. Duplicate costumes and dress-up clothes are frequently the impetus for spontaneous imitation and mirroring. On one occasion I observed a play group in a preschool setting where three expert players each slung an identical white purse over their shoulder and began to sashay across the floor in perfect unison. In an instant, a novice player grabbed a fourth white purse, slung it over her shoulder and joined them without missing a step.

Many novice players have been shown to be highly responsive to peers when they mimic or mirror the child's actions. There are numerous ways in which to enhance opportunities for this to occur that can be fun for both novice and expert players. Play guides might suggest or introduce some popular "copy-cat" games such as "Simon Says" or "Follow the Leader." One such activity involves pairing up the children so that they are standing face to face and mirroring the precise movements, gestures and expressions of the other (à la the opening theme to the "Patty Duke" show for those old enough to remember). In some cases this involves coaching the expert player to mirror the novice player, who may otherwise be inattentive and preoccupied. This frequently has the effect of arousing the novice player's curiosity to the point that he disrupts his routine and attends to the expert player.

Parallel Play

Creating conditions for children to play independently beside one another in a parallel fashion is another play guidance strategy that may be applicable for novice players at particular points in time. This strategy is especially appropriate for novice players who are increasingly able to tolerate proximity to peers, but are not yet ready to have direct contact with them. Supporting children in parallel play serves a number of important functions that ultimately lead to more interactive forms of play.

The goal is to find ways to naturally attract children to play alongside one another. The most logical approach is to engineer the play environment so that novice and expert players are drawn to play in close proximity to one another. In many cases this simply involves setting out play materials and activities within the same general physical space that are highly motivating to both novice and expert players.

To stimulate the children's social awareness and interest in one another's play, it is best to place similar, identical or related sets of toys and props within the same space. These should be logically arranged within a clearly delimited space. Table tops, small carpeted areas and large buckets are practical for this purpose.

A variety of play things naturally lend themselves to parallel play when laid out in this fashion. Hands-on types of play activities involving sensory exploration (e.g., water and sand play), construction (blocks and Legos) and arts and crafts (clay and play dough, drawing, painting, beadwork) are all examples. Certain commercially available products are also geared to parallel play. For example, water and sand play activity tables, Lego and Duplo table tops, and multi-sided art easels are all designed to accommodate several players. Finally, parallel play may also be stimulated by engaging children in more physically active play using larger props. For instance, setting up several large boxes in the same space will undoubtedly draw children to explore them alongside one another.

Joint Focus

Another play guidance strategy involves fostering opportunities for novice and expert players to establish a joint focus in play. This strategy is appropriate for novice players who are beginning to take an active interest in peers and their activities, but have not yet moved beyond playing independently beside them. The idea

PEER PLAY AND THE AUTISM SPECTRUM

is to guide novice and expert players to continue to play alongside one another by attending to separate parts of the same prop or play activity. While doing so, the children may be encouraged to informally exchange and take turns with materials that relate to the play.

Certain types of play materials and activities are particularly conducive to establishing a joint focus in play. A dollhouse is a prime example, as each child may attend to and interact with different props in separate rooms in the house. A miniature garage is a similar toy that may appeal to children who are interested in manipulating gears and such. Marble mazes offer the same type of appeal as children are able to play by dropping marbles in separate openings of the same toy. A musical instrument such as a xylophone is also likely to attract children to hit the different keys alongside one another. A tool bench that accommodates several players is great for children who are at any level of play – manipulation, functional or pretend.

On a larger scale, children may be drawn to explore different parts of a play structure that has separate openings, spaces and activities. For example, pop-up structures that connect cubes and tubes are commercially available. And it is simple to combine several big boxes to simulate a play house with different rooms or a train with several connecting railway cars.

It is also possible for children to establish a joint focus on a single play activity that is not as physically well defined as in the above examples. For instance, a novice and expert player may attend to different parts of a single doll whereby one child braids the doll's hair and the other child puts on the doll's socks. Given a large refrigerator box and a variety of paints and markers, children will likely be drawn to explore and interact with the box in different ways; some children may go inside and play, while others may decorate the outside of the box.

Joint Action

Many novice players reach a place in their development at which they require support to establish joint action in play with peers. This play guidance strategy is especially appropriate for children who actively show an interest in playing with peers, but have difficulty coordinating play activities. For many young and more involved children, an initial focus may be on guiding them to engage in a few brief reciprocal play exchanges involving joint action. For more advanced children, the focus may be on fostering more frequent and extended reciprocal play exchanges involving joint action.

There are a variety of ways to enhance opportunities for joint action. One way is introduce activities that stimulate joint action rituals. Many children delight in activities that follow "peek-a-boo" and "hide-and-seek" themes. Blankets and big boxes are especially appropriate for stimulating reciprocal play with variations on these themes. For instance, the children may take turns hiding in a large box and popping up like a jack-in-the-box. A number of sensory games are also conducive to joint action play. One of our favorites is the "human burrito." Here the children take turns lying on a blanket or large piece of spandex that is placed on the floor. They next add "imaginary" fixings (e.g., rice, beans, hot sauce) and roll the child up like a burrito. Variations include "human hamburgers" using large pillows as buns, and "human cookie dough" using large plastic or cardboard tubes as rolling pins.

Another way to stimulate joint action is to set out props and materials that are highly motivating and naturally lend themselves to this type of play. Trains are well suited for this purpose, as novice and expert players will need to coordinate their actions to set up the track, tunnels and bridges, and then run the train along the track. If there are two trains and two players, they will need to coordinate their actions to avoid running into each other (or perhaps to purposely crash into each other, as is often the case in true play). If there is only one train and two or more players, the children will need to take turns running the single train along the track. In this case, the other players may coordinate their actions with the train conductor by engaging in other parts of the activity, such as ringing a bell or lifting the railroad crossing sign at the appropriate moment.

Constructive play is also highly conducive to joint action play. Novice and expert players may be encouraged to combine separate structures or build a single structure together from the start. To combine separate structures, the play guide might suggest that the players add blocks to create a bridge from one building to the other. To build a single structure requires a more coordinated effort as the children must take turns adding blocks to the structure.

Another common approach to establishing joint action in play involves guiding children to formally take turns. There are many ways to stimulate turn-taking utilizing verbal, visual and physical cues or "turn-taking markers." The idea is to introduce rituals that are fun and easy for the players to follow and institute on their own. A most delightful approach developed by Beyer and Gammeltoft (1999) involves one child passing a hat to another to indicate whose turn is next in an activity or game. Another approach involves holding up a picture or sign that lets the players know whose turn it is. For example, an arrow may be pointed in the direction of the next player after each child takes a turn while playing a game.

Role Enactment

Role enactment is another play guidance technique that may be adapted for novice players. This strategy involves guiding children to carry out conventional actions with realistic props to portray real-life activities with peers. While it may be applied to virtually any novice player regardless of developmental level, this strategy has particular appeal to children who have developed functional play and are on the cusp of pretend play.

The idea of role enactment is to guide novice players to participate at their level of interest and ability in play themes that are essentially orchestrated by more experienced players. Play themes generally are based on familiar routines or events that children experience in daily life (e.g., shopping, birthday parties, eating a meal). Within the context of these themes, novice players may take on roles by performing simple scripts with realistic props directed to themselves, peers and/or dolls. For instance, taking on the role of a daddy by pushing a baby doll in a stroller, taking on the role of cook in a restaurant by stirring a pot on a stove or taking on the role of a Disney character by dressing up in a costume.

Any child is capable of performing in a role without actually having to pretend to do something or be someone else. Even a child who is predisposed to ritualistic object play may enact roles as a part of a more complex play theme. For example, a child who has a particular inclination to manipulate objects through ritualistic banging may enact the role of construction worker within the context of a larger play theme of building with blocks. In this case the child might be given a construction worker's hat to wear and a plastic hammer with which to bang on the blocks as the other players construct a block tower.

Role-Playing

Role-playing involves guiding novice and expert players to take on imaginary roles within jointly constructed play themes. This strategy is similar to role enactment but on a more advanced level. It is aimed at children who are capable of comprehending and engaging in pretend play, but require assistance in integrating and coordinating play scripts with peers.

Role-playing focuses on guiding novice players to fully participate in sophisticated play scripts with expert players with an emphasis on guiding novice and expert players to establish a shared pretend framework. This involves guiding the players to synchronize imaginary roles by performing actions, constructing narratives, engaging in dialogue and incorporating props in a coordinated fashion.

When children co-create and act out pretend play scripts, they are essentially immersed in stories. Some stories are easier than others for novice players to follow. Familiar scripts that include a distinct cast of characters and a simple plot with a clear beginning, middle and end may offer a logical starting point for supporting novice players in role-playing. Pretending to eat in a restaurant is an example of a rather straightforward script as each child acts out a part in the role of cook, waiter and customer.

As novice players gain experience, they may increasingly participate in co-constructing more complex play scripts that consist of evolving stories. These types of scripts are often complicated for novice players to follow as the story unfolds by deviating from its original theme. Evolving stories usually incorporate multiple characters, subplots and tangential elements that take on a life and logic all their own. For instance, the script may begin with eating in a restaurant and evolve with monsters invading and carrying everyone off to outer space. The novice player may still be pretending to be the cook while the others have taken off in their spacecraft.

When play scripts consist of evolving stories, expert players are often better equipped than adults to explain to novice players what is happening from one moment to the next. The play guide must therefore redirect the children to one another by asking questions, commenting and reframing the play event as needed (see Chapter 9). For instance, the play guide might reframe the event by mentioning that since not everyone made it on the spacecraft, the monsters need to go back and get the cook so he can feed them in outer space. At times the play guide may also need to coach the players to "freeze-frame" and replay particular scenes from the story script so that the novice player may follow along and participate more fully.

There are also times when novice players create their own subplots, but need support integrating them into a larger play theme. For instance, the child pretends to be lost in outer space and wanders away from the spacecraft where the other players are gathered. In such cases it is important to allow the child to build and refine his imagination, but to keep him connected to his peers using elements from the story. For example, the adult might suggest that a peer throw out an imaginary lifeline or send a rescue spacecraft to bring the lost space traveler back to the mother ship.

It is worth noting that some novice players (particularly children with Asperger Syndrome) are inclined to dictate how a pretend play script should be carried out in an attempt to literally recreate a familiar scene from a book or video. When handled appropriately, this can result in very positive experiences for all the players. For this to occur, however, a precedent needs to be set that is clearly understood by all players. Every child must be given an equal opportunity to be a director – no one child may direct all the time. Moreover, the director should have free reign to adapt or vary the script; she does not have to follow any set story. To reinforce this, it may be helpful to use a visual tool that denotes who is the director for a particular period of time, such as giving a child a megaphone or clapboard and a cap to wear as used by film directors.

An especially lovely example of a more sophisticated role-playing activity was carried out by a very talented speech and language therapist with an older group of children that included a 9-year-old boy with Asperger Syndrome. The focus of the intervention for this novice player was to establish common goals with peers as well as develop more flexibility, creativity and imagination. The children participated in activities that reflected a shared interest in television. They were first given the task of coming up with a plan to make a television out of a large refrigerator box. This involved writing out each of their roles and the steps they would take to draw, cut out and decorate the box. The children next wrote television commercials as an open-ended activity. In the end the children played in the box by taking turns putting on shows during which they presented the commercials. The following are examples of the expert and novice players' creations.

Expert Player's Commercial

Rid-a-Sis

Tired of your sister hogging the bathroom? Or being dragged to Mervyn's for a half-off shoe sale? We have a solution for you. Rid-a-sis can help.

We will take your sister and replace it with a brother that will obey your every command, and give you his allowance.

Just call 1-800-Rid-a-sis (from the makers of Rid-a-parents).

Or contact us at www.Rid-a-sis.com

Novice Player's Commercial

TripleStuf Oreo

Are you tired of Doublestuf oreo? Now you can get triplestuf oreo.

They're delicious and nutritious.

You can get Triplestuf oreo by calling 1-800-Triplestuf oreo or visit www.Triplestuf oreo.com

Are you tired of doublestuf? Take Triplestuf oreo now at stores everywhere.

Chapter Summary

This chapter focused on the practice of play guidance. This practice encompasses a variety of common-sense techniques that foster play within the child's zone of proximal development. Novice players are fully immersed in peer play experiences even if their participation is minimal. While participating in complex play events with more capable peers, they are able to practice and appropriate new and emerging skills. Play guidance techniques may be tailored to individual children and applied to a variety of social play situations. In the next and final chapter we will show how the practices of guided participation come together by presenting case illustrations of children in Integrated Play Groups.

CHAPTER 12

Case Illustrations of Children at Play

Chapter Highlights

This chapter shows how the practices of guided participation come together to support children in Integrated Play Groups. Three case illustrations will be presented featuring children of diverse ages and abilities:

▶ Luna's Play

▶ Max's Play

▶ Paulo's Play

Luna's Play

Luna is a 4-year-old girl who was diagnosed with autism at the age of 3. She concurrently receives special education support services in an integrated preschool and home-based program. She is described as having an aloof social style. She tends to ignore or avoid peers in social situations. She generally wanders on the periphery of peer groups when they congregate around play activities.

Luna has a particular fascination with water. She enjoys spending time in the bathtub pouring water in and out of containers. She also plays for long periods at the sink, running water through her fingers and over objects. Luna is nonverbal, but is beginning to use pictures to express her needs and make simple requests.

Luna participates in an Integrated Play Group at home with two expert players from her preschool class. The play groups meet twice a week for an hour in a play area set up in the living room. On sunny days they often move the group outdoors. Luna's mother and the home-based therapist alternate days taking the lead as play guide.

The focus of the intervention is on maximizing Luna's development in the following areas: (a) representational play with an emphasis on functional object play, (b) social play with an emphasis on establishing parallel play with peers, (c) social-communicative competence with an emphasis on establishing joint attention by initiating and responding more effectively and (d) expanding and diversifying her repertoire of play interests.

Table 12.1

Luna's Intervention

Play Scenario	Monitoring Play Initiations	Scaffolding Play	Social-Communi-cation Guidance	Play Guidance
The session opens with a ritual greeting and song. Luna's mother says, "It is sunny today, so let's play outside." She leads the children to the patio where a water table is prominently displayed. Floating in the water are several baby dolls, sponges, plastic bottles and containers of various sizes.	Recognize play initiation	Maximum Support – Directing and Modeling		Orienting
Pointing to the water table, Mother asks, "What do you want to play?" Melanie and Katie (expert players) immediately head to the water table and begin exploring the materials. Luna starts to head back inside to the kitchen sink.	Recognize play initiation	Intermediate Support – Verbal and Visual Cueing		Orienting

Play Scenario	Monitoring Play Initiations	Scaffolding Play	Social-Communication Guidance	Play Guidance
Mother says, "It looks like everyone wants to play with water. "Melanie and Katie, I think Luna might like to join you. Remember what we can do to get our friends to join us. Say 'Luna, look at the water in the tub.'" Melanie and Katie repeat this in unison, but Luna does not respond.	Interpret and respond to play initiation	Intermediate Support – Verbal and Visual Cueing	Reinforce cue – What to Say – "Look"	Orienting
Mother holds up a picture cue, "take hand," and models this by taking Luna by the hand and leading her to the water table and saying, "Look at the water." Katie follows by taking Luna's hand and leading her the rest of the way to the water table. Melanie calls out, "Look" while pouring water from a container.	Interpret and respond to play initiation	Maximum Support – Directing and Modeling	Reinforce cue – What to Do – "take hand" and What to Say – "Look"	Orienting
Luna immediately gravitates to the water table and grabs the container from Melanie's hand and begins pouring water over her fingers.	Recognize play initiation	Minimum Support – Standing By		
Mother says, "That's Luna's way of telling you that she likes playing in the water with you. Maybe you can get a different container and pour it over a baby doll – to wash the doll's hair."	Interpret and respond to play initiation	Intermediate Support – Verbal and Visual Cueing		Parallel Play/Joint Focus
Melanie and Katie both pick up baby dolls and pretend to wash them. Luna looks over and reaches out and touches Katie's doll.	Recognize play initiation	Minimum Support – Standing By		
Mother hands a doll to Luna and says, "Here's a doll for you. Do you want to wash the doll too?"	Interpret and respond to play initiation	Maximum Support – Directing and Modeling		Parallel Play/Joint Focus

Play Scenario	Monitoring Play Initiations	Scaffolding Play	Social-Communication Guidance	Play Guidance
Luna picks up the doll and dunks it head first in the water and repeats this action several times.	Recognize play initiation	Minimum Support – Standing By		
Mother says, "Look, the baby is diving in the water. Let's all make our baby dolls dive in the water like that."	Interpret and respond to play initiation	Intermediate Support – Verbal and Visual Cueing		Imitation-Mirroring
Katie and Melanie imitate Luna's actions. Luna takes notice and begins to giggle, which catches on – the three girls all giggle in unison as they dunk their baby dolls in and out of the water. Katie extends the script by saying that her baby is hungry. She pretends to feed the doll with a baby bottle. Melanie imitates Katie and feeds her doll with a second bottle. A moment later, Luna picks up a third baby bottle and holds it to her doll's lips.		Minimum Support – Standing By		

Max's Play

Max is a 7-year-old boy who was diagnosed with autism at the age of 4. He attends a special day class in a public elementary school. He has been described as having a passive social play style. Max rarely overtly initiates play with his peers. He has a tendency to remain isolated in social situations, but is beginning to show an interest in his peers. During free play he will watch and play beside other children, particularly when they engage in the few activities that are of interest to him.

Max has a limited repertoire of spontaneous play interests. He has a fascination with packaged and canned foods. He enjoys reading the labels on the packages, lining them up and sorting them by color and size. He often repeats television commercials and gazes at photographs of the products. Max's spontaneous communication consists primarily of immediate and delayed echolalia in which he repeats words and phrases.

Max participates in Integrated Play Groups with one other novice player from his class and three expert players from a third-grade general education class. His teacher is the play guide. The groups meet twice a week for 30 minutes in the afternoon.

The focus of the intervention is on extending Max's development in the following areas: (a) representational play (i.e., functional play) by enacting simple scripts around familiar routines with realistic props, (b) social play by establishing a common focus with peers, (c) social-communicative competence by increasing the rate of spontaneous initiations (using more effective verbal and nonverbal means) and (d) expanding and diversifying his repertoire of play interests.

Table 12.2

Max's Intervention

Play Scenario	Monitoring Play Initiations	Scaffolding Play	Social-Communication Guidance	Play Guidance
The session opens with a ritual greeting and a recap of the last session. The teacher asks the children to think of things they would like to play together. Max heads directly to the play grocery store and begins lining up tins on the shelf, reading aloud each package label. Ricky and Ute (expert players) gravitate to the grocery store and stand behind the cash register. Lisa and Nina (novice and expert players) say they would like to play dolls.	Recognize play initiation	Intermediate Support – Verbal and Visual Cueing		
The teacher suggests that Lisa and Nina go shopping with their babies while Max, Ute and Ricky work together in the store. Pointing to the picture cue, the teacher says, "Max and Ricky, why don't you take turns stocking the grocery shelves and stamping imaginary price labels on each item."	Interpret and respond to play initiation	Intermediate Support – Verbal and Visual Cueing	Reinforce cue – What to Do – "take turns"	Joint Action/ Role Enactment

Play Scenario	Monitoring Play Initiations	Scaffolding Play	Social-Communi-cation Guidance	Play Guidance
Together the boys line up tins, boxes and play food on the shelves. Using a plastic tube, Ricky pretends to stamp labels on some of the items, "Okay, 95 cents for Cocoa Puffs, 75 cents for Campbell's soup, 25 cents for spaghetti."		Minimum Support – Standing By		Joint Action/ Role Enactment
Pointing to a poster with a corresponding cue, the teacher tells Max to watch what Ricky is doing.		Intermediate Support – Verbal and Visual Cueing	Reinforces cue – What to Do – "watch"	
Max watches. Ricky next hands him a plastic tube and shows him how to "stamp" the rest of the items. Max takes the plastic tube and imitates the action by stamp-ing several new items and saying, "Cheerios, 25 cents, Rice-a-roni, 25 cents, Fritos corn chips, 25 cents … "		Minimum Support – Standing By		Joint Action/ Role Enactment
Meanwhile, Lisa and Nina begin loading a shopping cart with grocery items. Ute offers Max the role of bag boy while she runs the cash register. Max follows Ute and stands beside the cash regis-ter. Ute hands Max a paper bag and shows him how to hold it open. Max waits for further direction.	Recognize play initiation	Minimum Support – Standing By		
The teacher steps in and demonstrates each step of the check-out sequence. She suggests that Ute say "take" to Max, each time she gives him an item to put in the bag.	Interpret and respond to play initiation	Maximum Support – Directing and Modeling	Reinforce cue – What to Do – "take"	Joint Action/ Role Enactment

Play Scenario	Monitoring Play Initiations	Scaffolding Play	Social-Communi-cation Guidance	Play Guidance
The children establish a rhythm. Lisa and Nina take turns unloading the shopping cart one item at a time – Ute rings up each item on the cash register and hands the item to Max – Max puts each item in the grocery bag. When they finish checking out, Ute tells the shoppers, "Thank you for shopping at Lucky Supermarket, have a nice day." The shoppers say, "Thank you, bye-bye."		Minimum Support – Standing By		Joint Action/ Role Enactment
The teacher probes, "What should the bag boy say?" Ute tells Max to say, "Thank you, bye-bye, have a nice day," which Max repeats with a beaming smile.		Intermediate Support – Verbal Cueing	Introduce Cue – What to Say – "Thank you …"	Role Enactment

Paulo's Play

Paulo is a 9-year-old boy who was recently diagnosed with Asperger Syndrome. He is enrolled in the fourth grade in a private elementary school. He is described as having an active-odd social play style. He expresses a genuine desire for peer companionship, but has had little success in developing a mutual friendship. His peers frequently ignore his attempts to engage them for social interaction and play. Paulo tends to initiate in a one-sided and idiosyncratic fashion without consideration of his peers' perspectives. For example, he typically approaches peers by asking them if they have read a particular book, and then proceeds to recite lines from the book no matter what the response.

Paulo's play interests are consistent with themes generated from his most beloved books. His current favorite is the Harry Potter series by J. K. Rowling and he enjoys collecting figures and other paraphernalia represented in these stories. He spends much of his time organizing these toys and generating lists that depict the characters and key events. Paulo has also recently begun wearing Harry Potter eyeglasses that he picked up in a novelty shop.

Twice a week for 30 minutes Paulo participates in an Integrated Play Group with three of his classmates in an after-school program located on his school site. The play groups are facilitated by a speech and language therapist (SLP) as the play guide.

The focus of the intervention is on maximizing Paulo's development in the following areas: (a) representational play at an advanced level of symbolic pretend (to foster more flexible imagination and creative expression), (b) social play by establishing a common focus and common goals with peers, (c) social-communicative competence by establishing social reciprocity with peers by carrying on conversations and coordinating socio-dramatic scripts and (d) expanding and diversifying his repertoire of play interests.

Table 12.3

Paulo's Intervention

Play Scenario	Monitoring Play Initiations	Scaffolding Play	Social-Communi-cation Guidance	Play Guidance
The session opens with a ritual greeting and a recap of the last session. The SLP asks the children to come up with ideas and a plan for what they would like to play together. She prepares to write the different ideas on the board. Paulo immediately tells Lisa, Lori and Ray (expert players) that the plan for the day is to make Harry Potter books.	Recognize play initiation	Intermediate Support – Verbal and Visual Cueing		
The SLP reminds Paulo, "One of the goals of play groups is to 'cooperate.' That means each member may make a suggestion (which may be different from your suggestion). The next step is to make a plan together that everyone agrees upon. So Paulo, your suggestion is to make Harry Potter books. Why don't you ask the others what they'd like to play?" While facing the SLP, Paulo begins … The SLP quietly redirects him to the social-communication poster, "Don't forget that we need to face our friends when we talk to them." Paulo faces Lisa and asks, "What do you want to play?"	Interpret and respond to play initiations	Intermediate Support – Verbal and Visual Cueing	Reinforce cues – What to Do – "Face your friends when you talk to them" What to Say – "What do you want to play?"	Joint Focus

Play Scenario	Monitoring Play Initiations	Scaffolding Play	Social-Communication Guidance	Play Guidance
Lisa suggests putting on a puppet show. Lori says she'd like to do the same … Ray begins, but Paulo interrupts.		Minimum Support – Standing By		
The SLP points again to the social-communication poster and reminds the children to "take turns" when speaking. Ray continues, and suggests that they make a space station model. The SLP writes the different ideas on the board and asks the children if they can think of a way to combine their different ideas.	Interpret and respond to play initiations	Intermediate Support – Verbal and Visual Cueing	Reinforce cue – What to Do – "Take turns when speaking"	Joint Action/ Role-Playing
Ray suggests building a model of Hogwarts School instead of a space station. Lisa and Lori suggest making stick puppets of all the Harry Potter characters. Paulo adds that he will be Harry Potter and assigns the other children roles from the book. "Ray, you be Ron Weasly, Lisa, you be Hermione, and Lori, you be Professor McGonnegal."		Minimum Support – Standing By		
The SLP coaches Paulo to ask each of the others if they agree with their roles, which they do. The SLP next provides the children with markers and a pad of paper to write out the different steps of their plan. "What is the first thing you are going to do?" Ray and Paulo agree to make the model while Lori and Lisa make the puppets. A discussion continues on what materials they will need and how they will make their creations. After several minutes they come up with a simple plan.		Intermediate Support – Verbal and Visual Cueing	Reinforce cues – What to Do – "Face your friends when you talk to them"	Joint Action/ Role-Playing

Play Scenario	Monitoring Play Initiations	Scaffolding Play	Social-Communi- cation Guidance	Play Guidance
The SLP brings an assortment of art materials to the table and helps Ray and Paulo secure a cardboard base for the model.		Maximum Support – Directing and Modeling		Joint Action
The children spend half the session creating the model and puppets. The SLP occasionally interjects to guide the conversation by suggesting the children ask questions, make comments and exchange materials and ideas (e.g., What are you making? That looks cool! May I borrow that? Please, help me …).		Intermediate Support – Verbal and Visual Cueing	Reinforce cues – What to Do – "Take turns when speaking" What to Say – (see examples in play scenario)	Joint Action
They next begin acting out a simple script directed by Paulo. Lisa and Lori deviate from the script with protests from Paulo.	Recognize play initiation	Minimum Support – Standing By		Role-Playing
The SLP interjects by reminding the children (for Paulo's sake) that another goal of the play group is to be creative and use your imagination – that means it is okay to change the story so that it is different from the original. She suggests that next time they meet, the children write their own story script – Harry Potter can have new adventures.	Interpret and respond to play initiation	Intermediate Support – Verbal and Visual Cueing		Role-Playing
Ray suggests that Harry Potter can do magic to go into outer space. Paulo appears a bit uneasy but then adds, "Okay, Harry Potter can go to outer space, but only if he wears his invisibility cloak."		Minimum Support – Standing By		

Chapter Summary

This chapter concludes our discussion of guided participation. Guided participation as applied to the Integrated Play Groups intervention translates into a carefully tailored system of support. Case illustrations, featuring children of diverse ages and abilities, were presented to highlight the practices of guided participation. Play scenarios showed how play guides blended the practices of monitoring play initiations, scaffolding play, social-communication guidance and play guidance to promote skills within each child's zone of proximal development.

Phase IV Hands-On Activities

(See Phase IV Tools and Field Exercises)

Field Exercises

Conduct the following field exercises that correspond to Phase IV – Guided Participation in Play: IPG Intervention

- Field Exercise 12 – Social-Communication Cues
- Field Exercise 13 – Open-Ended Play Activity/Theme
- Field Exercise 14 – Role-Play Guiding an IPG Session

IPG Guided Participation Evaluation

As you begin implementing Integrated Play Groups, reflect on your practice by conducting an IPG Guided Participation Evaluation.

Self-Reflection Log for Play Guides

As you begin implementing Integrated Play Groups, reflect on your practice by recording your experiences using the Self-Reflection Log for Play Guides.

Phase IV Tools and Field Exercises

IPG Intervention Tools

- Guided Participation Evaluation
- Self-Reflection Log for IPG Guides

INTEGRATED PLAY GROUPS INTERVENTION TOOL
Guided Participation Evaluation

Play Guide:

Novice Player(s):

Date of Evaluation:

Reflect on how you are addressing the following objectives.

Objectives	Comments
• Fostering spontaneous, mutually enjoyed and reciprocal play • Expanding/diversifying the child's social and symbolic play repertoire • Enhancing peer-mediated play with minimal adult guidance	

Reflect on how you are applying the following practices.

Practices	Comments
Monitoring Play Initiations Recognizing, interpreting and responding to novice player's spontaneous play initiations: • Acts directed to objects, self and others • Conventional/unconventional acts • Overt-subtle-obscure forms of communication	
Scaffolding Play Systematically adjusting assistance to child/group: • Maximum Support – Directing and Modeling • Intermediate Support – Verbal/Visual Cueing • Minimal Support – Standing By	
Social-Communication Guidance Breaking down verbal/nonverbal cues for novice and expert players to: • Initiate play with peers • Respond to peer social overtures • Join/enter established play events with peers • Maintain/expand reciprocal exchanges in play	
Play Guidance Fully immersing novices in peer play events within "zone of proximal development" • Orienting • Imitation-Mirroring • Parallel Play • Joint Focus • Joint Action • Role Enactment • Role-Playing	

Wolfberg, P. J. (2003). *Peer play and the autism spectrum: The art of guiding children's socialization and imagination.* Shawnee Mission, KS: Autism Asperger Publishing Company.

INTEGRATED PLAY GROUPS INTERVENTION TOOL
Self-Reflection Log for Play Guides

Reflect on your experiences as a play guide. Note impressions, ideas, speculations, feelings, biases and concerns as you carry out Integrated Play Groups.

ENTRY DATE:

_____

_____

_____

_____

_____

_____

_____

ENTRY DATE:

_____

_____

_____

_____

_____

_____

_____

ENTRY DATE:

_____

_____

_____

_____

_____

_____

_____

Wolfberg, P. J. (2003). *Peer play and the autism spectrum: The art of guiding children's socialization and imagination.* Shawnee Mission, KS: Autism Asperger Publishing Company.

Phase IV Tools and Field Exercises

Field Exercises 12-14

- 12 – Social-Communication Cues
- 13 – Open-Ended Play Activity/Theme
- 14 – Role-Play Guiding an IPG Session

GUIDED PARTICIPATION IN PLAY
Field Exercise 12: Social-Communication Cues

Based on your preliminary assessment, generate at least two social-communication cues using visual supports that may be accessed by and adapted for both novice and expert players (please refer to Chapter 10).

Social-Communication Cue:

Social-Communication Cue:

Wolfberg, P. J. (2003). *Peer play and the autism spectrum: The art of guiding children's socialization and imagination.* Shawnee Mission, KS: Autism Asperger Publishing Company.

Field Exercise 13: Open-Ended Play Activity/Theme

Based on your preliminary assessment, generate at least one open-ended play activity or theme that is highly motivating for the novice and expert players and maximizes the novice player's social, communicative and symbolic development (please refer to Chapters 8-10).

Step 1	Identify an open-ended play activity or theme that corresponds to the novice player's play preference/initiation.
Step 2	List play materials and props needed to support the play; describe how these will be arranged and presented.
Step 3	Establish initial roles/partnerships for novice and expert players.
Step 4	Generate a list of ways to stimulate and extend the play, including actions, dialogue, questions, comments, visual cues.

Wolfberg, P. J. (2003). *Peer play and the autism spectrum: The art of guiding children's socialization and imagination.* Shawnee Mission, KS: Autism Asperger Publishing Company.

Field Exercise 14: Role-Play Guiding an
Integrated Play Group Session

With members of your team, role-play guiding an Integrated Play Group session from start to finish. Refer to the intervention tool, Guided Participation Evaluation, to reflect on your practice. Feel free to incorporate previous field exercises to support the role-play (please refer to Chapters 8-12).

Step 1	Choose a role and get into character (Hint: Novice and expert players may be based on actual children you know).
	Play Guide Novice Player(s) Expert Players
Step 2	Begin the play session with an opening ritual (please refer to Field Exercises 7, 8 and 9).
Step 3	Guide the players in an open-ended play activity/theme (please refer to Field Exercise 13).
Step 4	End the session with a closing ritual (please refer to Field Exercise 8).
Step 5	As a team, reflect on your practice by discussing the various components of the Guided Participation Evaluation.

Wolfberg, P. J. (2003). *Peer play and the autism spectrum: The art of guiding children's socialization and imagination.* Shawnee Mission, KS: Autism Asperger Publishing Company.

Epilogue

In my quest to bring this book to completion, I have been digging through the many artifacts I have collected from Integrated Play Groups over the past decade. Strewn across the floor are photographs of children and layers of their artwork (colorful designs and images of objects and people), creations used as tools in play (make-believe bank checks, admission tickets, birthday cards, awards) and the many stories and letters children have written. Alongside these are piles of documents collected from practitioners and families who have openly shared their experiences in their practice and day-to-day lives with children on the autism spectrum. Like Marcel Proust – whose stream-of-consciousness was sparked by the familiar taste of a Madeleine cookie *(À la recherche du temps perdu – Remembrance of Things Past 1913-27)* – I am flooded with visual images and narratives that transport me to the social and imaginary play worlds created by children in Integrated Play Groups and beyond. Knowing of so many children on the autism spectrum who have made their "passage to play culture" (see Wolfberg, 1999) is immensely fulfilling. It is my sincere hope that the information presented in this field manual will help to make this possible for many more children to come.

To offer inspiration to those who choose to embark on this journey, I'd like to conclude this book with the voices of novice and expert players, practitioners and families who have embraced the Integrated Play Groups model in the true spirit of play …

Novice Player Perspectives

I had fun playing grocery store. Yeah, I'm really sure, I guess I'm sure – okay.

> – 6-year-old girl with autism (personal communication)

I don't know what pretend is, but I like to do it.

> – 10-year-old girl with autism (Wolfberg, 1999, p. 13)

Play groups is learning about how to share, how to play new games we haven't done before. It also teaches us – explains to us about what it originally means to play daily in this school. Play groups explains how we play and expresses how our feelings – how we like to play … it perfectly describes this.

> – 9-year-old boy with Asperger Syndrome (personal communication)

Expert Player Perspectives

I help the children to make decisions on their own about what they'd like to play with. After they make their decisions, I play with them. Sometimes I have to help them take turns and share. When I first started play groups, I had a few problems playing with the children. I felt funny, and I was afraid of some of the children ... I stopped feeling funny and started to like them. We learned to play a special hide-n-go seek, and we learned to have patience with the children.

– 8-year-old neurotypical girl (Wolfberg, 1999, p. 157)

When I first started being a special friend it felt funny. It was really hard at first to play with all of the children. They ran away and did their own things. Later on it felt a little easier because they knew us better. Then ... we learned ways to communicate and play together. Th[at] was fun. A month later we were all good friends. I learned how to get along with all of them. I liked it very much because I never knew them before. I also learned to communicate with all the children.

– 8-year-old neurotypical boy (Wolfberg, 1999, p. 158)

Everyone wants to be in 'em [Integrated Play Groups] because it's fun.

– 8-year-old neurotypical boy
(Gonsier-Gerdin & Wolfberg, submitted for publication, p. 24)

Practitioner Perspectives

The past year [running Integrated Play Groups] has been a blast, and I know that all of the children have made positive gains from being involved in this program. The typical students have gained insight into autism, and have learned compassion and tolerance. All of the students involved have developed true friendships with their peers with autism. They are the first ones to sit by them at morning meeting, the first ones to pair up with them during gym class, and are protective of their friends. The benefits have clearly carried over into the mainstream setting. It truly is a passion ... (working with children with autism) ... It will be so nice starting the [next school] year feeling comfortable with what I am doing.

– Tara Tuchel – Special educator/SLP (personal communication)

Children are the guides to their growth process, and we are supporting them. Find your facilitative style, consider the age group, set the stage, and then proceed and try to let go of control.

– Special educator (O'Connor, 1999, p. 49)

[The Integrated Play Groups model has] added valuable tools to [my] bag of tricks.

– Special educator (O' Connor, 1999, p. 46)

Relax, trust the process, the model works.

– Special educator (O'Connor, 1999, p. 49)

Family Perspectives

[My 6-year-old son with autism] has made impressive progress in his social, communication and play skills [in Integrated Play Groups]. He is more responsive to other children and is gradually increasing his ability to initiate successful peer interactions. We've noted significant improvements in his cooperative play abilities, and he's beginning to develop symbolic/pretend play abilities. The teachers are convinced that the play groups have contributed significantly to the success of [his] kindergarten inclusion program, and at home we've seen a dramatic improvement in his ability to sustain playful interactions with visiting children. [He is] clearly enjoying peer interactions and play interludes far more than he did before the play groups began. His father and I feel that [he] is a much happier child than he was a year ago, and we're very pleased with the success of the program. I have developed tremendous respect for the efficacy of the Integrated Play Groups model, and I highly recommend this strategy for improving social, communication, and play skills in young children with autism.

– Parent of boy with autism
(reprinted from a newsletter with permission from the author)

Nina [7-year-old girl with autism] is still in part-time inclusion ... and doing VERY well – behaving saintly and loving being with her peers. Her language has grown considerably too.

Nina now has an expert playmate, Myra, we call her the play "stalker" – as all the tips you gave us make playdates with Nina highly valued by her peer classmates!

Myra demands playdates [with Nina] and upon arrival, Nina drops everything and announces "Let's play Barbies" – settles in to dress dolls and plays intensely! She also announces "It's time for pizza" – another ritual!

Her other friends, Cici and Lianne, still come regularly and the interactions definitely improve her behaviour and mood.

... Huh, and they say [children with autism] don't have any imagination ... Try telling that to a pair of my slacks, doubling as a river or the Tupperware top boat being bitten by a soft toy crocodile ... Ouch, it just bit me too ... time to go and play!

– Parent of 7-year-old girl with autism (personal communication)

Appendix A

Autism Institute on Peer Relations and Play - Center for Integrated Play Groups

► General Information

► Fact Sheet on Integrated Play Groups

The child shall have full opportunity for play and recreation, which should be directed to the same purpose as education; society and public authorities shall endeavor to promote the employment of this right.

United Nations Declaration of Human Rights, 1948, Principle 7

The AUTISM INSTITUTE ON PEER RELATIONS AND PLAY – CENTER FOR INTEGRATED PLAY GROUPS offers guidance and support to practitioners, families, researchers and others seeking to address the unique and complex challenges children on the autism spectrum experience in peer relations and play.

The aim of our institute (co-founded by Pamela J. Wolfberg, Ph.D. – author, educator, researcher – and Therese O'Connor, M.A. – education specialist, master play guide) is to expand national and international efforts to develop inclusive peer play programs for children based on the Integrated Play Groups (IPG) model.

Integrated Play Groups are designed to support children of diverse ages and abilities on the autism spectrum in natural play experiences with typical peers and siblings within school, home, therapy and community settings. Based on award-winning research, this model has been found to be effective in enhancing reciprocal social interaction, communication, play and imagination in children with autism, pervasive developmental disorder, Asperger syndrome and related social-communicative needs.

We offer a wide range of services and supports, including:

- Seminars – Courses
  Training – introductory, intermediate and mastery level
  Field Supervision

- Presentations

- General Consultation

- Evaluations

- Direct Intervention

- Research Activities

- Publications

- Resource Materials

For more information, contact

AUTISM INSTITUTE ON PEER RELATIONS AND PLAY
CENTER FOR INTEGRATED PLAY GROUPS

1882 – 22nd Avenue • San Francisco, CA 94122 • Phone: 415-753-5669
E-mail: pamela@wolfberg.com – thereseoc@earthlink.net
Web: www.wolfberg.com – www.autisminstitute.com

Wolfberg, P. J. (2003). *Peer play and the autism spectrum: The art of guiding children's socialization and imagination.* Shawnee Mission, KS: Autism Asperger Publishing Company.

Fact Sheet on Integrated Play Groups (IPG)

What are Integrated Play Groups?

The IPG model was created by Pamela J. Wolfberg, Ph.D. (author, educator, researcher), to address the unique and complex challenges children on the autism spectrum experience in peer relations and play. Integrated Play Groups consist of small groups of children on the autism spectrum (novice players) and typical peers/siblings (expert players) who regularly play together under the guidance of a qualified adult facilitator (play guide).

What is the purpose of Integrated Play Groups?

Research shows that peer play experiences are a vital part of children's learning, development and culture. Children on the autism spectrum face many obstacles playing and socializing with peers. Integrated Play Groups are designed to enhance children's social interaction, communication, play and imagination. An equally important focus is on teaching the peer group to be more accepting, responsive and inclusive of children who relate and play in different ways.

Who may participate in Integrated Play Groups?

Integrated Play Groups are customized as a part of a child's individual education/therapy program. The IPG model is appropriate for preschool and elementary-aged children (3 to 11 years).

Play groups are made up of 3 to 5 children, with a higher ratio of expert to novice players. Novice players include children of all abilities on the autism spectrum and with related special needs. Expert players include typical peers/siblings with strong social, communication and play skills.

Where and when do Integrated Play Groups take place?

Integrated Play Groups take place in natural play environments within school, home, therapy or community settings. Play groups generally meet twice a week for 30- to 60-minute sessions over a six- to twelve-month period. Sessions are carried out in specially designed play spaces that include a wide range of motivating materials and activities.

How does an Integrated Play Group work?

Play sessions are tailored to the children's unique interests, abilities and needs. The adult methodically guides novice and expert players to engage in mutually enjoyed play activities that encourage reciprocal social interaction, communication and imagination – such as pretending, constructing, art, music, movement and interactive games. Gradually the children learn how to play together with less and less adult support.

What are the benefits of Integrated Play Groups?

As demonstrated through award-winning research, novice players have benefited in the areas of social interaction, communication, language, representational play and related symbolic activity (writing and drawing). Expert players have benefited by showing greater self-esteem, awareness, empathy and acceptance of individual differences. Both novice and expert players have formed mutual friendships while having fun together.

For more information, contact

Autism Institute on Peer Relations and Play
Center for Integrated Play Groups

1882 – 22nd Avenue • San Francisco, CA 94122 • Phone: 415-753-5669
E-mail: pamela@wolfberg.com – thereseoc@earthlink.net
Web: www.wolfberg.com – www.autisminstitute.com

Wolfberg, P. J. (2003). *Peer play and the autism spectrum: The art of guiding children's socialization and imagination.* Shawnee Mission, KS: Autism Asperger Publishing Company.

Appendix B

Efficacy of the Integrated Play Groups Model: Research Highlights

► Research Focused on Novice Players (Children on the Autism Spectrum)

► Research Focused on Expert Players (Typical Peers)

► Research Focused on Play Guides (Practitioners)

► Research Focused on Families

► Summary of Benefits for Novice and Expert Players

The Integrated Play Groups model originated as a pilot project in an urban elementary school with the aim of guiding children with autism and related conditions to play and socialize with typically developing peers (Wolfberg, 1988). The model has since been transformed in an effort to keep pace with rapidly expanding knowledge about autism spectrum disorders and more than a decade of related research and practice (Gonsier-Gerdin, 1993; O'Connor, 1999; Wolfberg, 1988, 1994, 1999; Wolfberg & Schuler, 1992, 1993; Zercher et al., 2001). Research focused on novice players, expert players, play guides and families are summarized in the following tables.

Research Focused on Novice Players (Children on the Autism Spectrum)

Investigation	Focal Participants	Play Group Composition	Setting	Methods	Findings
Wolfberg, 1988 (pilot study)	4 novice players – 2 boys/2 girls (ages 9 to 10 years) with mild to severe autism	2 play groups of 5 children (2 novices/3 experts per group); mixed ages ranging from 8 to 10 years	30-minute IPG sessions/2 x per week for school term (9 months) in elementary school; led by special educator	Preliminary videotape observational analysis of social interaction and play with peers	Initial observations: • Gains in social interaction and play detected for each novice within first 3 months • Generalization to other social settings involving peers noted at end of school year Note: Tentative findings inspired large-scale investigation to field-test and refine the IPG model
Wolfberg & Schuler, 1992 (large-scale investigation)	38 novice players (ages 5 to 11 years) with mild to severe autism and related special needs	20+ play groups of 3 to 5 children (varied combinations novice and expert players), ages 5 to 11 years	IPG sessions with varied time frames carried out in 10 elementary school sites; led by teachers and speech and language therapists	Evaluation of 3-year model demonstration project using quantitative (see 1993 study) and qualitative (survey/interview) methods to validate IPG model and its impact on children with special needs	Teachers/SLPs reported: • Children interacted more naturally in IPGs than in other integrated situations • Novice and expert players become like a family • Greater reciprocity was found among novice and expert players • Certain novice players required extra support to "fit in" • Rituals are an important part of the play group experience for children • Play groups are therapeutic • Play groups offer children a "safe haven" to play with little outside pressure • Play groups provide more opportunities for social relationships than simply mainstreaming students in general education classes

Research Focused on Novice Players (Children on the Autism Spectrum) *continued*

Investigation	Focal Participants	Play Group Composition	Setting	Methods	Findings
Wolfberg & Schuler, 1993 (seminal study – part of 1992 large-scale investigation)	3 novice players – boys (age 7 years) – with moderate to severe autism	3 play groups of 5 children (2 novices/3 experts per group); all similar in age	30-minute IPG sessions/2 x per week for school term (9 months) in elementary school; led by special educator	Combined quantitative (multiple-baseline) and qualitative (observation/ interview) measures to investigate impact on social interaction, communication and play	Within first 3 months, each novice exhibited: • Decreases in isolate and stereotyped play • Increases in social play levels • Increases in functional and symbolic play • More diversified play End of term: • Language gains noted in two of the three children • Skills maintained when adult support was withdrawn after extended intervention • Skills generalized to other peers, settings, and social activity contexts
Wolfberg, 1994, 1999	3 novice players – 1 girl/ 2 boys (ages spanned 9 to 11 years while participating in IPG) – with mild to moderate autism	2 play groups of 5 children (2 novices/3 experts per group); mixed ages ranging from 8 to 11 years	30-minute IPG sessions/2 x per week for 2 school terms (18 months) in elementary school; led by special educator	Longitudinal ethnographic case analyses of social relations with peers and symbolic representation in play, language, writing and drawing	Novices showed similar developmental progression over time: • From isolate to more interactive/reciprocal peer play • From stereotyped/presymbolic to representational (functional/ pretend) play • Parallel symbolic transformations in language, writing and drawing • More diverse/complex forms of play in social vs. independent activity • Higher-level social capacities emerged before higher-level symbolic capacities • Combination of child characteristics (novice and expert) and social factors influenced changes

Research Focused on Novice Players (Children on the Autism Spectrum) *continued*

Investigation	Focal Participants	Play Group Composition	Setting	Methods	Findings
O'Connor, 1999	10 practitioners (7 preschool-kindergarten and 3 elementary special educators and speech and language therapists)	10+ play groups of 3 to 5 children (varied combinations novice and expert players); ages 3 to 11 years	IPG sessions with varied time frames carried out in preschool and elementary schools	As a part of a larger study, questionnaire/interviews included focus on play guide perceptions of benefits for novice players	Play guide perceptions of novice players: • Showed outward signs of sheer enjoyment while participating in IPG • Increases in eye contact, watching and imitating peers • Increases in social initiation and responsiveness • Increases in symbolic play levels • Increases in communication • Greater diversity of spontaneous play interests
Zercher et al., 2001 (replication of 1993 study)	2 novice players – twin boys (6 years) – with mild to moderate autism	1 group of 5 children (2 novices/3 experts); mixed ages ranging from 5 to 11 years	30-minute weekly sessions for 20 weeks in community-based setting (Sunday School class) led by doctoral student	Combined quantitative (multiple-baseline) and qualitative (observation/interview) measures to investigate impact on social interaction, communication/language and play	Novices exhibited: • Increases in shared social attention to objects • Increases in symbolic play acts • Increases in verbal utterances • Skills maintained when adult support withdrawn • Skills generalized to home setting

Research Focused on Expert Players (Typical Peers)

Investigation	Focal Participants	Play Group Composition	Setting	Methods	Findings
Wolfberg & Schuler, 1992 (large-scale investigation)	81 expert players (ages 5 to 11 years), who are typically developing	20+ play groups of 3 to 5 children (varied combinations novice and expert players); ages 5 to 11 years	IPG sessions with varied time frames carried out in 10 elementary school sites; led by teachers and speech and language therapists	Evaluation of 3-year model demonstration project using quantitative (see 1993 study) and qualitative (survey/interview) methods to validate IPG model and its impact on children with special needs	Play guides reported: • Children interacted more naturally in IPGs than in other integrated situations • Novice and expert players become like a family • Greater reciprocity was noted among novice and expert players • More acceptance of deviance was found than in other integrated contexts • Most students successfully incorporated use of strategies to engage in social interaction and play • Certain typical peers appeared to be more successful than others
Gonsier-Gerdin, 1993	11 expert players – 7 girls/ 4 boys (ages 6 to 9 years) – who are typically developing	3 play groups (1 to 2 novices/ 3 to 4 experts per group); mixed in ages	30-minute IPG sessions/2 x per week for 9 months in county-run class in elementary school; led by special educator	Semi-structured interviews (pre- and post), observations, and case study focusing on typical peer perceptions and experiences in IPG	Expert players: • Showed increased sensitivity, tolerance, acceptance of novice players' individual differences • Placed high value on expert player role involving a sense of responsibility to include novice players • Perceived play time as fun (as opposed to work) • Formed balanced/reciprocal relationships and mutual friendships with novice players that carried over to home/community • Identified, responded and incorporated novice players' unique play interests and idiosyncratic ways of relating/communicating into shared activities

Research Focused on Expert Players (Typical Peers) *continued*

Investigation	Focal Participants	Play Group Composition	Setting	Methods	Findings
Wolfberg, 1994, 1999	7 expert players – 4 girls/ 3 boys (ages 8 to 9 years) – who are typically developing	Participated in 4 play groups of 5 children (2 novices/ 3 experts per group); mixed ages ranging from 8 to 11 years	30-minute IPG sessions/ 2 x per week for two years in elementary school; led by special educator	Open-ended interviews with typical peers and observation as part of longitudinal ethnographic study	Expert player perceptions: • Retained identities as "kids" playing and having fun with added sense of responsibility to cooperate and include one another • Recognized need to put forth an effort to help novice players by adapting to their diverse interests and styles of communication • Perceived process of learning how to communicate and play together as growing easier as they gained familiarity and experience over time • Regarded novice players as "good friends" Expert players exhibited: • Different social play interaction styles and roles that afforded novice players different degrees of structure and support
O'Connor, 1999	10 practitioners (7 preschool-kindergarten and 3 elementary special educators and speech and language therapists)	10+ play groups of 3 to 5 children (varied combinations novice and expert players); ages 3 to 11 years	IPG sessions with varied time frames carried out in preschool and elementary schools	As a part of a larger study, questionnaire/ interviews included focus on play guide perceptions of benefits for expert players	Play guide perceptions of expert players: • Thoroughly enjoyed experience of participating in IPG • Increased self-esteem, confidence, assertiveness • Sense of pride in accomplishments • Increased awareness and acceptance of differences in others • More compassion, empathy and patience • Greater initiation and responsiveness toward the novice players

Research Focused on Play Guides (Practitioners)

Investigation	Focal Participants	Play Group Composition	Setting	Methods	Findings
Wolfberg & Schuler, 1992 (large-scale investigation)	19 special educators/ speech and language therapists	20+ play groups of 3 to 5 children (varied combinations novice and expert players); ages 5 to 11 years	IPG sessions with varied time frames carried out in 10 elementary school sites by teachers and speech and language therapists	Evaluation of 3-year model demonstration project using quantitative (see 1993 study) and qualitative (survey/interview) methods to validate IPG model and its impact on children with special needs	Play guide perspectives: • Guiding play groups gets easier over time • Play guides need to give up control stance to be effective • Play guides need to adopt the philosophy and values of the IPG model • There is a need for ongoing training and support • There is a desire to train others, but release time and support is needed
O'Connor, 1999	10 practitioners (7 preschool-kindergarten and 3 elementary special educators and speech and language therapists)	10+ play groups of 3 to 5 children (varied combinations novice and expert players); ages 3 to 11 years	IPG sessions with varied time frames carried out in preschool and elementary schools	Questionnaire/ interviews focusing on play guide perceptions of influences on own practice and competencies needed for success	Play guide perception of influences on own practice: • Better observation and assessment skills • More focused understanding of social and play goals • How not to underestimate the potential of children • How better to select and set up play activities • How to be more creative, facilitative and less directive/intrusive • How better to explain to parents what they might do to support their children in play Play guide recommendation for continued success: • Need for ongoing supervision and consultation following initial training • Creating collaborative Integrated Play Groups teams to meet and support one another on a regular basis • Providing opportunities to observe other play guides in action • Reflecting on one's practice by reviewing videotapes of oneself in action • Involving parents more to enhance generalization as well as to empower the families

Research Focused on Families

Investigation	Focal Participants	Play Group Composition	Setting	Methods	Findings
Wolfberg & Schuler, 1993 (seminal study – part of 1992 large-scale investigation)	Mothers of 3 novice players – boys (age 7 years) – with moderate to severe autism	3 play groups of 5 children (2 novices/ 3 experts per group); all similar in age	30-minute IPG sessions/ 2 x per week for 9 months in elementary school led by special educator	As a part of larger study, semi-structured interviews were conducted with parents of novice players participating in IPG to establish generalization and social validation	Parents noted observable differences in the play and social behavior of their children that carried over from the school to the home setting: • More diversified play repertoires • Socially appropriate attachments to dolls and stuffed animals that were not present prior to play groups • Formation of peer friendships • Improvements of sibling relationships • Reductions in aberrant behavior
O'Connor, 1999	10 practitioners (7 preschool-kindergarten and 3 elementary special educators and speech and language therapists)	10+ play groups of 3 to 5 children (varied combinations novice and expert players); ages 3 to 11 years	IPG sessions with varied time frames carried out in preschool and elementary schools	As a part of larger study, questionnaire /interviews included focus on play guide reports of feedback from parents of novice players	Play guides recounted parent reports: • Generalization of skills learned in IPG to the home • Increased levels of social and symbolic play in their children • More frequent and sustained play interactions with peers and siblings • Incidences of children showing greater tolerance for people and new social situations • Improvements in social and communication skills at home
Zercher et al., 2001 (replication of 1993 study)	Mother and father of twin boys (6 years) with mild to moderate autism	1 group of 5 children (2 novices/ 3 experts) mixed ages ranging from 5 to 11 years	30-minute weekly sessions for 20 weeks in community-based setting (Sunday School class) led by doctoral student	As a part of larger study, interviewed parents after viewing randomly selected video segments of novice players in baseline and intervention IPG sessions.	Parents noted that their children: • Ignored peers prior to intervention • Became more aware of presence of peers and what they were doing • Interacted more frequently with peers • Improved social skills • Played games and engaged in conversations with peers during intervention period

Summary of Benefits of the Integrated Play Groups Model*	
Novice Players	**Expert Players**
• More frequent and sustained social interaction and play with peers – decreased isolate play • Advances in representational play, developmentally/age-appropriate play – decreased stereotyped play • Advances in related symbolic activity (writing and drawing) • Improved social-communication skills • Improved language skills in verbal children • More diverse range of play interests • Higher degree of spontaneous social engagement (initiation and responsiveness) with peers • Increased affect – emotional expression • Sheer enjoyment – "fun factor" • Formation of reciprocal relationships – friendships with peers	• Greater awareness, tolerance, acceptance of individual differences • Greater empathy, compassion and patience for others • Increased self-esteem, confidence, sense of pride in accomplishments • Increased sense of responsibility to cooperate and include others • Ability to adapt to children's different play interests and ways of relating and communicating • Sheer enjoyment – "fun factor" • Formation of reciprocal relationships – friendships with atypical peers

*Based on the accumulated findings of Gonsier-Gerdin, 1993; O'Connor, 1999; Wolfberg, 1988, 1994, 1999; Wolfberg & Schuler, 1992, 1993; Zercher et al. (2001).

Appendix C

Resources

▶ Autism Spectrum Organizations

▶ Related Special Needs Organizations

▶ Play and Child Development Organizations

▶ Toys and Playthings

▶ Play Equipment and Environments

▶ Selected Books for Children

▶ Selected Reading on Autism, Play and Peer Relations

Autism Spectrum Organizations

Asperger Syndrome Coalition of the U.S. (ASC-US)
P.O. Box 351268
Jacksonville, FL 32235-1268
Web: www.asperger.org
Phone: (866) 4-ASPRGR

AASCEND
P.O. Box 591011
San Francisco, CA 94159-1011
Web: www.aascend.org
E-mail: autmon@hotmail.com
Phone: (415) 460-1662

Autism Links: Worldwide
Web: www.autismuk.com/index6.htm

Autism Network International (ANI)
P.O. Box 35448
Syracuse NY 13235-5448
Web: www.ani.autistics.org

Organization for Autism Research (OAR)
2111 Wilson Boulevard, Suite 600
Arlington, VA 22201
Web: www.autismorg.com
E-mail: OAR@autismorg.com
Phone: (703) 351-5031

Autism – PDD Resources Network
Web: www.autism-pdd.net

Autism Research Institute
4182 Adams Avenue
San Diego, CA 92116,
Web: www.autismresearchinstitute.com

Autism Society of America
7910 Woodmont Avenue, Suite 300
Bethesda, MD 20814-3067
Web: www.autism-society.org
E-mail: info@autism-society.org
Phone: (301) 657-0881 or (800) 3AUTISM

Autism Society of Canada
P.O. Box 65
Orangeville, ONT L9W
Web: autismsocietycanada.ca
E-mail: info@autismsocietycanada.ca
Phone: (519) 942-8720/Toll Free: (866) 874-3334

The Center for the Study of Autism (CSA)
P.O. Box 4538
Salem, OR 97302
Web: www.autism.tv

Families for Early Autism Treatment
Web: www.feat.org

**Friend 2 Friend: Helping Children Understand
Autism Spectrum Disorder**
Heather McCracken
596 Blueridge Avenue
North Vancouver, BC VTR 2J2
Web: www.members.shaw.ca/friend2friend
Phone: (604) 980-0881

Geneva Centre for Autism
250 Davisville Avenue, Suite 200
Toronto, ONT M4S 1H2
Web: www.genevacentre.com
E-mail: info@autism.net
Phone: (416) 322-7877

Maap Services, Inc.
P.O. Box 524
Crown Point, IN 46307
Web: www.maapservices.org
Email: chart@netnitco.net
Phone: (219) 662-1311

MIND Institute
UC Davis Medical Center
4860 Y Street, Room 3020
Sacramento, CA 95817
Web: http://mindinstitute.ucdmc.ucdavis.edu/
Phone: (888) 883-0961

National Alliance for Autism Research (NAAR)
99 Wall St., Research Park
Princeton, NJ 08540
Web: www.naar.org
E-mail: naar@naar.org
Phone: (888) 777-NAAR

National Autistic Society
393 City Road
London, EC1V 1NG - United Kingdom
Web: www.nas.org.uk
E-mail: nas@nas.org.uk
Phone: +44 (0)20 7833 2299

United Autism Alliance
1612 W. Olive Avenue, Suite #201
Burbank, CA 91506
Web: www.unitedautismalliance.org
E-mail: info@unitedautismalliance.org
Phone: (818) 953-3855

Related Special Needs Organizations

American Occupational Therapy Association
4720 Montgomery Lane
P.O. Box 31220
Bethesda, MD 20824-1220
Web: www.aota.org
Phone: (301) 652-2682/TDD: (800) 377-8555

American Speech-Language-Hearing Association
10801 Rockville Pike
Rockville, MD 20852
Web: www.asha.org
E-mail: actioncenter@asha.org
Phone (voice/TTY): Professionals/Students: (800) 498-2071
Public: (800) 638-8255

The Association for Persons with Severe Handicaps (TASH)
29 W. Susquehanna Avenue, Suite 210
Baltimore, MD 21204
Web: www.tash.org
E-mail: aswann@tash.org
Phone: (410) 828-8274

Circle of Friends
Centre for Integrated Education and Community
24 Thome Crescent
Toronto, ONT M6H255
Phone: (416) 658-5363

**Council for Exceptional Children
(CEC)**
1110 North Glebe Road, Suite 300
Arlington, VA 22201-5704
Web: www.cec.sped.org
Phone: (888) CEC-SPED/(703) 620-3660/TTY: (703) 264-9446

Easter Seals
Office of Public Affairs
700 Thirteenth Street, N.W., Suite 200
Washington, DC 20005
Web: www.easter-seals.org
E-mail: info@easter-seals.org
Phone: (202) 347-3066

Hanen Centre: Family-Focused Early Language Intervention
Suite 403 – 1075 Bay street
Toronto, ONT M5S 2B1
Web: www.hanen.org
E-mail: info@hanen.org
Phone: (416) 921-1073

Interdisciplinary Council on Developmental and Learning Disorders
4938 Hampden Lane, Suite 800
Bethesda, MD 20814
Web: www.icdl.com
Phone: (301) 656-2667

National Information Center for Children and Youth with Handicaps (NICHCY)
P.O. Box 1492
Washington, DC 20013-1492
Web: www.nichcy.org
E-mail: nichcy@aed.org
Phone: (Voice/TTY) (800) 695-0285/(202) 884-8200

Play and Child Development Organizations

Association for Childhood Education International (ACEI)
17904 Georgia Avenue, Suite 215
Olney, MD 20832-2277
Web: www.udel.edu/bateman/acei/
E-mail: aceihq@aol.com
Phone: (800) 423-3563/(301) 570-2111

Association for Play Therapy, Inc.
2050 N. Winery Avenue, Suite 101
Fresno, CA 93703
Web: www.iapt.org
E-mail: info@a4pt.org
Phone: (559) 252-2278

High/Scope Educational Research Foundation
600 N. River Street
Ypsilanti, MI 48198-2898
Web: high/scopeglobal.com
Phone: (800) 442-4329
E-mail: info@highscope.org

Childswork/Childsplay
135 Dupont Street
P.O. Box 760
Plainview, NY 11803
Web: www.childswork.com
Phone: (800) 962-1141

**National Association for the Education of
Young Children (NAEYC)**
1509 - 16th Street, N.W.
Washington, DC 20036-1426
Web: www.naeyc.org
Phone: (800) 424-2460

**International Association for the
Child's Right to Play (IPA)**
U.S.A. Web: www.ipausa.org
Global Web: www.ipaworld.org

U.S.A. Representative:
Rhonda Clements
Graduate Physical Education
240 Hofstra University
Hempstead, NY 11548
Phone: (516) 463-5176
E-mail: hprrlc@hofstra.edu

International Representative:
Dr. Marcy Guddemi
CTB/McGraw-Hill
20 Ryan Ranch Rd.
Monterey, CA 93940
E-mail: mguddemi@ctb.com
Phone: (800) 538-9547 x7807

The Association for the Study of Play
Web: www.csuchico.edu/phed/tasp/
E-mail: mmfryer@aol.com
Phone: (301) 656-9479

Society for Research in Child Development (SRCD)
University of Michigan
3131 South State Street, Suite 302
Ann Arbor, MI 48108-1623
Web: www.srcd.org
E-mail: srcd@umich.edu
Phone: (734) 998-6578

Toys and Playthings

BRIO Corporation
P.O. Box 1013
N120 W 18485 Freistadt Road
Germantown, WI 53022
Web: www.briotoy.com
Phone: (888) 274-6869

Constructive Playthings
13201 Arrington Road
Grandview, IL 64030
Web: www.constplay.com
Phone: (800) 448-1412

Discovery Toys
P.O. Box 5023
Livermore, CA 94551
Web: www.discoverytoysinc.com
Phone: (800) 426-4777

HearthSong
Processing Center
P.O. Box 1050
Madison, VA 22727-1050
Web: www.hearthsong.com
Phone: (800) 325-2502

IKEA
Catalog orders/International site index
Web: www.ikea-usa.com
Phone: (800) 434-4532

Imaginarium
On-line orders/store locations
Web: www.imaginarum.com
Phone: (888) 696-5649

Lakeshore Learning Materials
2695 East Dominguez Street
Carson, CA 90749
Web: www.lakeshorelearning.com
Phone: (800) 428-4414

Learning Materials Workshop
274 North Winooski Avenue
Burlington, VT 05401
Web: www.learningmaterialswork.com
E-mail: info@learningmaterialswork.com
Phone: (800) 693-7164

Lekotek
2100 Ridge Avenue
Evanston, IL 60201
Web: lekotek@lekotek.org
Phone: (800) 573-4446

Manhattan Toy Group
430 First Avenue North, Suite 500
Minneapolis, MN 55401
Web: www.manhattantoy.com
Phone: (800) 541-1345

Purciful's Magical Toys
2350 34th Street
Lubbock TX 79411
Web: www.purcifuls-toys.com
E-mail: purcifuls@yahoo.com
Phone: (806) 239-2927

Play Equipment and Environments

Grounds for Play
1401 E. Dallas Street
Mansfield, TX 76063
Web: groundsforplay.com
Phone: (800) 552-7529

Leathers & Associates
Custom Designed Community-Built Projects
99 Eastlake Road
Ithaca, NY 14850
Web: www.leathersassociates.com
Email: leathers@leathersassociates.com
Phone: (607) 277-1650

Planet Earth Playscapes
P.O. Box 852
Ithaca, NY 14851
Web: www.earthplay.net
E-mail: mail@earthplay.net
Phone: (607) 273.5069

Play for All
Myrabluan Bunnan
Via SCONE, NSW 2337, Australia
Web: www.e-bility.com/playforall/home.htm
Email: kbishop@bigpond.com
Phone: (02) 6545-4260

Selected Books for Children

Amenta, C. A. (1992). *Russell is extra special: A book about autism for children.* New York: Magination Press.

Autism Society of America. (1999). *Growing up together: A booklet about kids with autism.* Bethesda, MD: Author.

Berry, R. (unpublished book). *Hearts and hands together.* Redwood City, CA: Redeemer Lutheran School and Developmental Pathways for Kids (www.developmentalpathways.com).

Bleach, F. (2001). *Everybody is different: A book for young people who have brothers or sisters with autism.* Shawnee Mission, KS: Autism Asperger Publishing Company.

Edwards, B., & Armitage, D. (illustrator). (1999). *My brother Sammy.* Brookfield, CT: Milbrook Press.

Gagnon, E., & Myles, B. (1999). *This is Asperger Syndrome.* Shawnee Mission, KS: Autism Asperger Publishing Company.

Gartenberg, Z. M., & Gay, J. (photographer). (1999). *Mori's story: A book about a boy with autism.* Minneapolis, MN: Lerner Publications.

Gerland, G. (2000). *Finding out about Asperger Syndrome, high-functioning autism, and PDD.* London, UK: Jessica Kingsley Publishers,

Gold, P. T. (1975). *Please don't say hello.* New York: Human Sciences Press.

Hoopman, K. (2001). *Blue bottle mystery: An Asperger's adventure.* London: Jessica Kingsley Publishers.

Katz, I., Ritvo, E., & Borowitz, F. (1993). *Joey and Sam: A heartwarming storybook about autism, a family, and a brother's love.* Northridge, CA: Real Life Storybooks.

Lears, L., Mathews, J., & Ritz, K. (illustrator). (1998). *Ian's walk: A story about autism.* Morton Grove, IL: Albert Whitman & Company.

Leonard-Toomey, P. (Ed.). (1996). *In our own words: Stories by brothers and sisters of children with autism and PDD.* Fall River, MA: Community Autism Resources, Adsum, Inc. (www.adsuminc.org).

Martin, A. M. (1990). *Kristy and the secret of Susan.* (Baby Sitters Club #32). New York: Scholastic Publications.

Messner, A. W. (1996). *Captain Tommy.* Stratham, NH: Potential Unlimited Publishing.

Meyer, D. (Ed.). (1997). *Views from our shoes: Growing up with a brother or sister with special needs.* Bethesda, MD: Woodbine House.

Peralta, S. (2002). *All about my brother.* Shawnee Mission, KS: Autism Asperger Publishing Company.

Schnurr, R. G., & Strachan, J. (illustrator). (1999). *Asperger's, huh? A child's perspective.* Gloucester, Ont., Canada: Anisor Publishing.

Simmons, K. L. (1996). *Little rainman.* Arlington, TX: Future Horizons, Inc.

Thompson, M. (1996). *Andy and his yellow frisbee.* Bethesda, MD: Woodbine House.

Twachtman-Cullen, D., & Sassano, D. (illustrator). (1998). *Trevor, Trevor.* Cromwell, CT: Starfish Press.

Watson, E. (1996). *Talking to angels.* New York: Harcourt Brace & Co.

Selected Readings on Autism, Play and Peer Relations

Beyer, J., & Gammeltoft, L. (1998). *Autism and play.* London: Jessica Kingsley Publishers

Bretherton, I. (Ed.). (1984). *Symbolic play: The development of social understanding.* Orlando, FL: Academic Press.

Cohen, D., & MacKeith, S. A. (1991). *The development of imagination: The private worlds of childhood.* London: Routledge.

Corsaro, W. A. (1985). *Friendship and peer culture in the early years.* Norwood, NJ: Ablex.

Fuge, G., & Berry, R. (in preparation). *Pathways to play: Theme based activities for therapists facilitating sensory integration and integrated play groups* (A Companion Guide to Integrated Play Groups Field Manual) www.developmentalpathways.com

Gagnon, E. (2002). *Power cards: Using special interests to motivate individuals with Asperger's and high-functioning autism.* Shawnee Mission, KS: Autism Asperger Publishing Company.

Garvey, C. (1977). *Play.* Cambridge, MA: Harvard University Press.

Gray, C. (2000). *The new social story book.* Arlington, TX: Future Horizons, Inc.

Gray, C. (1993). *Taming the recess jungle: Socially simplifying recess for students with autism and related disorders.* Jenison, MI: Jenison Public Schools.

Greenspan, S. I., & Wieder, S. (1998). *The child with special needs: Encouraging intellectual and emotional growth.* Reading, MA: Addison-Wesley.

Gutstein, S. E. (2000). *Autism-Aspergers: Solving the relationship puzzle.* Arlington, TX: Future Horizons Inc.

Linder, T. (1993). *Transdisciplinary play-based assessment: A functional approach to working with young children.* Baltimore, MD: Paul H. Brookes Publishing Company.

Linder, T. (1993). *Transdisciplinary play-based intervention: Guidelines for developing a meaningful curriculum for young children.* Baltimore, MD: Paul H. Brookes Publishing Company.

Meyer, L. H., Park, H. S., Grenot-Scheyer, M., Schwartz, S., & Harry, B. (1998). *Making friends: The influences of culture and development.* Baltimore, MD: Paul H. Brookes Publishing Company.

Mouritsen, F. (1996). *Play culture: Essays on child culture, play and narratives.* Odense University, Denmark.

Odom, S. L. (Ed.). *Widening the circle: Including children with disabilities in preschool programs.* New York: Teachers College Press, Columbia University

Paley, V. G. (1990). *The boy who would be a helicopter: The uses of storytelling in the classroom.* Cambridge, MA: Harvard University Press.

Perske, R. (1988). *Circle of friends: People with disabilities and their friends enrich the lives of one another.* Nashville, TN: Abingdon Press.

Quill, K. A. (Ed.). (1995). *Teaching children with autism: Strategies to enhance communication and socialization.* New York: Delmar Publishers, Inc.

Quill, K. A. (2000). *Do-Watch-Listen-Say: Social and communication intervention for children with autism.* Baltimore, MD: Paul H. Brookes Publishing Company.

Rubin, K. H., & Ross, H. S. (Eds.). (1982). *Peer relationships and social skills in childhood.* New York: Springer Verlag.

Singer, D. G., & Singer, J. L. (1990). *The house of make-believe.* Cambridge, MA: Harvard University Press.

Staub, D. (1998). *Delicate threads: Friendships between children with and without special needs in inclusive settings.* Bethesda, MD: Woodbine House, Inc.

Sussman, F. (1999). *More than words: Helping parents promote communication and social skills in children with autism spectrum disorder.* Toronto, Canada: Hanen Centre.

Taylor, M. (1999). *Imaginary companions and the children who create them.* New York: Oxford University Press.

Weiss, M. J., & Harris, S. L. (2001). *Reaching out, joining in: Teaching social skills to young children with autism.* Bethesda, MD: Woodbine House.

Winner, M. G. (2000). *Inside out: What makes the person with social-cognitive deficits tick?* Arlington, TX: Future Horizons.

References

American Psychiatric Association. (2000). *Diagnostic and statistical manual of mental disorders-IV.* Washington, DC: Author.

Autism Society of America. (1999). *Growing up together: A booklet about kids with autism.* Bethesda, MD: Author.

Baron-Cohen, S. (1995). *Mindblindness: An essay on autism and theory of mind.* Cambridge, MA: MIT Press.

Baron-Cohen, S. (1987). Autism and symbolic play. *British Journal of Developmental Psychology, 5*(2), 139-148.

Baron-Cohen, S., Leslie, A. M., & Frith, U. (1985). Does the autistic child have a theory of mind? *Cognition, 21,* 37-46.

Bartlett, A. H. (1999, August 15). The scheduled child. *San Francisco Examiner Magazine*, p. 11/31.

Bauminger, N., & Kasari, C. (2000). Loneliness and friendship in high-functioning children with autism. *Child Development, 71,* 447-456.

Beckman, P. J., & Kohl, F. L. (1984). The effects of social and isolate toys on the interactions and play of integrated and nonintegrated groups of preschoolers. *Education and Training of the Mentally Retarded, 19,* 169-175.

Berry, R. (unpublished book). *Hearts and hands together.* Redwood City, CA: Redeemer Lutheran School and Developmental Pathways for Kids.

Bloom, L., & Tinker, E. (2001). The intentionality model and language acquisition: Engagement, effort, and the essential tension in development. *Monographs of the Society for Research in Child Development,* Series No. 267, *66*(4), 1-104.

Boucher, J. (1999). Interventions with children with autism-methods based on play (editorial). *Child Language Teaching and Therapy Journal, 15*(1), 1-5.

Bronfenbrenner, U. (1977). *The ecology of human development: Experiments by nature and design.* Cambridge, MA: Harvard University Press.

Charman, T., & Baron-Cohen, S. (1997). Brief report: Prompted pretend play in autism. *Journal of Autism and Developmental Disorders, 27*(3), 325-332.

Cohen, D., & MacKeith, S. A. (1991). *The development of imagination: The private worlds of childhood.* London: Routledge.

Corsaro, W. A. (1985). *Friendship and peer culture in the early years.* Norwood, NJ: Ablex.

Corsaro, W. A. (1988). Routing in the peer culture of American and Italian nursery school children. *Sociology of Education, 61,* 1-14.

Corsaro, W. A. (1992). Interpretive reproduction in children's peer cultures. *Social Psychology Quarterly, 55,* 160-177.

Dawson, G., & Adams, A. (1984). Imitation and social responsiveness in autistic children. *Journal of Abnormal Child Psychology, 12,* 209-225.

Dewey, D., Lord, C., & Magil, J. (1988). Qualitative assessment of the effect of play materials in dyadic peer interactions of children with autism. *Canadian Journal of Psychology, 42*(2), 240-260.

Dodge, K. A., Schlundt, D. C., Schocken, I., & Delugach, J. D. (1983). Social competence and children's sociometric status: The role of peer group entry strategies. *Merrill-Palmer Quarterly, 29,* 309-336.

Dyson, A. H. (1991). The roots of literacy development: Play, pictures, and peers. In B. Scales, M. Almy, A. Nicolopoulou, & S. Ervin-Tripp (Eds.), *Play and the social context of development and early care and education* (pp. 98-116). New York: Teachers College Press.

Eckerman, C. O., & Stein, M. R. (1982). The toddler's emerging interactive skills. In K. H. Rubin & H. S. Ross (Eds.), *Peer relationships and social skills in childhood* (pp. 41-71). New York: Springer-Verlag.

Eisen, G. (1988). *Children and play in the Holocaust: Games among the shadows.* Amherst: The University of Massachusetts Press.

Elkind, D. (1981). *The hurried child, growing up too fast.* Boston: Addison-Wesley.

Ferrara, C., & Hill, S. (1980). The responsiveness of autistic children to the predictability of social and nonsocial toys. *Journal of Autism and Developmental Disorders, 10,* 51-57.

Frith, U. (1989). *Autism: Explaining the enigma.* Oxford, England: Blackwell.

Frost, L., & Bondy, A. (1994). *The picture exchange communication system (PECS) training manual.* Cherry Hill, NJ: PECS.

Fuge, G., & Berry, R. (in preparation). *Pathways to play: Theme-based activities for therapists facilitating sensory integration and integrated play groups* (A Companion Guide to Integrated Play Groups Field Manual). www.developmentalpathways.com

Gardner, H. (1982). *Art, mind and brain: A cognitive approach to creativity.* New York: Basic Books.

Garvey, C. (1977). *Play.* Cambridge, MA: Harvard University Press.

Gonsier-Gerdin, J., & Wolfberg, P.J. (submitted for publication). *Elementary school children's perspectives on peers with disabilities in the context of Integrated Play Groups: "They're not really disabled. They're like plain kids."*

Goodall, J. (1971/1988). *In the shadow of man* (rev. ed.). Boston: Houghton Mifflin, Co.

Gray, C. (1995). Teaching children with autism to read social situations. In K. A. Quill (Ed.), *Teaching children with autism: Strategies to enhance communication and socialization* (pp. 219-241). New York: Delmar Publishers Inc.

Hanson, M. J., Wolfberg, P. J., Zercher, C., Morgan, M., Gutierrez, S., Barnwell, D., & Beckman, P. (1998). The culture of inclusion: Recognizing diversity at multiple levels. *Early Childhood Research Quarterly, 12*(4),185-209.

Harris, P. (1993). Pretending and planning. In S. Baron-Cohen, H. Tager-Flusberg, & D. J. Cohen (Eds.), *Understanding other minds: Perspectives from autism* (pp. 228-246). Oxford: Oxford University Press.

Hartup, W. W. (1979). The social worlds of childhood. *American Psychologist, 34,* 944-950.

Hartup, W. W. (1983). Peer relations. In M. Heatherington (Eds.), *Handbook of child psychology* (pp. 103-196). New York: John Wiley & Sons.

Hay, D. F. (1985). Learning to form relationships in infancy: Parallel attainments with parents and peers. *Developmental Review, 5,* 122-166.

Hohmann, M., & Weikart, D. P. (1995). *Educating young children: Active learning practices for preschool and child care programs.* Ypsilanti, MI: High/Scope Press.

Howes, C., Unger, O., & Matheson, C. C. (1992). *The collaborative construction of pretend.* Albany: State University of New York Press.

Jarrold, C., Boucher, J., & Smith, P. (1996). Generativity deficits in pretend play in autism. *British Journal of Developmental Psychology, 14,* 275-300.

Khalsa, G. S., & Murdock, L. (2003). *Joining In! A program for teaching social skills.* Shawnee Mission, KS: Autism Asperger Publishing Company. [Video]

Koegel, R. L., Dyer, K., & Bell, L. K. (1987). The influence of child-preferred activities on autistic children's social behavior. *Journal of Applied Behavior analysis, 20,* 243-252.

Leslie, A. M. (1987). Pretense and representation: The origins of 'theory of mind.' *Psychological Review, 94,* 412-426.

Lewis, V., & Boucher, J. (1988). Spontaneous, instructed and elicited play in relatively able autistic children. *British Journal of Developmental Psychology, 6*(4), 325-339.

Lewy, A., & Dawson, G. (1992). Social stimulation and joint attention in young autistic children. *Journal of Abnormal Child Psychology, 20,* 555-566.

Libby, S., Powell, S., Messer, D., & Jordan, D. (1998). Spontaneous play in children with autism: A reappraisal. *Journal of Autism and Developmental Disorders, 28,* 487-497.

Lord, C., & Magill, J. (1989). Methodological and theoretical issues in studying peer-directed behavior and autism. In G. Dawson (Eds.), *Autism: New directions in diagnosis and treatment* (pp. 326-345). New York: Guilford Press.

McCracken, H. (2002). *Friend 2 friend: Helping children understand autism spectrum disorder* (brochure). North Vancouver, B.C., Canada: Author.

McCune-Nicholich, L., & Bruskin, C. (1982). Combinatorial competency in symbolic play and language. In D. J. Pepler & K. H. Rubin (Eds.), *The play of children: Current theory and research* (pp. 30-45). Basel, Switzerland: Karger.

McCune-Nicholich, L. (1981). Toward symbolic functioning: Structure of early pretend games and potential parallels with language. *Child Development, 3,* 785-797.

Meyer, L. H., Park, H., Grenot-Scheyer, M., Schwartz, I. S., & Harry, B. (Eds.). (1998). *Making friends: The influences of culture and development.* Baltimore, MD: Paul H. Brookes.

Mouritsen, F. (1992). Child culture – play culture. In S. H. Rossel (Ed.), *A history of danish literature* (pp.1-34). Lincoln: University of Nebraska Press.

Mouritsen, F. (1996). *Play culture: Essays on child culture, play and narratives.* Odense, Denmark: Odense University.

Mundy, P., Sigman, M. D., Ungerer, J., & Sherman, T. (1986). Defining the social deficits of autism: The contribution of non-verbal communication measures. *Journal of Child Psychology and Psychiatry and Allied Disciplines, 27*(5), 657-669.

National Research Council. (2001). *Educating children with autism.* Committee on Educational Interventions for Children with Autism: Division of Behavioral and Social Sciences and Education. Washington, DC: National Academy Press.

Odom, S. L., Zercher, C., Marquart, J., Li, S., Sandall, S., & Wolfberg, P. J. (2001). Social relationships of children with disabilities and their peers in inclusive preschool classrooms. In S.L. Odom (Ed.), *Widening the circle: Including children with disabilities in preschool programs* (pp. 61-80). New York: Teachers College Press, Columbia University.

O'Connor, T. (1999). *Teacher perspectives of facilitated play in Integrated Play Groups.* Master's thesis, San Francisco State University.

Page, L. G., & Smith, H. (1985). *The foxfire book of toys and games: Reminiscences and instructions from Appalachia.* New York: E.P. Dutton.

Paley, V. G. (1990). *The boy who would be a helicopter: The uses of storytelling in the classroom.* Cambridge, MA: Harvard University Press.

Parten, M. B. (1932). Social participation among preschool children. *Journal of Abnormal and Social Psychology, 27,* 243-269.

Peck, C. A., Schuler, A. L., Tomlinson, C., Theimer, R. K., & Haring, T. (1984). *The social competence curriculum project: A guide to instructional communicative interactions.* Santa Barbara: University of California, Special Education Research Institute.

Phyfe-Perkins, E. (1980). Children's behavior in preschool settings: A review of research concerning the influence of the physical environment. In L. G. Katz (Ed.), *Current topics in early childhood education* (pp. 91-125). Norwood, NJ: Ablex.

Piaget, J. (1962). *Play, dreams, and imitation in childhood.* New York: Norton.

Remes, L. (1997). One day with my sister Aimee. In P. Leonard-Toomey (Ed.), *In our own words: Stories by brothers and sisters of children with autism and PDD* (pp. 4-5). Fall River, MA: Community Autism Resources, Adsum, Inc.

Rogoff, B. (1990). *Apprenticeship in thinking.* New York: Oxford University Press.

Ross, H. S., & Kay, D. A. (1980). The origins of social games. In K. H. Rubin (Ed.), *Children's play* (pp. 17-31). San Francisco: Jossey-Bass.

Rubin, K. H., Fein, G. G., & Vandenberg, B. (1983). Play. In E. M. Hetherington (Ed.), *Handbook of child psychology: Socialization, personality, and social development* (pp. 694-759). New York: John Wiley & Sons.

Rutter, M. (1978). Diagnosis and definition. In M. Rutter & E. Schopler (Eds.), *Autism: A reappraisal of concepts and treatment* (pp. 1-25). New York: Plenum Press.

Schopler, E., & Mesibov, G. (Eds.). (1986). *Social behavior in autism.* New York: Kluwer Academic – Plenum Publishers.

Schuler, A. L., & Wolfberg, P. J. (2000). Promoting peer socialization and play: The art of scaffolding. In A. Wetherby & B. Prizant (Eds.), *Language issues in autism and pervasive developmental disorder: A transactional developmental perspective.* Baltimore, MD: Paul H. Brookes.

Selmer-Olsen, I. (1993). Children's culture and adult presentation of this culture. *International Play Journal, 1,* 191-202.

Siegel, B. (1996). *The world of the autistic child: Understanding and treating autistic spectrum disorders.* New York: Oxford University Press.

Sigman, M., & Ruskin, E. (1999). Continuity and change in the social competence of children with autism, Down syndrome, and developmental delays. *Monographs of the Society for Research in Child Development, 64,* 1-114.

Sigman, M., & Ungerer, J. (1981). Sensorimotor skills and language comprehension in autistic children. *Journal of Abnormal Child Psychology, 9,* 149-165.

Singer, D. G., & Singer, J. L. (1990). *The house of make-believe.* Cambridge, MA: Harvard University Press.

Smilansky, S. (1968). *The effects of sociodramatic play on disadvantaged preschool children.* New York: Wiley.

Smith, P. K. (1963). *Games and songs of American children.* New York: Dover Publications.

Smith, P. K., & Connolly, K. J. (1980). *The ecology of preschool behavior.* Cambridge, MA: Cambridge University Press.

Smith, P. K., & Vollstedt, R. (1985). On defining play: An empirical study of the relationship between play and various play criteria. *Child Development, 56,* 1042-1050.

Sorce, J. F., & Emde, R. N. (1981). Mother's presence is not enough: The effect of emotional availability on infant exploration. *Developmental Psychology, 17,* 737-741.

Szatmari, P. (1992). The validity of autistic spectrum disorders: A literature review. *Journal of Autism and Developmental Disorders, 22,* 583-600.

Taylor, M. (1999). *Imaginary companions and the children who create them.* New York: Oxford University Press.

Tiegerman, E., & Primavera, L. (1981). Object manipulation: An interactional strategy with autistic children. *Journal of Autism and Developmental Disorders, 11*(4), 427-438.

Tilton, J. R., & Ottinger, D. R. (1964). Comparison of toy play behavior of autistic, retarded and normal children. *Psychological Reports, 15,* 967-975.

United Nations. (1948). *Declaration of the rights of the child.* (Adopted 1959). Office of the United Nations High Commissioner for Human Rights. Geneva, Switzerland (www.unhchr.ch/).

Van der Beek, A., Buck, M., & Rufenachm, A. (2001). *Kinderraeme bilden: Ein Ideenbuch fuer raumgestaltung in kitas.* Berlin: Herman Luchterhand Verlag.

Vandell, D. L., & Wilson, K. S. (1982). Social interaction in the first year: Infants' social skills with peers versus mother. In K. H. Rubin & H. S. Ross (Eds.), *Peer relationships and social skills in childhood* (pp. 187-208). New York: Springer Verlag.

Vygotsky, L. (1966). Play and its role in the mental development of the child. *Soviet Psychology, 12,* 6-18. (Original work published in 1933).

Vygotsky, L. S. (1978). *Mind in society: The development of higher psychological processes.* Cambridge, MA: Harvard University Press.

Watson, J. S. (1976). Smiling, cooing, and 'the game.' In J. S. Bruner, A. Jolly, & K. Sylva (Eds.), *Play: Its role in development and evolution* (pp. 268-276). New York: Basic Books.

Westby, C. E. (2000). A scale for assessing development of children's play. In K. Gitlin-Weiner, A. Sandgrund, & C. E. Schaefer (Eds.), *Play diagnosis and assessment* (2nd ed.) (pp. 131-161). New York: Wiley & Sons.

Wetherby, A. M., & Prutting, C. A. (1984). Profiles of communicative and cognitive-social abilities in autistic children. *Journal of Speech and Hearing Research, 27,* 364-377.

Williams, E., Reddy, V., & Costall, A. (2001). Taking a closer look at functional play in children with autism. *Journal of Autism and Developmental Disorders, 31*(1), 67-77.

Wing, L., & Attwood, A. (1987). Syndromes of autism and atypical development. In C. Cohen & A. Donnellan (Eds.), *Handbook of autism and pervasive developmental disorders* (pp. 3-19). New York: John Wiley & Sons.

Wing, L., & Gould, J. (1979). Severe impairments of social interaction and associated abnormalities in children: Epidemiology and classification. *Journal of Autism and Developmental Disorders, 9,* 11-29.

Wing, L., Gould, J., Yeates, S. R., & Brierly, L. M. (1977). Symbolic play in severely mentally retarded and autistic children. *Journal of Child Psychology and Psychiatry, 18,* 167-178.

Wolfberg, P. J. (1988). *Integrated play groups for children with autism and related disorders.* Unpublished master's thesis, San Francisco State University.

Wolfberg, P. J., & Schuler, A. L. (1992). *Integrated play groups project: Final evaluation report* (Contract # HO86D90016). Washington, DC: Department of Education, OSERS.

Wolfberg, P. J., & Schuler, A. L. (1993). Integrated Play Groups: A model for promoting the social and cognitive dimensions of play in children with autism. *Journal of Autism and Developmental Disorders, 23*(3), 467-489.

Wolfberg, P. J. (1994). *Case illustrations of emerging social relations and symbolic activity in children with autism through supported peer play* (Doctoral dissertation, University of California at Berkeley with San Francisco State University). Dissertation Abstracts International #9505068.

Wolfberg, P. J. (1995). Enhancing children's play. In K. A. Quill (Ed.), *Teaching children with autism: Strategies to enhance communication and socialization* (pp. 193-218). New York: Delmar Publishers Inc.

Wolfberg, P. J. (1999). *Play and imagination in children with autism.* New York: Teachers College Press.

Wolfberg, P. J. (2000, May-June). Making make-believe: Enhancing communication and social skills through Integrated Play Groups (Edited by Veronica Palmer). *Autism-Asperger's Digest* (pp. 12-17). Arlington, TX: Future Horizons.

Wolfberg, P. J., Zercher, C., Lieber, J., Capell, K., Matias, S. G., Hanson, M., & Odom, S. (1999). "Can I play with you?" Peer culture in inclusive preschool programs. *Journal for the Association of Persons with Severe Handicaps, 24*(2), 69-84.

Zercher, C., Hunt, P., Schuler, A. L., & Webster, J. (2001). Increasing joint attention, play and language through peer supported play. *Autism: The International Journal of Research and Practice, 5,* 374-398.

Index